DOING FAMILY THERAPY

Also by Robert Taibbi

Doing Couple Therapy:
Craft and Creativity in Work with Intimate Partners

Doing Family Therapy

*Craft and
Creativity in Clinical Practice*

THIRD EDITION

Robert Taibbi

THE GUILFORD PRESS
New York   London

© 2015 The Guilford Press
A Division of Guilford Publications, Inc.
370 Seventh Avenue, Suite 1200, New York, NY 10001
www.guilford.com

Printed in the United States of America

This book is printed on acid-free paper.

Last digit is print number: 9 8 7 6 5 4 3 2

The author has checked with sources believed to be reliable in his efforts
to provide information that is complete and generally in accord with the
standards of practice that are accepted at the time of publication. However,
in view of the possibility of human error or changes in behavioral, mental
health, or medical sciences, neither the author, nor the editors and publisher,
nor any other party who has been involved in the preparation or publication
of this work warrants that the information contained herein is in every
respect accurate or complete, and they are not responsible for any errors or
omissions or the results obtained from the use of such information. Readers
are encouraged to confirm the information contained in this book with other
sources.

Library of Congress Cataloging-in-Publication Data

Taibbi, Robert.
  Doing family therapy : craft and creativity in clinical practice / Robert
Taibbi. — Third edition.
      pages cm
  Includes bibliographical references and index.
  ISBN 978-1-4625-2120-3 (paperback : acid free paper) —
ISBN 978-1-4625-2121-0 (hardcover : acid free paper)
  1. Family psychotherapy.   I. Title.
  RC488.5.T33 2015
  616.89′156—dc23
                                                        2015015537

About the Author

Robert Taibbi, LCSW, has more than 40 years of experience as a clinician, supervisor, and clinical director, primarily in community mental health, and is currently in private practice in Charlottesville, Virginia. He is the author of several books, including *Doing Couple Therapy*, as well as over 300 magazine and journal articles, and writes a column entitled Fixing Families for *Psychology Today* online. He provides training both nationally and internationally in couple therapy, family therapy, brief therapy, and clinical supervision.

Preface

*A*s I finish this new edition of *Doing Family Therapy*, it seems as though much has changed since the previous edition. The family therapy field continues to grow and morph, incorporating the creative concepts and techniques of practitioners, as well as accommodating more specialized populations and problems. And the larger therapy landscape has changed too. Clients are no longer left to quietly ask close friends for referrals; technology has taken over. They are going online looking at scores of local clinician profiles, comparing and contrasting styles and qualifications. They show up in your office with clear ideas of what they are looking for and are knowledgeable, thanks to proliferating websites and self-help books about the therapy process and options. This is all good news for the field; the process is less hierarchical than it was 20 years ago—when the therapist knew best—and much more collaborative.

But just as the field has changed, so have I. In the past few years I've been particularly interested in brief models of therapy and have become more behavioral in style. I've also been traveling nationally and internationally, providing training to a wide variety of practitioners. I've had wonderful opportunities not only to hear what clinicians in the field want, but, through teaching, to clarify my own evolving thoughts and to put them into clearer and more concrete terms.

All of these changes are reflected in this edition. In addition to some chapter reorganization, I have added more conceptual and practical information—more detailed guidelines for assessments, multiple ways of viewing problems, concrete treatment maps for adolescent issues, characteristics of the three stages of family treatment, and more detailed suggestions on the dos and don'ts of guiding and shaping the session process. This last item is and always has been at the heart of therapy, the place where change unfolds in the space between family and therapist, and it is where beginning family therapists understandably struggle the most. I hope all of this new information will give you something solid to bounce your own ideas and style against, and help you hit the ground running.

In spite of these changes, however, the unifying concept of this book remains the same as it was 20 years ago—that is, the realization that there are multiple paths to families and their problems, and that the most effective therapist is the one who can blend his or her values, personality, and skills to create a unique therapeutic style.

Finally, I want to thank those who have been generous with their comments—social workers, psychologists, and counselors in workshops who remember using my book in graduate school; professors who provided helpful feedback; readers across the country and across the world who sent e-mails; and all of those who have been kind enough to tell me how the book has shaped their clinical work in some small way. My humble gratitude to all of you.

Contents

DOING FAMILY THERAPY

chapter 1

Family Therapy

Welcome to Oz

*T*hey shuffle into your office without saying a word; it's the first appointment and nobody is happy. The 6-year-old boy immediately goes for your desk chair; the mother, a large woman in a faded green dress, nails him before he can hit the seat—"A. J., that's the lady's seat. Come sit over here." She rocks back and forth on the chair without standing up and stretches out one of her massive arms toward him; her tone is moderately firm. A. J. hesitates for a moment, then shrugs his shoulders and sits next to her with his head down. She reaches over and rubs his back.

The father is sitting across the room from the mother, and has pulled his chair back so that it's almost in the corner. In contrast to his wife, he's as thin as one of the chair legs. He looks like he just got off work. His work boots still have mud on them and his uniform looks dusty. The name on the pocket says Ed. He doesn't look up at you but surveys his fingers, then begins to pick at some dirt under one of his nails.

Next to you is the daughter, a blond-haired, attractive girl, 13, maybe 14. She's chewing gum and jiggling her foot, looking straight ahead, staring, it seems, at the molding behind the couch.

"So," you say, "thanks for coming. Glad to see you were all able to make it." You smile and try to make eye contact with everyone in the room. No one meets your eyes except for the mother, who is now sitting at the edge of her seat.

"Momma, I gotta go to the bathroom." A. J. tugs on his mother's sleeve and wiggles in his chair. The mother gives him a quick glance, raises her index finger to her lips, and pats his knee.

"Momma, I gotta go now."

"A. J., sit still!" You're startled by the loud thud of a command from the father, who is now staring at his son.

A. J. ignores him. "Momma, Momma." His voice is getting whiny; he's tugging at his mother's sleeve again and has shifted from wiggling to bouncing up and down on the chair.

"Now, you can just wait a few minutes, A. J., while we talk to this lady." The mother's voice has a strained sweet tone to it; she reaches over and starts rubbing his back again.

"Damn it, Lynn, why didn't you get him to go before we came?"

Time to get to work. "Ed, it seems—"

"Because he didn't need to, that's why." Lynn glares and stretches out her neck and words at the same time toward her husband. Then she turns to A. J., and her voice shifts back to its saccharine tone. "Go ahead, honey, if you need to go. Just ask the lady if it's all right."

"He can wait!" Ed slams both hands down on the arm of his chair.

"Momma—"

"A. J., shut up!" Ed hooks his hands around the chair arms, threatening to get up.

You try again. "Ed, how—"

"The boy's got to go, Ed!"

"Hold it, everybody," you say, raising your voice. Things are starting to get out of control.

"Listen, you're the one who dragged me down here to talk to some stranger," says Ed, flicking his hand toward you, "all because of your precious little boy who—"

"Well, Ed, I sure as hell don't want him to turn out like you!" Lynn is now screaming, waving her arm. "Like you, Ed!"

"Momma, I got—"

"Okay, everybody," you croak, "let's—"

"I swear I don't need this!" Ed stands up and kicks his chair back against the wall. "And I don't need you, bitch." In a flash he swings the door open, stomps out, and slams it shut.

"Momma, I got to go."

The daughter keeps staring at the molding.

SWEPT AWAY

This, of course, is one of a family therapist's worst nightmares. The family that breaks out the guns and knives before you even get the fee set. The family that stages a mutiny and gangs up on you: "Do *you* have children?"; "Are you telling me that I should let him run around 'til three in the morning?"; "We tried being nice, we tried being tough, but it doesn't help"; "You don't understand, young lady, I have bad nerves." And worst of all, perhaps, the family that just won't talk.

Individual therapy always seems easier. One on one, no distractions, the quiet intimacy of the therapeutic relationship. As you listen deeply, soaking in both what is said and not said, the client's internal world, layer by layer, slowly unfolds. The vulnerable and fearful are named, and by naming are known.

Couple therapy offers a different challenge and requires a different skill set. Here, like a tightrope walker, you're always struggling to maintain balance in the room, moving within the triangle of relationships. You want to make sure that Tom doesn't feel left out, or that Kate doesn't feel you are taking her husband's side. But there can be waves of intimacy, where partners are stepping out from behind their walls, where you seem not to be in the room, but, of course, it is only because you are there that they are able to step out at all.

If you do your job well, family therapy too can create these same powerful experiences, but getting there can seem particularly tough at times. Like Dorothy in *The Wizard of Oz*, you're swept up and suddenly dropped into a realm that seems strange, bewildering, and intimidating. Even though it's your office, you're the outsider. Six people talking at once, each wanting your attention, each testing the limits ("Psst, Johnny, hand me that basketball"; "I want to go to the bathroom"; "Can I go get a Coke from the machine?"), everyone talking at once, blaming someone else or waiting for you to blame them, wanting you to tell them what to do to fix the problem 5 minutes after they sit down. A group of people with their own history, culture, and language. Secret signals—the biting of a lip, a quiet laugh, the shaking of a head, the clenching of a fist—that suggest pools of stored resentments, private grudges, and painful conflicts touched off by the most innocent of questions; a chain reaction that can spiral out of control before you have a chance to glance up from your notes or catch your breath.

That's how it seems to go in family therapy; so much can speed by outside your control or even your awareness. The sigh that hung in the air and seemed so poignant in individual therapy is now quickly swallowed up by the stepfather's smirk. The intimate conversation between the caring but frightened mother and her lonely and awkward adolescent daughter suddenly dissolves when the 4-year-old decides she can't handle it and insists that she's going to throw up right there and then. Instead of being a guiding sage, you're more often like a traffic cop stuck in the middle of a busy intersection doing your best to keep the verbal traffic flowing— "Hold on, Dad," you say, holding up your hand, "let Sara finish"; "Okay, Dad," now beckoning him on, "what did you want to say?"

And then there are the stories—he said . . . , she said . . . , they said . . . , today, last Friday, 30 years ago. Stories of the past, stories about people long dead yet strangely alive and powerful, stories of hurt, and stories that show just how bad things can get or how good they can possibly be. That 50-pound heap of facts that partners in couple therapy will each dump in your lap in order to make their case to you that the other guy is the crazy one can now in family therapy feel like 500 pounds, all of it falling down on your head at once, enough to quickly drown even the best family therapist.

OF LEADERSHIP, PRAGMATISM, AND COURAGE

Family therapy is not for the weakhearted; even if you're a seasoned therapist, it can feel like you are flying by the seat of your pants at times. To be able to navigate the family therapy terrain, and be both grounded and creative, requires an interlocking of three qualities: leadership, pragmatism, and courage. Without any one of these, family therapy never gets off the ground and families leave sessions feeling more hopeless about change and therapy itself. Let's look at each quality:

Leadership

Lacking the built-in intimacy of individual therapy or the greater control and easier focus of couple therapy, family therapy requires that you step up and actively guide the process throughout the session. You can't afford to sit on your hands, nod your head, and simply ask "And how does that make you feel?" If you allow an argument to go on and on, or permit a mother to dominate the conversation, the other family members will interpret your passivity as permission to continue doing what they are doing, your silence as condoning their stance. And they will leave feeling the same way they did when they came in—miserable and angry—but now more entrenched and thinking they could have done all of this at home for free.

So it starts with you. You are the role model and the coach. You, as the outsider, are the one who can see in which new direction the family needs to go or can go, and the one who can guide them toward it. As you do this they will simultaneously come to understand what family therapy—and your style of family therapy—is all about. You cannot shape the process, but you can deliberately choose how you will do it.

To help offset the performance pressure this responsibility may understandably create, realize that your success and failure as a family therapist come less from knowing what exactly to do at each step along the way, and more from your willingness to push family members out of the behavioral and emotional comfort zones that fill their lives and hold their problems. Your most basic of goals is to challenge families to approach rather than avoid their anxiety, and then steer them through the change process. And while you are doing this, your leadership allows them, paradoxically, to feel safe sensing that someone is in charge and able to calm the chaos in the room and in their minds. They see that if they stick it out and get through that minefield of fear about the unknown, good things can be found on the other side.

Families more often expect exactly this. In an age of quick advice, technological immediate gratification and quick results, and in a time of limited services and insurance restrictions, many start their first session believing that things will be different by the end of it. If it doesn't happen, and they spend their time essentially replicating the patterns and problems that they know so well and play out every day, they won't come back. Leadership is the rudder that steers the therapy ship.

Pragmatism

Family members often come in believing that they are right, or that you will tell them who is right, or that you will have the right answer, yet another reason for you to feel pressure to have to deliver all of the above. But the problem with right is that it implies a wrong, which implies mistakes that, as everyone knows, you should avoid. This type of thinking and expectation is not good for you or the family. The worry over right will make you tentative or cause you to scramble like them to stack up facts and evidence. Such reactivity will undermine your leadership and derail the family therapy process.

Instead, you want to step out of this right/wrong box and help families to do the same. Mistakes, you want to help them understand, are something we can decide only after the fact, rarely before. Forty years ago Steve Jobs woke up one morning with a crazy vision of making a computer small enough to fit on people's desks. It all could have been a mistake: He could have sold none; people could have said who needs a machine on my desk when I have paper and pencil and a secretary who already can do all kinds of things for me. If he only had acted with a guarantee that his idea would indeed work, he could have dropped the entire idea and the vast changes that ultimately came about would have perhaps never come to fruition or been delayed at best.

There is the common phrase: "ready, aim, fire." Much of therapy in general, and good family therapy in particular, operates on a variation of that rubric: ready, fire, aim. You give a homework assignment and from the results decide what needs to be done next. You make an interpretation and when it fails to resonate with the client, you back up and try a different approach. Family therapy requires a trial-and-error, do-and-fine-tune, acceptable-risk mindset. Change begins not with what is right but with trying something different, not about a myopic and anxious focus on means, but rather a focus on ends.

By doing things differently; by living in the present rather than constantly worrying about the future; by assuring families that the best they can do is to only do the best they can do right now; by adapting an attitude of flexibility and a willingness to try, and then see what happens next, the therapist leads and encourages the family along the path of change. By overriding the fear of mistakes or a rigid mind-set of right, you and the family are free to be actively creative and active, rather than reactive, cautious, and potentially stuck.

Courage

While few of us would list therapy up there among the world's most dangerous professions—there are no James Bond-like high-speed chases, no balancing on the edge of roof tops, no handling of dangerous heavy machinery—we recognize that the inner journey can be just as perilous as the outer. It's no surprise that clients often talk about feeling as though they are perched at the edge of a cliff or that there is a bomb inside of them ready to explode—their sense of personal danger is absolutely real. It's fear, after all, not foolishness or ignorance that usually keeps our lives stuck and stagnant. In families it's the interlocking of each family member's fears that compound upon themselves to make any change ever-more difficult. Courage is the antidote and what powers the other two qualities. Without it there is no leadership or pragmatism.

Being courageous, however, doesn't mean you take foolish chances, but instead that you are able to approach rather than avoid your and the family's anxiety. This means confronting the mother who appears so fragile and makes others, including you, believe that she can't handle confrontation; talking to a child about the terrible things that happened to him or her without getting lost in your own grief and anger; or saying nothing at all so that the person across from you can finally say what he has been holding back for a long time. It means moving against the family's natural inertia; raising the thorny issues that no one wants to talk about; and resisting all the pressure you feel inside to fix people, take sides, and do everything right.

This is the everyday courage that doing therapy demands: pushing yourself to use your theory and skills creatively, mindfully. It's the courage of not only putting your own philosophy into practice but of helping others to define, refine, and eventually live theirs. It's acknowledging both the gift of seeing much of your own life in the life of others, and the danger of becoming confused over who you are trying to help. It is the willingness to try something in order to move ahead, even if you aren't exactly sure where it will lead. It's the simple courage of honesty.

Good therapy requires control but is not controlling, constantly facing the unpredictable while constantly predicting that the unpredictable will come, fostering intimacy while keeping clear limits on that intimacy, and being committed but being willing to stop when it seems an end has been reached or will never come. Good therapy is a seeming hodgepodge of contradictions and qualifiers that require that you walk a thin line between too little and too much, between reaching out and holding back. Courage is the stuff that glues the contradictions together; keeps you steady on the line; and gets you moving until the skill, knowledge, and self-trust can take over. Without it the families you see are penned in, confined to the narrow range of your own comfort; with it they can begin to experience their lives in the new way.

These three qualities, then, determine the success of your work with families. We will explore them in myriad forms as we survey the landscape of family therapy together.

THEORY: SOMETHING TO HOLD ON TO

The triad of leadership, pragmatism, and courage form the personal core and challenge of doing family therapy; together they serve as a ballast to help hold you personally steady. Having roots in a particular theory is what can keep you intellectually steady. While too many theories can overwhelm you and the wrong kind can constrict you, have none and you are set adrift in a vast ocean of facts and observations. A theory of therapy gives you something to hold on to. It can be as simple or complex as you like, and what a theory says is less important than what it can give to you and allow you to do.

Theories fulfill several important functions. First, they are by definition, tools for organizing. They are the Peg-Board on which we hang what we see and hear; they show us where to look and what to listen for. Events that once seemed random are now seen as connected. A father's hunting trip with his son is no longer just a family folktale, but when hung on the theory is an example of role modeling, an attempt to resolve and repair some split from the past, or yet another way of avoiding growing tension within the marriage. A daughter's unexpected running away from home is not the ridiculous ending to a stupid argument about shoes, but an understandable, even predictable way of coping with undisclosed sexual abuse, a response to the father's life-draining depression, or part and parcel of the larger cycle of addiction. With your theory as a lens, behavior and words suddenly have meaning and merit. Seemingly unrelated events and reactions are now linked to a larger family process, a deeper layer of problems that not only explain what has happened but tell what can happen in the future. Most important, your theory can provide a road map for changing it.

With the organization that theory provides comes an increase in your personal sense of control. Think back to your first interviews with families, couples, or even individuals. In the middle of it you probably felt swamped by the tidal wave of facts and emotions coming at you, and no doubt left the session bleary-eyed and exhausted. With the theory's ability to help us bundle facts together and dismiss others entirely, anxiety that potentially can make us ineffective is reduced. When we fear becoming overwhelmed in the process of the session—by the conflicting stories about what happened last Thursday, the building emotions of Dad's anger, or Mom's sadness—we can lean on our theory to tell us what to ask or do to gather the information we need. As we read the intake sheet we use our theory to help us start filling in the blanks, formulating a hypothesis that we can take into the initial session with us. The theory becomes then not only a tool but a support, an internal security blanket, a place we can always return home to. With it we have the courage to walk into the unfamiliar world of the family; we feel prepared, rather than confused and apprehensive.

Theory not only helps you, it helps your clients as well. Through the filter of your theory old behaviors are suddenly seen with new eyes. Neutral words replace those laden with anger and blame: "I can understand, Ms. Smith, why you are feeling frustrated, but Davon isn't just trying to give you a hard time. He is hyperactive and it is harder for him to sit still than it is for Shameka"; "Did you all see what just happened? Mom, you made a suggestion, Dad, you disagreed, you both start to argue, and Mary whines as a way to distract you and get you to stop. This pattern is one that you all easily fall into, and it can automatically sweep you up. Every family has patterns, and this is one of yours."

By seeing their problem in such a new light, by "reframing" the problem, and by talking to themselves with different words, the family discovers ways out of the psychological and emotional mental ruts in which they were constantly spinning. New, more creative solutions become possible: "My son isn't a bad kid who needs to be punished, but has a biochemical disorder that makes it hard for him to do certain things"; "I'm not really going crazy, I just need to talk to someone about my sadness"; "Our relationship isn't lousy simply because we're both stubborn, but because our needs over the years have changed." The theory opens new doors to the solving of problems, the process of healing.

What can make this all the more difficult, especially for those new to the field, is the bewildering array of approaches from which to choose. Over the years traditional family therapy approaches—structural, strategic, narrative, multisystemic, solution focused—have morphed and been reshaped by changes in the workplace, culture, and larger therapy field. Managed care; client-directed treatment; the push for best-practice models; the growing sensitivity to the effects of multiculturalism, racism, sexuality, and class; and attachment research, as well as brain research and increased use of medications, have had their impact and increased the number of perspectives available to the family therapist.

While research, evidence-based approaches, and sensitivity to the subtle but important aspects of human dynamics always need to be considered in order to bring high-quality services to those you serve, you must be careful not to dismiss another important ingredient in the process: namely, you. There is enough research that shows it is within the fine connections between therapist and client that effective therapy takes place. Choose what is effective and proven, but also choose one that best fits you. This means that you shouldn't just settle on a particular theory just because it's what you were exposed to in school. You shouldn't choose one because it intellectually appeals to you, is popular with your colleagues, or even seems to work with certain problems.

The best theory for you is the theory that meets you halfway. It should fit your personality, strengths, and personal philosophy: your assumptions, values, and notions of what life is and the role people and problems play in it. When there's that kind of a match— a close fitting of the basic you and the theory you embrace—it supports you rather than you supporting it. It underscores your natural instincts and intuitions. Rather than feeling constricted or constrained, you feel empowered.

BOOK GOALS AND OVERVIEW

This book is not set to be a survey course in family therapy theories or an in-depth presentation of any particular model. Instead it
is intended, whether you're new to the therapy field or a seasoned
practitioner new to family therapy, to serve as a guidebook of sorts
on core family therapy concepts, skills, and tools that can help you
get through those early tough times, and help you feel less intimidated and more empowered in doing family therapy. With this
foundation the hope is that you will not only learn how to think like
a family therapist, you'll be able to stay grounded whenever you
begin to feel overwhelmed. On this foundation you can build your
own personal style of family therapy.

That is the other goal of this book: While theory is important,
you don't want to obsess about following the chapter and verse of
any particular one; instead, incorporate your own personality and
creativity into your thinking, and shape it into a unique therapeutic
style. If staying anchored means learning to rely on a basic core of
concepts, staying creative means realizing that there isn't only one
approach to any family.

This is the pragmatism that we've already discussed, and it is
this individualized approach to family therapy that we'll be focusing on together. Through case examples we'll look at options—the
multiple ways of tackling a family's concerns—so that you can learn
to map out alternative routes that not only keep you and the family
both moving when a particular path seems blocked but also fit your
skills and the family's resources. Working in this way not only helps
families receive what you most have to offer, namely, more of yourself, but in the long run keeps you energized and sane.

This book is divided into three parts. In Chapters 2–7, we map
out the terrain of family therapy; the basic skills that keep you
afloat; the obstacles and dangers; and the ways to handle them in
the beginning, middle, and end stages of treatment.

In Chapters 8–13, we look at a variety of cases and problems.
Here's where we talk about applying the basic skills, explore clinical options, and begin to sort out your own preferences and style.
Through this process you'll learn to think creatively and make use
of your intuitions.

Finally, in Chapter 14, we discuss some practical tips for dealing with the pressures of the work, especially in agency settings; ways of staying emotionally healthy over the long haul, and ways of managing the daily wear and tear of the work. We also step back and explore work in the larger context of your everyday living, the role of work and therapy in the light of your beliefs and values, what it means to have a calling, and what it takes to have integrity.

Along the way there are exercises for you to try that can help you see how the concepts of the chapter may apply to your personal and professional life. These will give you a chance to further define your strengths, skills, and values.

Looking Within: Chapter 1 Exercises

At the end of each chapter you will find a number of exercises and questions designed to make the material in the chapter more personally relevant, and to ground the concepts within your own practice. It may be tempting to just read these and not actually do them, but try to give some time to them. If after starting, an exercise seems redundant or irrelevant, go ahead and move on to the next. But if the exercise stirs your curiosity, or better yet, your anxiety, give it a try. You have nothing to lose, and you may be surprised at what you find.

1. Here are some questions to help you uncover some of your own core beliefs, philosophies, and values. Try writing down the answers to as many as catch your interest. See if you can develop a short, concise personal statement of life, values, and work.

    What is the most important thing in life? (Trust the first thing that comes to your mind.)

    What is the purpose of life? What is the purpose of *your* life? What can only you give, create, do?

    What is the meaning of relationships, of families? What is our responsibility toward others?

    Why do relationships change? How much can people change? How do we know when change is necessary?

    What are the limits of relationships? When should relationships end? What does commitment mean?

    What is the relationship between doing for yourself and doing for others?

    What does it mean to love someone or something?

    What should parents most teach their children? What are the limits of the parents' responsibility, involvement?

What is the role of emotions in our lives?
What is the purpose of work?
How much of our life is controlled by our past?

2. Here's a short imagery exercise. Go to a quiet place for a few minutes where you know you won't be disturbed. Sit comfortably in your chair. Take a few deep breaths, and for a few moments just concentrate on your breathing. Begin to feel relaxed.

   See if you can envision a meadow in your mind's eye. It is a bright, warm, sunny day; the grass is green, flowers are in bloom and the air smells sweet with their fragrance, a slight breeze blows. And there you see yourself, walking along, feeling relaxed, the sun warm on your back. As you are walking you see ahead of you the edge of a wood. You decide to walk toward it.

   As you approach the wood, you begin to hear in the breeze the sound of a name, the name of a person of the same sex as you. As you near the edge of the wood and peer into the darkness of the trees you are aware that someone is there in the shadows, the person whose name you heard. You become curious, you begin to wonder who this person is, what he is like. Then you listen and can tell that this person is coming toward you.

   A person emerges from the trees. Notice how he looks and imagine yourself starting a conversation with this person. Imagine asking all the questions that you are curious about, finding out all you want to know that will tell you just what this person is like. Take as much time as you need talking to this person.

   When your conversation is over, the person waves good-bye and walks back into the wood. You turn around and begin to walk back toward the meadow, thinking about all that you have just heard. When your fantasy feels over, just sit for a few minutes and relax.

   It is important to hold within ourselves (and help create for families) a vision of what we can be. This imagery exercise is designed to get you in touch with your ideal self. This may have been easy for you to do, or you may have had some difficulty. Perhaps you had sensations or recalled memories, or heard dialogue, but had trouble creating the images. Don't be concerned. You can try again another time, and will probably have a different response.

   Be aware of the person you saw, not only his or her appearance but his or her personal qualities, dreams, and attitudes toward others and life. Notice the gap between the way you see yourself now and the person you imagined. Is there anything that surprised you? Is there a particular quality that you would most like to develop? What would it take to do it?

3. You don't need to take karate lessons or Outward Bound courses to increase your sense of courage. Simply begin by taking small risks, not just in your work but elsewhere in your life. Practice approaching your fear: walk up to that neighbor on your block who you've seen a few times and start a conversation, ask a question in a group even though you know it sounds foolish, try something physically different even though you feel clumsy or know you're not good at it. Avoid telling lies for a couple of days and see what happens.

A half-dozen times during the week, as you become aware of approaching the edges of your own anxiety, go forward, do whatever is scary, and then pat yourself on the back. The goal is not to be without fear, but to be able to act in spite of it.

chapter 2

Core Concepts

Process, Patterns,
Problems, and Resistance

What are we doing when we are doing family therapy? This is the question we focus on in this chapter, and the answer brings us to the core concepts of family therapy: process, patterns, problems, and resistance. Let's take them one by one.

PROCESS

Process and content. Focus on the flow of water versus the water itself. Examine the root of the complaining versus the complaints themselves. Process and content are two sides of the same coin that make up therapy and form the whole of what happens in the room. And you are like the movie director, panning in and out, back and forth between content (What did the doctor say?; What is Dad's specific worry about Karen's dating?; What is the family's history of depression?) and the process (the fact that Dad is dominating the conversation, that Mom always sounds hesitant, that the family changes the subject when you bring up the grandfather, or that Andy is sitting silently in the corner). While content provides the skeleton of the problem, process is the problem and problem solving in motion.

Initially, however, you and the family are likely talking two different languages: the family speaks of content (the what) and you, at least a good part of the time, on the process (the how). The family members usually each come armed with their facts, their stories, their versions of the situation, the problem, and the "reality," and like most of us their content rides up and down on their scale of emotions. The more upset they become, the more they begin to heap on fact after fact to make their case—describing significant past events, material evidence like school reports and checkbook stubs—in order to show everyone in the room that they are right. And often their expectation is that you will arbitrate, be the judge, sort through all of this content and decide there and then whose reality is correct, who really has the problem and needs the therapy.

You want to allow each person to present his "opening statements" to get things off his chest to reduce some of the initial tension, and by your active listening to begin building rapport. But at some point your leadership and theory need to kick in. If you just listen and not lead, if you have no mental map to help you sort out what is and isn't important out of all the facts coming at you ("And you said your dog's name is . . . what was that again?"), you'll not only begin to get lost in the woods of details, worse, you'll begin to feel like the family is overwhelmed and reactive. You may feel that all their problems are just falling down on your head. And, you'll think the only way out is to try and solve all the separate problems "out there," rather than looking at where family members get stuck in the problem-solving process, and what keeps them from solving these problems on their own.

This is where process comes in and what therapy is really about. The client world outside of therapy that you are feeling pressure to shape can be managed only in the "right here, right now" during the session. Your influence and power are limited to what you do and say and can create right there in the room within the microprocess of interactions between you and your clients. You assume that elements of the client's world and problems are encapsulated in the patterns and interactions right there before you: The way that the mother dismisses her husband's suggestion that they come in as a couple next session is the same way she dismisses his concerns about the child's school grades; the way the teenager turns her chair away from you and stares at the ceiling is the same shutdown response she gives her parents when they ask who is the friend she is going to the concert with.

This is all you can work with and have available to work with: exploring what is under the mother's dismissive tone or encouraging her husband to speak up even though his instincts are to remain silent and nod his head, talking gently to the teen about how she feels when questions are lobbed in her lap. This is where your skills are concentrated and applied: changing the conversation, unearthing new emotions, defining the intention behind the behavior, and the worry behind the anger. Everything else—whether the client follows your advice, pays the rent, or controls his temper with the kids at home—is out of your immediate control. Your challenge is to shape the time, space, and interactions in the immediacy of the moment to create something new.

This is often a difficult perspective to absorb and, at times, to maintain. When we feel frustrated or overwhelmed, we need to remind ourselves of both the limits and concentration of our power; these two abilities are present and in the room. By doing this, we teach families to do the same: to think and act now, rather than wait for the future. They learn to move against the grain of their hesitations, avoidance, self-doubt, and self-criticism, and speak clearly about what is in their hearts. We convey to them that the work of good relationships over the long term is more about having healthy ways of tackling problems and changes, and less about the content or outcome of any specific one. Finally, they learn that life happens in the present and can be measured in the quality of our interactions and what we do and say next, namely, the process.

PATTERNS

If the process is problems in motion, it is also the raw material of patterns. Patterns are the process solidified and cut into anxiety-binding shapes, chunks of predictable interactions. Some are positive (supportive, anxiety reducing) while others are dysfunctional (interactions that invariably get stuck in the emotional mud rather than move along a path of understanding, problem solving, and compassion). In systems theory the belief is that the patterns are always more powerful than the individuals; the patterns create their momentum and autopilot response. As Susan Johnson, the creator of emotionally focused therapy says, it is the pattern that is the enemy, not the other guy.

The fact that the patterns are contained in what the family presents doesn't necessarily mean they're easy to see. The family doesn't usually think and talk in terms of patterns; they talk in terms of separate, isolated behaviors and events: Eric fights all the time, my husband is always yelling at me. If clients do link events, they're usually individual, sequential ones (Johnny starts to complain, then he wails, then he starts kicking, then he falls on the floor) rather than the horizontal, interactional, bouncing-off-each-other patterns you are looking for.

There are two basic ways of finding these patterns. One is to ask "What happens next" questions that help the client map the patterns for you: "So after Johnny starts to complain, what do you generally do? And when he wails, what do you do then?" By doing this, both you and the client are able to see the ping-pong of moves, the connection between the behavior of one and the behavior of the other. Generally, the pattern runs until there is a shift in emotion (the mother swats Johnny and he starts to cry, or the mother stomps into her bedroom and slams the door), setting off a new pattern of reconciliation.

The other way of detecting patterns is to see them in the room in the process. Mom tells Susan to sit up straight, Susan slumps even more, Dad tells Susan to listen to her mother, Susan snaps at her father, Mom shrugs and looks away, Susan sits up a bit, slumps again, and it's over. This may be repeated with different content: Mom asking Susan to tell what happened yesterday, Susan saying there's nothing to tell, Dad scolding Susan, and so on. If the pattern isn't automatically reenacted there in the room, ask them to enact for you what happens at home. Ask Dad and daughter to discuss right now a curfew time, ask Mom and son to negotiate a chore list, and watch what unfolds. As it does, you can begin to point out the pattern you see, in a calm, nonaccusatory way: "It's interesting. I notice that when Susan does _____, you, Mom, always do _____, and then, Dad, you seem to do _____." You're introducing the family to the ways in which their reactions have become set.

By thinking and looking in terms of patterns you cognitively move away from the swamp of content details and help the family do the same. Rather than arguing over whether it was Tuesday or Wednesday, with your help they can begin to see that the conversation is going nowhere and that they are falling back yet again into the same emotional potholes of evidence and blame. The key to making things better lies in helping them realize when they are falling into their patterns, learning to get themselves out, and coaching them toward moving in a more positive direction.

PROBLEMS

Problems, of course, are what bring clients in: the child who won't sleep; battles over money; the grief over a miscarriage; or the worry about the sister who lives in the basement, rarely comes out, and seems massively depressed. And we go into action: defining, deconstructing, reframing, redefining, and hopefully, ultimately helping to solve the problems that clients most want to fix.

But problems are never what they seem. Even on first glance what would be a problem everyone would define—say, a flat tire—may seem overwhelming to a couple scrambling to get the laboring wife to the hospital as quick as possible, while the businessman smiles knowing he's found the perfect excuse to miss the meeting he's been dreading. This is the nature of problems; they are truly uniquely our own, handpicked and labeled so by our psychology. They are truly in the eye of the beholder.

What seems initially difficult about family therapy is that the family members are offering competing problems for your attention, each with differing owners and levels of severity. Your job is to sort and sift this all out, present some new perspectives to replace the family's old worn-out ones, and teach them that how they think about problems ultimately determines what they do with them. Here are some lenses that you can try on and try out when sizing up problems:

Your Clinical Theory

As mentioned earlier, your clinical theory shapes what you see and redefines presenting problems into something else. If you follow a structural approach, the model will direct you to look at the difference between the ideal family structure—strong hierarchy, parents working together—and how the family presents. Presenting problems are set within this frame. If, on the other hand, you are using a multisystemic approach with a teen, you will be looking at the extrafamilial systems in which the family is embedded, ways of moving away from those that are negative influences, and strengthening the positive ones. By offering the family this new lens, you stir new questions, new emotions, and hopefully new motivation and hope.

Learning Problems versus Problems about Learning

These terms were developed by Ekstein and Wallerstein (1958) in their seminal book *The Teaching and Learning of Psychotherapy*. Basically, they said that client problems can be boiled down to one of two types: learning problems and problems about learning. Learning problems have to do with skill. I have never raised a baby and have no idea of how to diaper one. This is a skill problem. Once someone shows me how to do it and I practice it, it will no longer be a problem. Problems about learning, on the other hand, are those situations where I have the skill—that basically I'm a good parent and know how to raise my kids—but my emotions override what I know and create the "problem": Every time my teenage son acts defiant, puts his hands on his hips, and gives me that "look," I forget everything I know I should do, and instead feel like wringing his neck.

So, say Ekstein and Wallerstein (1958), what we need to sort out at the top is whether a client's problem is a learning problem or a problem about learning. Is this family struggling over money because they really don't know how to set up a budget or balance a checkbook, or is it about emotions and control: the dad emotionally acts out by going on spending sprees, that the argument isn't about how to pay off the credit card but who decides what should and should not be charged on it? As we'll be emphasizing, you do not need to have the answers to these questions, you merely need to ask the questions. You start by asking yourself: skill or emotion? With this question you have a quick and handy assessment tool, as well as a way of helping families see where their problems may lie.

Problems as Bad Solutions

Because of the tight relationship between problems and their owners, what often seems, especially to outsiders, a problem is really just a bad solution to another problem beneath; this is our next level of

thinking about problems. For example, Sam's wife m
has a drinking problem because he drinks a quart of $\jmath$
every night, but Sam, most likely, doesn't think he has ι
For Sam his drinking is a solution, albeit not a particula
one perhaps, to another problem: that he is depressed, or
about his business going bankrupt, or that he's preoccupi⟍ ⟋ oy
some trauma of the past. Similarly, we can also look at the spending
spree, the teen who runs away from home, and the angry outburst
that results in the police being called as bad solutions. The assumption here is that people are most often doing the best they can at any
given moment, however dysfunctional it may seem to you or other
family members. As a family therapist it means asking yourself "If
this problem is really a bad solution, what's the problem beneath it?"

Again, your job isn't to have the answer. Instead, you ask Sam
how he thinks about his drinking differently from how his wife
does, and see what he says.

Problems Arising from Childhood Wounds and Outmoded, Limiting Coping Styles

Problems as bad solutions and problems about learning neatly fold
into our last way of thinking about problems: problems arising from
worn-out coping styles and their origin in childhood wounds.

Here's the concept: Regardless of our parents' best intentions,
we all walk out of our childhood with some emotional wounds.
If my father, for example, was critical of me, I became sensitive to
criticism; if my mother was depressed, preoccupied with her own
problems, or lacked mothering skills, I often didn't get the attention
I needed and became sensitive to feeling abandoned and neglected.

As a child our ways of coping with these injuries and unmet
needs were limited; we weren't apt as a 6-year-old to initiate an adult
problem-solving discussion with our parents about improvements
we wanted them to make. Instead, we relied—based on personality,
how our siblings were coping, what was modeled by our parents—
on one of three basic options to cope: withdraw, be good (always
do what we thought others expected of us), or become angry and
defiant.

Not surprisingly, these coping styles and injuries carry into
adulthood: If you were wired to be sensitive to criticism, you probably will read more into your supervisor's curt response to your

question than a colleague might. If you are sensitive to neglect, you will likely feel anxious and hurt and mentally question when your partner seems to pull away when he claims he is tired. When these situations arise, you once again feel like that wounded 10-year-old and feel rewounded, and respond in your learned way of coping: withdrawing from your supervisor or trying hard to be accommodating to her, or angrily accusing your partner of being selfish and insensitive.

Buddhists have a phrase—"How you do anything is the way you do everything"—the notion that our personality and primary coping styles infiltrate all the nooks and crannies of our lives. By combining these concepts of emotional wounds and childhood coping styles it's easy to see how problems are both activated and maintained. Relationship issues that touch on the edge of an old wound often become the acute issues that families, individuals, and couples define. The way out is difficult because of the limits of one's coping style. It is child based, too narrow, and too inflexible for the larger, more complex adult world. It is like running outdated software in a new computer.

As a family therapist you are looking for "how clients do": the old software in place, the way clients respond to stress and manage relationships, and the specific issues to which they are particularly sensitive. Your goal then becomes helping them recognize these automatic responses, assisting them to upgrade the software, and guiding them to respond in a more flexible, adult-like way. Often the process involves clients taking the seemingly simple yet emotionally difficult risk of doing the opposite of what they tend to do: to speak up rather than withdraw, determine what they want rather than scrambling to discern what others want, and self-regulate to reduce the anger but then use it as information to tell themselves and others they need most. By moving against their grain clients are able to step out of their childhood potholes; by having a variety of coping skills, they are less likely to be emotionally stuck when problems arise.

You too have a variety of ways of looking at problems and several lenses through which you can define and approach a family's problems. What you are curious about is: What keeps this family from solving their problems on their own?; Is it a question of skill—they don't know specific communication or parenting skills?; Is it a question of emotions overriding these skills in specific situations?;

Is it a matter of a deeper problem under the presenting problem that is not being addressed?; Is it a matter of old wounds being activated and their overall approach to stressful situations? These lenses also require family members to go against their grain, step out of their comfort zones, and stop being on autopilot. We're back to the pragmatism that we discussed earlier of doing different rather than right, the approaching of anxiety rather than avoiding it.

RESISTANCE

Problems and a family's resistance—to do what is needed to solve the problems they are presenting—seem to go hand in hand in clinical literature, though different theoretical models place varying emphasis and slant on it. Traditional psychoanalytic models, for example, assume that resistance is not only part of the work but, in fact, the focus, while behavioral approaches tend to talk little about it (Anderson, 1983). Apart from the either/or camps is the notion that resistance makes sense in that clients are likely to always have mixed emotions about stepping outside their comfort zones, adapting new perspectives, or even engaging in the therapeutic process itself.

If we assume that people are always doing their best, that by walking into your office and giving up their time and money at least some part of them is desiring change and the solving of a problem, here are, for your consideration, four basic sources of "resistance," all of which tie into our core concepts and also happen to fall onto the therapist's lap:

• *No agreed-upon problem.* If there is unclarity or disagreement about what the actual presenting problem is (the court believes the parents need couple therapy, the couple feels that the court is just harassing them) and if the ends and means are tangled (the court orders therapy, the couple would rather talk to their minister or grandmother), the clients aren't motivated and seem resistant.

• *Faulty expectations regarding the process.* Clients cannot help but have expectations about therapy—about what the therapist will do (listen, give advice, decide who is right), the focus (for example, see my child rather than the family), what will occur in a session (ask about my past, listen to my story, ask a lot of questions)—or about the length of treatment (two sessions rather than 2 months). If therapists don't meet these expectations or are not able to change them quickly, the family is likely not to return.

• *Poor pacing.* This is also about process and often pragmatism. You give a family a homework assignment (for example, for the parents to create a reward chart for a child's behavior) and they show up next week without having done it. This seems like resistance. But maybe it's because they didn't understand how to do it, or felt it was too overwhelming, or didn't understand how it would help their child do better in school. The clinician is moving too fast, making too many assumptions, and the parents are having trouble learning the skills, feel overwhelmed, and need more support or information.

• *Replicating a family role.* Here the therapist creates roadblocks by unintentionally igniting emotional wounds (for example, the therapist comes on too strong with a teen and is seen by the teen much like the teen's pushy father; the therapist works too hard to rescue the family and fix all the problems, and everyone becomes passive). The therapist in these situations has become inducted into the system. Rather than being an outside change agent, she is caught up in a role that ultimately maintains dysfunction, and interferes with the family learning new skills.

I hope you notice that all of these derailments are not about the client but about you. Try thinking of "resistance" as a bad solution to another problem in the therapeutic relationship or process. By keeping these four sources in mind when clients dig in their heels and don't follow through, you can uncover the problem under the problem and address it. We'll talk more about this in the following chapters.

So back to our opening question: What are we doing when we are doing family therapy? What we are doing is toggling among these four core concepts:

1. Focusing on process. The *how* rather than just the *what*—not only so that we don't get overwhelmed by the family's content, but to begin to help the family see the process and understand that it is the medium for change.
2. Defining patterns. Stopping dysfunctional ones and helping

families do the same, so that they break out of patterns' grip, and take conscious action to move in a more positive direction.

3. Approaching the stated problems. Doing this with new perspective in order to begin to define and deconstruct the problem and give us a foothold in understanding it.

4. Resistance. Clearing out obstacles that arise along the way that prevent the family from moving forward.

So here you have the core concepts that form the foundation for family therapy and upon which everything else is built. In the chapters ahead we look at the skills and techniques that you need to put these concepts into operation.

Looking Within: Chapter 2 Exercises

1. When you look back over your own past, what emotional wounds have you incurred? What are you most sensitive to in your relationships with others? Are there any themes (for example, "I always wind up feeling . . . ")? How do you cope when these wounds are triggered? How do you tend to cope with stress overall?

2. Are there certain problems that you struggle with due to lack of skills? Does this occur in therapy when handling emotional situations—the aggressive clients, for example—simply because you don't know the skills of how to respond to such people? Are there other persistent problems in your life that could be improved by learning the skills to adequately tackle them?

3. Being able to shift between process and content is a matter of practice. In nontherapeutic situations—talking to a friend, for example—see if you can practice switching between both modes. When watching a movie, see if you can identify each mode.

4. Are there problems under your problems? One good way of sorting this out is asking yourself the "five whys." Initially developed by Toyota as a way of drilling down to automobile manufacturing problems, you can apply this practice to problems in your personal life. Write out the problem, ask yourself why, and see what answer comes up next. Then ask why again and see what arises. Continue through the five whys but feel free to go even deeper.

chapter 3

The Basic Six

*P*rocess, patterns, problems, and resistance are the core concepts that form the heart of family therapy and the clinical work on which you can build your therapy approach and style. In this chapter, we look at the extensions of these four and examine the Basic Six: those elements that are the heart of the therapy session to which you can always return to keep you grounded. When you start to feel overwhelmed by content, when the family unravels problem after problem with no end in sight and shifts their burden directly onto your lap, and when the family is paralyzed by powerful emotions that not only evaporate whatever new and fragile sense of hope you try to create, you need ways of refocusing and recentering.

Recentering is the important word here. If you've ever learned meditation, you were probably told to focus on your breath or on a one-word mantra. And you were also probably told that whenever you "caught" yourself lost in meddlesome thoughts, you didn't need to feel concerned or guilty or worry about doing it right, but merely to stop and return back to the breath or mantra. In the beginning it was easy to wander off into the forest of your own plans and worries—the argument you had with your husband that morning, the list of items you needed to get at the grocery store, the upcoming deadline on the report or paper you needed to do—without even being aware of it. And in the beginning it probably seemed that you were returning to the mantra more than you were actually saying it. But if you kept it up long enough with practice, this changed; you were more able to stay with the mantra before wandering off.

So it is with family therapy. When you find yourself lost in the family—overwhelmed by their words, questions, and emotions—don't panic and don't kick yourself for messing up. Simply keep in mind the basic skills outlined in this chapter for navigating the process, and get recentered. They can help you stay on track through the most difficult sessions. In the beginning you may find yourself seemingly always going back, but with practice your forays into the thick of the family will increasingly go further. Even with a lot of experience you'll sometimes get overloaded, and it's good to know you can always go back and start again. Once you feel comfortable with these six basic skills you can use them as the basis for improvisation. Mix and match these, the way a good chef mixes and matches her favorite ingredients, to create your own style, your own unique approach to a particular problem or family.

1. DETERMINE WHAT
IS THE PROBLEM/WHO IS THE CLIENT

"I just haven't been feeling myself lately."

"The teacher says my son is acting up in class, and he has been giving me a hard time at home. I wonder if you could talk to him and straighten him out."

"The judge ordered me to come here for counseling until you say I don't have to. I don't think I need to; it's my ex-wife who's the one with the problems."

"My husband and I agree that our daughter has a problem with her attitude, but personally, I think the real problem is that my husband is never home."

People come to you because of problems and, as brief, solution-focused approaches and managed care have emphasized, it is vital that you know exactly what the problems are. This means having a clear understanding of just what the client is talking about and struggling with: What do "haven't been feeling myself," "acting up in class," or "a problem with her attitude" mean? At face value, these are not solvable problems because the behaviors, emotions, and symptoms they indicate are vague and undefined. By helping clients become clearer and more precise about what they are saying, you help them become clearer and more precise about what they are thinking and feeling. This not only begins to bring the problem into the room and to create a clearer picture of what is wrong, but also helps you begin formulating a clear, positive vision of what the solution can be.

You also need to be clear about who has the problem. Sometimes, especially when the client is a self-referred adult, the client in the room and the client with the problem are one and the same, and it's all pretty simple: "I feel depressed; I'm here so you can help me"; "My kids are running all over me, I need to learn how to handle them better." Other times, however, it's not quite so easy. Often the only person with the problem is the person who is seeing a problem in someone else: the mother who thinks her son should find new friends, but the son thinks his friends are just fine; the father who thinks the mother should be tougher, but the mother feels she has a close relationship with her daughter and the father is just jealous; the wife who wants her husband to stop drinking so much, but he says that he only has a beer now and then and it isn't a problem for anyone but her. If only this other person would change, each says, I would feel better.

When they all show up in your office, with everyone pointing the finger at someone else, it's important to pair problems and people carefully. The mother and teacher who are having problems with the boy may be the only ones having problems; that is, the boy and father may not be. The man referred by court doesn't have a problem except perhaps with the court order itself; so far the only person with a problem is the judge or probation officer. The father has a problem with his daughter, but the mother has more of a problem with the father. Whoever sees or feels the problem owns it and is ultimately responsible for solving it.

When the problem behaviors seem so obvious—the husband is falling-down drunk every night, the little boy is fighting everyone in the neighborhood, the teenager is refusing to go to school—it's easy for you to get caught up in everyone's concern and to join forces with them in trying to convince the identified patient (IP), the one who everyone is pointing their fingers at, that a problem really does exist. It's an awkward role that you need to avoid. You are stepping out of the service role, rapidly becoming an enforcer, and the IP generally starts to respond to you with more and more resistance. From her point of view, she simply doesn't have a problem, at least not the problem that everyone is so concerned about, and your siding with the others only dismisses you more quickly.

Rather than wrestling with the IP over the problem, you can have those who feel there is a problem come in together with the IP and talk with different words and a different emotional tone (thanks to you) about their worry and fears about the IP's behavior and see if this helps motivate the IP to look at the problem. If the person defining the problem—the probation officer, social service worker, teacher, or generally some other representative of an agency or institution—isn't planning on being present at that first meeting, invite her to come in. I'm concerned, says the teacher, that if you don't settle down in class and pay attention, you'll be left back. I'm worried, says the mother, that if you don't stop arguing with me at home, you won't behave well with your aunt and shouldn't go to see her this summer. If you don't get counseling to help you control your anger, says the probation officer, not only will you possibly be sentenced to jail time but you could lose custody of your daughter. Your job here is to make sure the communication is clear, that the IP is able to understand the others' concerns, and that the IP can explain why the problem is not his.

Another approach to this conversation is to explore with the IP any problem that he is concerned about: If you could have any change at home, school, or in your life, what would it be? This is where the boy, it turns out, is actually very upset that his mother seems to be spending all of her time with the new baby; or he feels like his teacher is always on his back and never gives him credit for what he does well; where the man agrees that maybe he does have a problem with his temper, but he's gotten a lot worse since he lost his job, and he feels like no one is willing to help him get into job training. You're moving toward the problem as a bad solution, uncovering the problem under the problem. You now have a point of engagement and motivation for change, and since it often doesn't matter where you start but rather that you start, you have a green light to go forward.

But what if the IP won't engage, absolutely states that there is no problem, and that therapy is a waste of time? You leave the IP alone and help the other person see what he can do about his problem. Thank the son for coming in, set up a time to meet with the mother alone to talk about parenting, and have her sign a release for you to talk to the teacher so that they can coordinate how they will handle the boy's behavior. Tell the client that you'd be happy to tell the court that the IP doesn't see a need for coming and that he needs to consider some other option. Tell the man that you're not sure whether he has a drinking problem, but suggest to the wife that she attend an Al-Anon meeting or offer to help her figure out what she can do if the drinking continues.

Again, your job is not to take sides but to clarify just what the sides are: the parents' problem and the kid's problem, the agency's problem and the client's problem, the husband's problem and the wife's problem. It's common in family therapy to have a laundry list of problems simply because there are several people, each with their individual yet interlocking struggles and versions of reality. In order to manage them all you start by drawing lines of responsibility around each one, and then do one of several things. You may decide to handle each one separately: "This session we will talk about ways of using time-outs with Sam, and next week we can talk about that holiday depression that you're worried about"; "Let's work on deciding what to do about Chloe's school behavior, and then we can work on some of those marital issues you are concerned about."

You can also move to a different level, harness the family's energy, and use systems theory to show the family how two or more problems are connected: "Susan, you don't like Jesse going out with the guys so much, and Jesse, you feel that Susan's always involved with the kids and doesn't want to spend time with you alone. Maybe one problem dovetails into the other"; "John, you're worried about Tom always provoking his younger brother, and Tom, you're mad at your dad for ignoring you; I wonder if your bothering your brother is a way to let your dad know that you're mad and get him to pay attention"; "Manuel, you are worried about Teresa's school work. Teresa, you are upset about your parents arguing so much. I'm thinking that the tension at home may be making you feel depressed and stressed, Teresa, and making it hard to do your work."

This way of connecting one problem to another helps the family members begin to see that their behaviors are not independent but interrelated, with one problem becoming an attempted solution to another, with actions and reactions interconnecting to form patterns. Once the connection is made and accepted by the family, the focus shifts from arguing over who has the problem to finding ways of breaking the pattern. It also builds on the motivation already present, as the change in one member's highest concern is indelibly linked to the concerns of the other.

Finally, rather than taking turns working on separate problems and linking problems, it is often possible to collapse several problems into one new one. Joseph, for example, is referred by the school for truancy and comes to the first session with his parents. It is quickly revealed that the father has started gambling heavily again after years of restraint, and the mother reports that for the past 6 months she has been suffering with chronic back pain, and doctors have done little to help. While on the surface you can look at these as separate problems, it is no coincidence, perhaps, that they have all erupted since the sudden death of Joseph's 6-year-old sister of leukemia last year.

In this light it is useful to see that the family members' problems are different (albeit not necessarily adaptive) ways of coping with the grief that they all share. By exploring and defining this underlying shared trauma, the seemingly separate problems become one, namely, the sadness and grief that each feels. With your support, the focus shifts from the specifics of their behaviors to unraveling the emotional knot of grief that both links and handicaps them.

Similarly, Ann is referred for breaking probation and staying out past curfew. The mother also complains that 12-year-old Brandon is fighting all the time with his younger brother Dan. All these separate problems are linked, you believe, to the parents' struggle to create structure and consistent limits within the home, and this, in turn, stems from the parents' differing views on the way the children should be handled. Again, the separate problems are boiled down to a different primary one, namely, the couple's relationship and difficulty working together. This becomes the focus of the therapeutic contract.

Giving the family a new problem and a new perspective to replace the old, worn-out ones they are stuck on psychologically frees and stimulates new energy and creativity for solving them. The only tricky part for you as the therapist is making sure that the family members agree with the connection you are making between this new problem and their old one. Everyone needs to agree that there really is a link among the grief and Joseph's truancy, Dad's gambling, and Mom's back pain, or among the marital strain, Ann's behavior, and the boys' fighting. You can do this through psycho-education by exploring and showing the problem in the room (for example, pointing out how the parents are disagreeing right there and how the kids are acting up or not listening), by the weight of your own expertise, and by their desire to hear your opinion. Some-times this notion that seemingly disconnected problems are, in fact, linked can be a hard sell, and you may have to work on the prob-lems separately until you can gather more evidence to convince the family that the connection really exists.

Being clear about who the client is and what the problem is out-lines the starting point for developing a therapeutic contract. It is also what you can return to when you begin to feel overwhelmed by the variety of problems that the family presents.

2. LOOK FOR WHAT'S MISSING

There is a Sherlock Holmes story about a horse that's stolen from a barn one night. Holmes declares to Watson that the key to the case is the barking dog. But, says Watson, there was no barking dog. Precisely! says Holmes. The fact that the dog didn't bark meant that whoever came that night was not a stranger, but someone who the dog knew well.

You too need to think like Holmes. You need to see not only what the family presents but what they don't: to look for what is not being said, what is not happening, and what is missing in the picture the family creates of themselves in front of you. These are the holes in the fabric of the family—the father who doesn't come to the appointment, the good things that Michael can do, talking about the time the mother was in jail, the affair the wife had 3 years ago, anger, sadness, the oldest brother's ongoing depression, laughter, lit-eral pats on the back, and physical affection—all the things different members of the family can't do, avoid, and aren't aware of.

Or what they can't quite say. This is the subtle awareness of language: the way the father mentions "problems" or "things in the past," how the mother stops and shifts gears in midsentence—"And then he . . . but the teacher said"—or simply trails off. To be aware of this is to see language working as protection. To talk about "a problem" rather than specifically describing the behavior or situation is to put a protective glaze over the emotions. To stop in mid-sentence and shift course is literally to "not go there." So go there! Ask "What problems?"; "What things?" Ask the client to go back and finish the sentence. The more specific the language becomes, the more defined the emotions become.

We're back to talking about comfort zones, ingrained ways of coping and wounds, and the intimacy of problems. The parents know the story of Michael and his problems with his attention-deficit/hyperactivity disorder (ADHD); they can give you a run-down of all the problems they have had with him since he was young and can talk about it for hours. Similarly, the mother knows anger, uses it as a default emotion regardless of the situation, while the father can demonstrate there in the room his quick accommodation when his wife gets the slightest critical edge in her voice. We're looking for what we don't see or hear: the emotions, behaviors, topics, and the language. We are asking ourselves—Where does this family get stuck?; What can't this family do?—and the answer lies in what is not in the room. This is what you, as the outsider, can see that they cannot: these blind spots, this uncharted territory of new emotions and behaviors where both their anxiety and ultimately their solutions and healing lie.

And then you guide them there. Since often the most important conversations are the ones that the family avoids, try having them and see what happens: "Tom, you're always so quiet, and I wonder if Ann thinks you just don't care. Can you tell Ann what you're thinking about what she said?"; "It seems you all have never talked about your father's death. Maybe we can all talk about it, even for a few minutes"; "Helen, you are always in charge of putting Thomas in bed. How about you let John be in charge of doing it this week?"; "Angie, you made a comment about your jail time. Can you tell me more about that?"; "Chris, it's clear you're angry about your daughter's relationship with her boyfriend, but what are you most worried about if it continues?"

You may move toward these unspoken topics at times because you need to better understand and filter through the content that the family presents, but more importantly and more often you raise these questions to challenge family members to move away from the familiar. You use your leadership to shift the process and conversation, and by doing so assess their tolerance for anxiety, to provide them with a slightly different perspective of one another, and even a small experience of change.

How do you learn to see and hear what is missing, rather than only what is present? By training your eye, ear, and mind. As you listen to an audiotape, listen for what is not mentioned, and for what is only vaguely said. As you watch a videotape, notice what the individuals and the family as a whole are not doing. When you hear emotions or see behaviors ask yourself what would be the opposite, or like Sherlock Holmes, ask yourself what you would expect to see or hear that you're not. With practice, what's presented will become an automatic springboard for zeroing in on what's not there—what can these individuals and family not do?

And when you feel overwhelmed or unfocused in a session, look for what's missing right there in the room (what is not being talked about, what emotions are being avoided, what secret is lying somewhere in the corner of the family's past) or focus once again on the holes you may have already mapped out (the mother's anger, the father's sadness, the child's inability to say what he or she feels). You are the change agent and guide. Step forward so the family can do the same.

3. BLOCK THE DYSFUNCTIONAL PATTERNS

As mentioned earlier, patterns are the heart of family therapy, the way of organizing what you see, the complement to what you don't see. The missing elements of family interactions—unexpressed emotions, undiscussed secrets, and so forth—point to anxiety that is too great for the family to handle. On the other hand, dysfunctional behaviors or routines signal that the family has found a way to contain the anxiety provoked by underlying problems. If the family's anxiety is found in what's missing, the family's anxiety is contained in the patterns.

Just as you can learn to look for what's missing, you can also train yourself to notice patterns. Again, watch videotapes of sessions, movies, or even sit back and observe what you notice at a family gathering, or a couple at a restaurant. In the initial session you want to give the family the space to not only tell their stories but to allow the patterns to unfold: that Mom repeatedly interrupts the daughter, the daughter snaps back, the father tells the daughter not to talk to her mother like that. The father observing his child playing with the toy house, makes suggestions—to notice the toy dog at the corner of the table—and the child says that he doesn't want to play with the house anymore. The elderly parents try and talk to their grown son about his seeming isolation and gaming addiction, and he always retorts by pointing out problems the couple used to have in their relationship.

Once you figure out what the pattern is, your next step is easy: *block the pattern*. It's easy for many newcomer clinicians to family therapy to go into a panic because they worry that they need to have a healthy pattern already on deck to replace the dysfunctional one. You can have a plan in mind, of course, and noticing what's missing will give you a direction. But even if you can't think on your feet, by blocking the pattern you will force the family to do something different.

So you ask Mom to try and not interrupt her daughter or the father to stay out of their exchange. You ask the father to just watch what his son does in play rather than making suggestions. Hold up your hands like a traffic cop when the parents begin to double-team their son with criticism yet again, and see what happens. While their first reaction is likely to be to ignore you, or to slide back into the safe zone within 2 seconds, if you persist, continuing to cut them off at the pass, the anxiety of the moment will push them to try a new and different way of relating. This places them in the position of creating their own change and allows you once again to simply fine-tune it, and with your help begin to recognize the pattern themselves.

4. TRACK THE PROCESS

As mentioned in Chapter 2, content and process are the two sides of therapy you will move between throughout the session. Both are sources of information. Your clinical theory may stress one over the other. Traditional cognitive-behavioral theory, for example, starts with content and always returns to it: John may feel rejected, but he can learn to tell himself that it doesn't mean that he is a *bad* person or did anything *horrible*. Tim's failing summer school is a *problem*, not a *disaster*. Mike doesn't *always* blow up, but only when he feels that people are misunderstanding how important his career is to him. We may not be able to choose our emotions, but, say cognitive-behavioral therapists, we can choose our thoughts, and the medium of thoughts is language. It's the language of our self-talk that locks, binds, and limits; its distortions create a warped reality and negative emotions. By remaining alert to this dysfunctional language and consciously changing it, we can directly shape our emotions and change our actions. More experiential therapies—the externalizing of narrative therapy, the empty-chair work of Gestalt, and the enactments of structural therapy, on the other hand—push process more to the fore.

Whatever you focus on, particularly in those opening sessions, is teaching a family about what you think is important in the therapy process and what they themselves need to focus on. If you get too caught up in detailed questions about facts—What exactly did grandma say on the phone?; How do you know that Jake was late for school on Tuesday?—you're training the family to think that this is important for you to know, that these content details matter. They'll be ready at the next session to give you a verbal transcript of the phone conversation, they will have noticed what time Jake left the house. What you say and choose to talk about comes to shape what the client thinks about.

Process needs to be part of this mix from the start and you want to track it closely to keep you from getting lost in the details, enable you to detect patterns, and teach families that process itself is important. Many families can't see it, ignore, or separate it from content—"Stop interrupting me!" they snap—before sliding back into their story. Content, in fact, is most valuable, most potent, and most heard when it can merge with the process itself: "I'm hesitating and fumbling because I'm afraid that if I say the wrong thing you're going to get mad"; "I hear what you are saying but don't really understand what you're saying; tell me again with different words why my going out last weekend hurt your feelings." This matching of content and process in the moment is the basis of Carl Rogers's concept of authenticity; of Zen consciousness, self-awareness, reflection, and esteem; and the key to absolute honesty and living in the present. Powerful stuff.

One helpful metaphor for helping families understand process is to describe how having a conversation is like driving a car. There are two parts to driving a car. The first is knowing where you want to go before you set out. Before you start a conversation, decide what is the one thing—the content—you most want the other person to understand (for example, that it feels disrespectful to me when you look through text messages while I am talking); the one problem you want to solve (for example, to come up with a chore list for the children). The other part is keeping the car on the road—the process—and this is where most families get into trouble. Within minutes they are no longer talking about text messages or the chore list, but are getting angry and talking about Christmas 2012 again, the time Sally lied, who decides whether chores are important at all. The conversation has gone into a ditch.

When this actually happens in the session, like patterns, you want to initially wait and see if the family can get the car back on the road: "We don't need to talk about Christmas 2012 again right now," says the dad, "let me explain why privacy about my phone is important to me." If they can't—if Christmas 2012 rapidly spirals off into your mother, your stupid brother, that time you did such and such—step in, stop the pattern, and change the process by pointing out the process: "Hold on everyone. Can you tell that this conversation is going nowhere, that the car has gone off the road and getting stuck in a ditch?" Their first response will likely be to ignore you, say yes but then continue where they left off. You'll need to be persistent and point out the process repeatedly until they can begin to do it on their own.

You're also tracking the process to catch the mismatch among words, emotions, intent, medium, and message. This is usually done with questions ("John, you're talking about the good times of the past, but looking mighty sad. How are you feeling right here, right now?") or statements ("Mary, I'm trying right now to offer a suggestion and I feel like you're ignoring me"). The client, be it one individual or the entire family, has to shift, and is forced to stop and think about what just happened and is happening right then. This shift in focus creates the opportunity for the family members to move from meaningless content to meaningful, honest content that fully incorporates the underlying emotions.

Again, the first times you point out these mismatches, clients will often resist you in order to reduce their anxiety. "I *was* listening," Mary mumbles back, both denying the reality in the present and avoiding the confrontation. But if you stick with the process ("Did you just feel like I was scolding you?" said in a gentle voice) and help the client to stay focused on what's happening in the present, cutting her off from slipping back into the same content, the client not only plows new emotional ground in her relationship with you but begins both to discriminate content from process and to learn to move between them.

Finally, you want to track the process like a bloodhound in order to make sure that you and the family are staying in lockstep together. As we discuss in the next chapter, this is particularly important in the first session. What this means is that you don't want to go forward unless the family is with you. You want to correct any blips in the process as they arise. So if you ask the father to try and just watch how his child plays and not make suggestions, but he continues to do so, you want to stop then and there and address it: "I was suggesting that you let Jacintha play on her own just to see better what she herself decides to do, but you seem to be having some trouble doing that. I'm wondering why."

Similarly, if you make an interpretation: "It sounds like your supervisor reminds you of your mother," and the client makes a face or "I'm wondering aloud whether Harold seems to be having trouble paying attention in school because he may have attention-deficit/hyperactivity disorder," and you get back a weak, look-away, whatever "I guess so," from the mother, you need to stop and find out what is happening. "You just made a face and it seems like you don't agree. Tell me how you think about your supervisor differently." "I'm thinking Harold may be at risk for ADHD because of your family history, but it seems like you're thinking about this differently."

Catching these out-of-step moments allows you to repair missteps in the interaction and the relationship. You can explore the problem under the problem of the father's difficulty in leaving his daughter alone; you can explain to the client why there is a parallel between her reaction to her supervisor and her history with her mother; you can educate the mother about what ADHD means, or find out what about it bothers her the most. By catching these moments as they unfold, you are fixing the problem in the room that is interfering with moving forward and implementing the treatment plan. If you let it go, miss or disregard the father's continued interruption, the client's facial expression, or the mother's weak response, they may say at the end of the session that this was really helpful, promise to do the homework you gave them, but then they will cancel the next appointment and tell you they'll get back to you, or show up and not have completed any of the homework.

By tracking the process both you and the client can learn to tackle problems and derailments—the hurt feelings and the misunderstood comment, which are sources of resentment in the therapeutic and family relationships—right there and then, directly and immediately as they unfold. The therapy stays on course, and the family sees how to confront problems quickly and effectively. By staying aware of and on the growth edge, you and the client can avoid creating and lapsing into your own stale patterns of behavior that can bind anxiety and blunt the change making.

All of this requires the courage we talked about at the start. Your job is to always turn up the corners of content to see what lies underneath; to talk about the elephant in the room that no one wants to acknowledge; and to confront the client who too quickly dismisses your well-thought-out, well-grounded sage advice, interpretation, intervention, and diagnosis. You want to bring up what is missing, say aloud what they are possibly thinking, and ask the hard questions that they in the moment are afraid to ask. It seems easier to let it go, rationalize that you can circle back "at a more appropriate time" later, or like the family, deflect and focus on content—"So what did you do on your vacation?"—to relieve the building tension.

Resist the urge to do this. Instead stay with the process, move forward, and say what you see.

5. EXPERIENCE BEFORE EXPLANATION

Who and what is the problem tells you what you most need to focus on and fix, and what the family's expectations and goals are. The focus on process, patterns, and what's missing helps you link what you see happening in the room with what goes on in the family's life outside the room. That focus helps you formulate the creation of the problem and a possible solution, and also helps the family see therapy as a viable and active means of changing the problem, rather than merely talking about it.

What ties these two foci together is the clinician's skillful use of that set of twins: experience and explanation. *Experience*, the close cousin of process, is the one that runs through the room intent on what happens; like questions, experience raises anxiety and energy.

Explanation, the close cousin of content, is the one, like statements, that smoothes and soothes, that makes sense out of what experience has just done, and connects it to the family's problem and needs.

Just as you need to learn to confidently move between content and process, you also need to learn to move between the twins of experience and explanation. And like toggling content and process, a good balance is important. Let experience run too wild, too long, and the family feels overwhelmed, shaky, fragmented, and frightened; everything is in shambles, their anxiety goes through the roof, and more often than not they run away and don't come back. Lay down too much explanation and the family goes to sleep. Like its cousin content on a bad day, explanation bores the family to death; the words wash over them, leaving them unchanged.

Explanation's strength is its calming presence, immensely valuable when what you want is to lower anxiety. This is what the doctor does when she tells the frightened little boy that she is going to give him a shot in his arm and it's going to sting for a minute, or describes to the obsessing patient exactly what will happen in surgery tomorrow, and what it will be like after surgery while he is in the hospital. This is what you do in the first session when you talk to the family about what therapy can or cannot do regarding the problem, or what the format will be for the session.

Psychodynamic approaches devoted a great amount of attention to beefing up explanation's power and ability to mobilize change. These explanations were renamed in their vocabulary as "interpretations," and like the puny David facing Goliath, their lack of experience's kinetic power was compensated by impeccable timing. Properly timed interpretations are, in the psychodynamic process, an art form. When hurled at just the right moment these explanations strike the client right between the eyes, crystallizing all that the client has been moving toward in awareness. They shine a light on the vague shadows that the client has been slowly groping through; suddenly, the shadows dissolve into something clear and hard. The client has more than an explanation; she has an "insight," an "aha" experience that can then spill over into emotions and behaviors. Good interpretations transform explanations into experience.

The downside to this approach is the length of time it takes. The less directive role of the psychodynamic therapist means that he is essentially waiting for Goliath to approach, waiting for the unconscious process to build and take hold. The directive role of the family therapist speeds up this process; rather than waiting, he marches forward into the fray and begins to stop the patterns, and pushes the family to see what's missing. These actions raise anxiety and open up the possibility of change.

All of this leads us to the fifth basic concept: experience before explanation. If the primary goal is to get the family moving, to ride on the motivation that brought them into the office, they need, to paraphrase Fritz Perls, the founder of Gestalt therapy, an experience, not an explanation. Bring the problem alive, get them to try something different, talk about what they don't want to talk about, have them taste something new, and then mop up with explanation. What you're then doing is exactly what the psychodynamic therapist has been waiting to do for months: providing an explanation that crystallizes and shapes the anxiety that you have just generated. If explanation walks into the room with a bucket and mop too soon, while everything is still orderly and set, it stands in the corner and melts into the woodwork. Everyone wonders why it's there.

By marching ahead with experience you're not only breaking up the patterns but desensitizing the family to the experience of change, to the taking of risk. Rather than (yet again) retreating from new situations, or, out of fear, seeing the new as only another example of the old, the family approaches their anxiety with your help; when they do so they increase both their self-esteem and courage.

Of course, you, as the clinician, are once again the best person to model this courage. Armed with your theory and philosophy, you are the one best able to push into the holes that you see the family cautiously walking around, that you sense by feeling the edges of your own anxiety. While this may sound daunting, it needn't be. Here are some examples of experience before explanation:

This mother is angry. For the last 6 months her 11-year-old son has been driving her crazy: getting into fights at school, earning failing grades, arguing with her all the time. She thinks the problem is the new kid in his class who he has been hanging around with. "Had anything happened 6 months ago?" you ask. "No," she says, then hesitates. "Well," she says matter-of-factly, "His grandmother, my mother, died back during the summer, but she had been ill for a long time, and we all knew it was coming." "Tell me about your mother," you say. She begins to describe her, and as she does her eyes become teary. "Do you miss her?" you ask quietly. The wall around her grief begins to break, and she quietly begins to sob for many minutes; you sit with her and wait. When she finally calms down and looks at you again, you ask, "Do you think your son feels the same way you do?" "I don't know, I guess, but we never talk about it," she responds. "I wonder," you say, "if the way he has been acting is connected to all this sadness and the way you both have been feeling."

At the urging of the school teacher, Jim brings in his 8-year-old daughter, Jenny, who has lately become moody and withdrawn. He is not so much concerned about why, but what he should do about it. The parents have been divorced for several years, but, Jim assures you, they continue to have a good relationship, and Jenny has handled it well. Jim has been steadily and recently dating a woman named Cathy. He swears that Jenny likes Cathy, though Jenny says little to anyone, including you. You ask Jenny to draw a picture of her family, and with some prodding she does. You show it to the father. There, clearly labeled in her 8-year-old scrawl, is a picture of her mother and father holding hands with a smiling Jenny standing right in the middle of them.

It's the classic marital argument. Lisa starts complaining about how Phil is always criticizing her, and Phil snaps back, saying that Lisa never follows through on what she agrees to do. Quickly they escalate, using sarcasm, making faces, yelling, and bringing up old wounds and stories of the past. You hold up your hands and ask them both to stop. You ask Lisa to turn her chair toward you, and ask her to say more about what bothers her when Phil seems to be criticizing her. She becomes teary and says she feels pushed away and lonely, much like she felt when her father did the same thing when she was growing up. You talk briefly about the power of triggers from the past and ask her to tell Phil how she would like him to speak to her when he is frustrated.

Again we see the other basic concepts coming into play: clarifying the problem, focusing on process, moving toward what's missing, breaking patterns. What each example also shows is the creating of experience in order to set the stage for explanation. You may have guessed the moment that the mother mentioned the death of her mother that the grief may be trickling beneath the boy's acting out. You could have cut to the chase and explained this to the mother, who most likely would have nodded her head, but emotionally disagreed and discounted what you were saying simply because of the anxiety it created.

But by gently leading the mother into her grief, the telling of the story of her son and her mother flow together. Only after she is emotionally aware of her grief can she consider it resting within her son as well; only then does your linking them together and redefining the problem in new terms now make sense and seem relevant to her.

The same is true with the father and daughter. The father wanted to know what to do, and you could have quickly given him a list of behavioral things to try at home. What's missing, however, is the content of the daughter's silence and his own reluctance to look underneath the changes in his family, or at the impact of his new relationship. The daughter's picture powerfully and directly says to him what your explanation would not.

Finally, it's easy to see how the couple's verbal and nonverbal behavior is fueling old patterns of destruction. Rather than giving a mini-lecture on their poor communication (and possibly replicating the criticizing process), you break the patterns and give Lisa a chance to talk and Phil to listen, without all the nonverbal and verbal triggers. More important, you help them create a different, positive interaction right there in the room that you can then map out for them so that they can replicate it at home. Should it not work— should Phil fail to listen or dismiss what Lisa says—you can see where and how it breaks down, and try something else.

What each of these examples has in common is the shift in the emotional climate in the room. It is said that one can't solve a problem with the same emotion that fostered it or with the same consciousness that created it. Only by changing the emotional climate in the room is the family able to see what you see and fully absorb the new ideas you have to offer, which in turn can help them change their perceptions of the problem.

If you are moving too quickly and notice that the client's anxiety is rising too high and creating resistance (for example, not paying attention, distracting, outright refusing to try what you suggest), you can use explanation as a brake: "Lisa, I'm asking you to look at me rather than Phil so that you can say what you think without getting distracted by his nonverbal behavior"; "Jim, I asked Jenny to draw a picture because it is usually easier for kids to say how they feel through art or play"; "Mrs. Johnson, I'm asking about your mother because I'm wondering how much the loss of his grandmother may be bothering your son even though he doesn't talk about it. Often children's sadness comes out as behavior problems." Statements like these put a frame around the experience and make it just enough less threatening that you can continue to go forward.

There's always the temptation, especially when you feel overwhelmed or frustrated, to use explanations like a blanket to smother the fires of anxiety (yours and the family's) before it gets out of control. But the better way to look at anxiety is to see it as a tightrope that you and the family walk across together. Explanations are the balancing pole that you hold in your hands and gently shift from side to side in order to stay upright and moving along the line. With practice as you move through experience, your skill in using the balancing pole increases; explanations become more and more part of the experience itself.

6. BE HONEST

Honesty is what runs through the other five skills. It keeps you moving in the right direction. Honesty is the essential ingredient of leadership and your default position. It enables you to define problems, track the process, see the patterns, and approach what's missing. When you fear that things have drifted off course, when you are not sure what is going on or what you are going to do, when you feel confused and worry that you made a mistake (gulp!), being open and saying this to the family—that we've moved off course, I'm feeling confused, I'm not sure what to say in response—keeps you responsible, models authenticity, and reduces the pressure to do it right or have all the answers. You are not giving up your leadership, you are merely telling the family that it's time to regroup and check the map.

For those new to family therapy, this can seem like a difficult stance to take. It's all too easy to feel that you need to have all the answers, that the family will see you as incompetent, that if you say what you think, they'll get angry, they'll get even more depressed, and they won't be able to handle it. But remember that the beauty of family therapy is that you don't have to work so hard, you don't have to be the one to crack the case, to get something absolutely right. By changing the process and patterns you are solving the problem. If you have a question and don't have the answer, don't panic, you're not alone. Throw it back to the family and ask them to figure it out with you. If you feel stuck, ask if they feel the same; see if anyone has any ideas. Family therapy has the potential to become good group therapy; your job is to guide the process and keep everyone on task.

This is where your own values, principles, and philosophy come into play. Mine tell me that it is better to show integrity and to match my words, actions, and emotions; that my honesty encourages others to be honest as well; and that supporting greater integrity and honesty is, when you think about it, what therapy really is all about.

There you have it, the basic six of family therapy, the skills that can keep you on track and sane. Match them not only against your own conception of family therapy but against your own personality and values. In the next four chapters we explore how these basics are applied to the beginning, middle, and end stages of family therapy.

Looking Within: Chapter 3 Exercises

1. It is easier to develop skills when you're not under performance pressure. Increase your sensitivity to what's missing by looking for it in others outside the clinical sessions. Sit back and watch what emerges over the next couple of staff meetings or consults with other therapists. Track your own emotions and behaviors: which are hard for you to show, feel, and see? Try showing, feeling, and seeing them and watch what happens.

2. Try being honest outside the clinical room—not big honesty in the form of confession, but small honesty in the form of staying attuned to your own inner process as you interact with someone, matching your words and inner feelings. Undoubtedly you do this well already with certain people in your life (your daughter, your spouse, your best friend); try building courage with someone where it is less comfortable (a stranger, your supervisor, one of your parents). Be sure to pat yourself on the back for the effort regardless of how you think it turns out.

3. Practice tracking the process. In a conversation, focus less on content

and more on the process. When the other person trails off in a sentence, ask him to pick it up again and finish it. When he uses some abstract word, ask him to give you an example to make it more precise and concrete, and see what happens emotionally. If he makes a face when you make a comment, ask the person about his reaction: "It seems like you don't agree," or "You're getting quiet. Are you bored, am I talking too much?" Again, the content is not important; focus instead on the process.

chapter 4

In the Beginning

Great Expectations

*M*eeting someone new is always so awkward. It's easy for you to worry about what may happen: "Will the family start arguing?"; "Will they expect me to tell them how to fix their child's encopresis in the first session?"; "What if the teenager refuses to talk or stomps out?" On top of that you're already feeling a bit frazzled because your car decided to break down in the middle of the interstate, and then the director has just come around *again*, not too subtly reminding everyone how billing income is down and that, by the way, your performance evaluation is coming up next month. Ugh.

But from the family's side of the room, they have anxieties of their own: "Will I be liked?"; "Will the kids misbehave and embarrass us?"; "Will I have to talk about my abortion?"; "Is Meg going to bring up that one time I got drunk and slapped her?"; "Is this guy going to think that this is all my fault?"

Yes, beginnings are always difficult for everyone, and even if you're a seasoned clinician, it's easy to feel a flutter of anxiety when a new family first walks into the office. And as mentioned earlier, the clients of today are much different from those of 10 or 20 years ago. Through websites, television, and media, clients are more knowledgeable about the therapy process; with online therapy shopping they have more choices and come with clearer expectations. With insurance restricting sessions, limited sessions due to waiting lists, and the instant gratification of technology, they and you are often seeking quick results. So the pressure is there, especially in the first session, to hit the ground running. You can't afford to spend a large chunk of the session filling out paperwork or nodding your head and simply listening. Clients need to feel and think differently at the end of the first session than at the beginning or they won't come back. By the time those butterflies have subsided on both sides of the room, both you and the family need to begin to share a vision of what can be, and experience the feeling that this therapy might actually work.

In this chapter we present a map for the first session, defining the goals, tasks, and tools. In the following chapter we look at the process: how to actually conduct the first session and pull these elements together to create a successful beginning and firm foundation.

FIRST-SESSION GOALS

Allen and Terry Adamson come in with their two sons, Daniel, age 12, and Brian, 10. The boys are constantly at each other's throats, says Dad, are doing poorly in school, and to cap it all off Daniel was recently caught breaking into a neighbor's house with a couple of his friends. Both parents agree that the boys haven't gotten along since Brian was old enough to crawl, but things have been especially difficult over the last 6 months. They had tried therapy once before, a few months back, but only went one time. All the therapist did, they said, was ask a bunch of questions, gave no suggestions, and only seemed interested in scheduling another appointment. They thought it was a waste of time.

Here you have your presenting problem. Your mind is probably already racing ahead—formulating, based on your theory—possible hypotheses and questions to ask. But before you start scrambling let's map out what you need to accomplish in the first session.

Think about the last time you went to see your primary care physician. Maybe you woke up with some ugly rash on your arm and you had no idea how it got there. You Googled rashes, went on WebMD, saw all the terrible pictures of rashes that looked a bit like yours, and read dire prognoses of the rash spreading all over your body in 24 hours. So you go to see your doctor, feeling more than a bit anxious. And what does he do? The doctor listens to what you have to say, looks at the rash with a magnifying glass, maybe does some quick blood work to see if there is anything unusual, and asks you questions: "What have you been doing in the last 24 hours?"; "What did you eat?"; "Were you in the woods?"; "Do you have any other symptoms?" Then the doctor gives you feedback: No, it is likely not the skin rot you read about online, but a contact dermatitis, and if you use the cream he prescribes for 5 days, it should clear up. If the rash is not better in 3 days, give her a call.

Do you feel better when you walk out, less anxious, more hopeful? Absolutely, and the doctor does this in 15 minutes. The Adamsons and most families are looking for exactly the same experience: less anxious, more hopeful, a clear path toward making things better. So what do we need to accomplish in that first session to get there? Here are our goals:

- Build rapport.
- Create new/deeper conversations.
- Assess the problem and the family.
- Change the emotional climate in the room.
- Offer a new view of the problem and a preliminary treatment plan.

Let's take a look at these one by one.

Build Rapport

You can ask all the smart questions in the world, but it won't matter if Allen and Terry think you don't understand, don't care about how they feel, or think that you are incompetent. The same is true with you and your family doctor. Rapport is the matter of building the relationship, conveying competence and trust, and being sensitive to the family's needs and fears as you gently lead them in and out of their anxiety. Without rapport, without an emotional connection to you, your clients will be too frightened and will refuse to move. They'll shut down or not come back. Rapport and safety go hand in hand.

So how do you build rapport? Some simple techniques follow:

Courtesy

Address everyone by name, invite them to sit down, apologize if you were a few minutes late. Listen to what each person says, give each a chance to speak, and show you're listening by not interrupting and by making eye contact.

Matching Body Posture, Voice Tone, Language, and Perceptual System

You can mirror the body posture of the person talking: crossing legs, leaning forward. You can also match the tone: the energy of the 6-year-old, the quiet hunched-over sound of the teen. If the father throws in cuss words, throw in a couple yourself; if the mother is a scientist, talk about research findings. Use the skills of neurolinguistic programming and talk the language of each person's perceptual system: "Allen, how do you *see* the problem?"; "Terry, how do you *feel* about what Brian just said?"; "Daniel, how do you *handle* it when your dad blows up at you?"

Being Conscious of Dress

Your clothing reflects an impression, like it or not. You want to appear professional, but not cause your clients to feel uncomfortable or out of place. That doesn't mean you need to wear construction boots when seeing the dad who is a carpenter, but you also don't want to wear the three-piece power suit unless there is a particular reason that you want to appear more authoritative. Sometimes you do (hence, the white coats of doctors), to meet client expectations, but at times to bolster your own self-confidence. The important point is to be mindful—don't throw on whatever just because you forgot to do the laundry.

Being Sensitive to Differences

In recent years much has been written about culture and its impact on clinical practice. All of us know that the clients' racial, ethnic, religious, and cultural backgrounds shape their expectations of therapy, family structure and family values, the role of the parents and their children, and the ways decisions are made and priorities are set. Familiarizing yourself with these cultural differences is an important foundation for your work. But you don't need an encyclopedic knowledge of various cultural values as much as a respectful attitude. This means raising differences rather than dismissing them, showing inquisitiveness and interest in their uniqueness. You can demonstrate this simply by asking questions: "You mentioned that you are Hindu (or Muslim or Jewish or born-again Christian)—can you tell me how your religious beliefs shape your family values?"; "Every family is different—what are some of the values or beliefs that you feel make your family unique and special?"; "Because I am not Latino myself, I wonder if you can tell me how your heritage has influenced your family values." Families appreciate the opportunity to discuss their particular view of life. By asking and listening carefully, you are showing respect for their views and a willingness to incorporate them in your working partnership.

Actively Listening

You show that you understand not by saying "I understand," which can often sound phony. By inviting clients to explain more in order to help you understand—"I'm not quite sure I understand. Can you tell me more . . . ?"—you acknowledge the emotions underlying their statements: "Allen, it must be really frustrating for you"; "Terry, you sound really worried about Daniel"; "Daniel, I bet you feel like your folks are always on your back."

Actively listening is probably the most basic and powerful means of building rapport: the fact that the individual feels heard. This is what the good family physician does when she asks what's wrong and takes the time to sincerely listen to what you have to say.

You can take this one step further by listening for clues that tell what not to do as well. The Adamsons said they thought their last experience with therapy wasn't helpful because the clinician only asked questions and gave no feedback. Note to self: Make sure you give feedback. Similarly, if a teen says that his parents are always lecturing him, you want to be careful that you don't sound like you're lecturing when talking with the teen. If the mother makes a quick reference to her critical father or husband, you want to be careful that you don't sound like yet another male who is critical.

Therapy at some basic level is being the ideal parent or spouse. Give people what they didn't get or need most: sensitivity, support, encouragement, safety, and appreciation. Hearing how they describe past and present relationships tells you what wounds and wounding to avoid and how to best resonate with clients. Actively listening is not being manipulative or insincere, it's sensitive and deliberate, combining your own empathy with your clinical judgment and skill.

Create New/Deeper Conversations

There is nothing that could be more exasperating for a family than to spend 15 minutes filling out forms, and then another 35 minutes answering question after question, some of which seem to them totally unrelated to the problem ("So how do you get along as a couple?"; "Any complications during pregnancy?"), only to have the therapist suddenly look at his or her watch and say, "Wow, looks like we ran out of time. Let's continue this next week. How about the same time?" and send the family on their way. As soon as they hit the hallway, they're thinking, "Continue what? Wasting my time?!" No surprise when they don't show up the next week.

Just as you are expecting to walk out of your doctor's office with something—hopefully a prescription, at most some lab work, tentative diagnosis, and a referral to a specialist—before that first session ends, families like the Adamsons are expecting not only to be heard, but also to hear something useful: what you think is going on, who really has the problem, what fancy test you're going to do next time to tell what is really going on, what they should do this week when the fighting breaks out again, something. To walk out feeling that they just covered the exact same ground they did with the other therapist leaves them wondering what's different this time, why they bothered to come.

To say you need to create new, deeper conversations means that you are essentially starting treatment in that first session. We all learn about assessment and treatment—Act 1, Act 2—one following from the other. While this seems to make logical sense, it's better to think of treatment as not coming after assessment as much as running alongside it. Treatment, in fact, becomes part of the assessment process. By asking the mother to say something positive to her daughter, rather than constantly criticizing, right there in the room you are able to see how willing she is to follow your suggestions, how hard it is for her to actually do it, and whether switching from nagging to praise actually helps change the daughter's reactions. By making a homework assignment, for example, you not only give the family a way to work on the problem, you give yourself a way of finding out what works or doesn't work with this particular family.

You create deeper conversations and start treatment by focusing on the basics. You determine who has and what is the problem: Terry is worried about Brian, Allen is mad at Daniel, Daniel is upset about school. You block the dysfunctional patterns. If the Adamsons's complaint is that the boys are fighting too much at home, you don't want to allow the boys to argue for too long in the office, or have the parents repeat over and over again their ineffective way of handling it, such as scolding the boys but not stopping them. If dysfunctional patterns continue for too long in the session, the family is going to feel that therapy isn't much different from what they do at home for free. You ask questions about what's missing: "You mentioned 'things' in the past—what kind of 'things' are you talking about?"; "You're understandably focusing a lot on your son—can you tell me something about your daughter?" You have the courage to ask the hard questions, to move into areas that in everyday conversation others stay away from, that they think about but are afraid to bring up: "Do you worry that your wife is going to eventually get fed up and possibly leave if things don't change?"; "Are you afraid that your son will struggle as you did?"; "Do you feel that the school is too involved and that they need to mind their own business?" You carefully track the process by asking Allen and Terry to describe how they each handle Daniel and point out how easily they disagree. You seek to create an experience by asking Allen to sit next to Daniel and express to him his feelings about the break-in.

Throughout it all you demonstrate honesty and leadership to help everyone feel safe, so that your silence is not mistaken for consent. The family learns that therapy is an active process of working together to solve problems, rather than just answering your questions and getting advice. By creating these deeper conversations you begin to change the story that each holds on to, and you create the vision of what can be, countering their fear that things will always remain the same.

Assess the Problem and the Family

Deeper conversations are the beginnings of treatment and the medium for assessment. In the course of family therapy you will shift back and forth between (1) time spent in sessions finding out about something you need to know (for example, Bobby's school history, why the parents got divorced, the grandmother's problems with depression, how well the behavioral chart worked last week) and information that helps you better understand the problem and develop or fine-tune a treatment plan; and (2) time spent within the session helping the family reach their goals: providing information about the problem, helping them learn and practice new skills (for example, the father listening to his son instead of criticizing, the oldest daughter staying out of the fights between the parents), gaining new insights (for example, helping the mother see how she is treating her oldest daughter more like an adult friend than a teenager), and discussing in a safe environment issues important to them (for example, the big fight over the weekend or the couple's sexual problems). Most of what you do will be of the latter type—helping the family reach their goals—most of the information gathering obviously takes place in this beginning stage.

However, deciding what you need to know and finding it out can seem overwhelming. Here are some key questions to ask yourself and their implications for treatment.

What Keeps This Family from Solving These Problems on Their Own?

What this question raises is the difference between learning problems and problems about learning. Not all problems have to be complex and convoluted, and sometimes what the family needs is just some information and instruction. Eight-year-old John was recently diagnosed with ADHD and placed on medication, but the physician suggested the parents see you for help with everyday management. Here you talk about the need to set structure and routines at home, to define the expectations about John's behavior in Walmart while they are still sitting in the Walmart parking lot, about coordinating homework assignments with his teachers, and so on. Sometimes what the family is doing is already on target, but just needs to be tweaked—their use of time-outs with the 4-year-old; the father's combination of Alcoholics Anonymous (AA) meetings and increased exercise for his recovery; the time-outs need to be shorter or in the child's bedroom; the father needs to increase his meetings when under stress or have daily contact with his sponsor—to make what they are already doing more effective.

But sometimes sorting whether it is a learning problem or problem about learning is not so easy. Is this mother struggling with her teenage daughter because (1) the mother doesn't know how to communicate with a teen and offer more choices, and instead is micromanaging her daughter the same way she did when she was 8; or (2) the daughter gets explosive and the mother, who has a history of being in abusive relationships, gets emotionally triggered and battles with her more as an adult than as a parent? Are these parents having trouble getting their children to get to bed because (1) they don't understand the importance of routines for young children, or (2) when the mother is out of town on business, the children whine, push the father to let them stay up later, and he gives in?

Skills, emotions, or both? Again, you don't have to know the answer, but you ask yourself the question and then ask them: "So you both had an argument yesterday about what your daughter was going to wear to school. I'm wondering why. Does this happen every morning? Do you feel, Mom, that you should have a say about what your daughter wears to school, or was yesterday different? How? Why do you think this turned into a big argument?" Or "It sounds like you both agree that the kids should have a set bedtime, but Dad, it sounds like when you are home with them on your own, they begin to give you a hard time and push to stay up later. I'm wondering why. Do you maybe feel that bedtimes don't need to be so set, or is it something else—that their whining rattles you and you give in, or that when your wife is away you don't have to be so strict?"

Sorting this out helps you know what to do next. If it is about parenting skills, you can provide some education and give specific steps to put new behaviors in place. If it is more about emotional triggers, take the time to unravel them: What does the mom begin to feel and think when her daughter gets angry, what about the whining rattles the dad so much, or how does he think about rules and routines differently when his wife is not there?

What Are the Family's Strengths?

With so much of the focus on problems and dysfunction it's easy to overlook your other partner in healing, namely, the family's strengths. When we think of strengths we often think of the obvious—they are economically stable, show insight and compassion, have external supports—the hold-the-line grandmother, the concerned teacher, the church group that is more like an extended family. But often the simplest and most potent sign of strength is that the family comes to see you: they are willing, albeit in varying degrees, to sit together in your office; talk to a stranger about their worry that their children will struggle as they did; or that their own childhoods will some- how haunt those of their children. They sit with the hope that things can be better.

Often they cannot articulate or define these strengths. The tun- nel vision of their problems and depression, and the expectation of your judgment gets in the way. You can articulate the strengths, and one of your jobs is to underscore what they are doing well, to draw out those stories of resiliency, define the good intentions beneath the not-so-good behaviors, and commend them for their willing- ness to reach out for help. By affirming them you are building on the small but decisive step that they have taken.

How Well Can the Family Members Communicate with One Another?

Lots of screaming is not good, nor is shutting down, turning away, stomping out, or waving fingers. Good communication is, of course, the elementary process that binds both good family life and good therapy, and where families often struggle. Your job is to assess by watching, educating, and teaching skills—letting everyone speak, not interrupting, making "I" statements, talking about feelings rather than facts, and so on—and by politely pointing out to the family members when basic rules of communication are being vio- lated and getting them back on track. This in itself works like a tow truck to get them out of the verbal ditch, and begin solving their problems on their own more effectively. In the first session, facilitating good *communication is often a priority and the first step in treatment.*

Are There Cracks in the Family Structure?

One of the ways your family doctor assesses your presenting prob- lem is by comparing your signs and symptoms against a healthy norm. He checks your urine and finds out that your pH is higher than it should be, or takes your blood pressure and finds that it is 30 points above the normal range. By having a healthy range to measure against, the doctor has a starting point for a diagnosis and treatment.

You can do the same by comparing the family in the room against a healthy family structure. Here we move into structural family therapy models that we can represent with the following diagram:

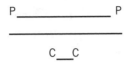

The parents are represented by P and the children by C. There is a hierarchy in that the parents are on top having more power and control, the children are on the bottom having less, and the solid line in between indicates that there is a clear boundary between the adult and child worlds. The solid line between the parents indicates that they have a solid adult relationship and that they are on the same page in terms of parenting. Even though their styles may be different they agree to expectations, consequences, and so on in managing the children. And if there is a single parent, the same hierarchy is still in place. Finally, the solid lines between the children mean that even with age differences and some amount of sibling rivalry, they can get along and can support each other.

By comparing your family against this model you have a quick means of assessing problems. A few of the common less healthy variations are shown below.

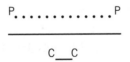

The dotted lines between the parents indicates that they are not working together as a team, are on different pages regarding parenting, and in extreme cases are polarized in that one parent who is strict causes the other parent to compensate by being overly lenient. What happens in these situations is that the children are constantly testing because expectations are not clear or are playing one parent against the other to get their way. What needs to be fixed? The parents need to work together as a team.

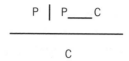

The vertical line between the parents indicates that they are disengaged and the move of one child to the parent's side indicates a surrogate relationship. Here we could imagine one parent using a teen as a confidant and treating her more like an adult; the hierarchy is broken and the teen then feels entitled. Often, too, the other parent may have his own form of solace in an affair or addiction: alcoholism or workaholism. Again, what needs to be fixed? The walls in the marital relationship need to come down, and the child needs to be bumped back down to the child group.

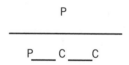

What we see is that one parent is alone and in charge, and the other parent is joined below with the children. Essentially this parent has no power, is treated as one of the children, the children treat this parent as a peer, and sometimes the disempowered parent will be a ringleader for the children leading periodic attacks against the other parent. While the controlling parent has power, what the diagram clearly shows is that she is isolated and alone. What needs to be fixed? The other parent needs to move up and regain power, and both parents need to work together as a team and have a good adult relationship.

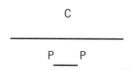

Finally, in some ways this is a worst-case scenario. Here we have not a parent on top but a child or usually a teen. He is emotionally and/or physically running the family rather than the parents. Sometimes this occurs because the teen is filling in for incapacitated parents—there may be severe illness or addiction that keeps the parents from fulfilling their roles. In the more dysfunctional version, the child acts out, sets the emotional tone, the parents feel helpless, and the teen feels entitled to do whatever he wants. What needs to be fixed? In either scenario the child needs to be bumped down. If the child is filling in for the parents, often some sort of foster care situation needs to be created or the parents get the support or treatment they need to fulfill their roles as caretakers; if the child is acting out and entitled, often the courts need to get involved to put limits on the child.

So, like the physician in that first session, you compare what the family presents against where they should be. You take into consideration cultural and ethnic differences—a certain role for the father or mother, or, for example, a more child-centered structure based on their values—to see how structure fuels the presenting problems. And then you can ask questions and make observations such as the following to help you determine where the gaps lie:

Even though their styles may be different, do both parents agree on rules and expectations for the children? Are there areas they disagree about? How do they handle them?

Do the parents feel they are able to get the support they need from each other? Do they do things together as a couple?

How do the parents feel the children get along with each other?

How do the children feel they get along with each other?

Do the parents disagree in the room about managing the children? Do they describe themselves being polarized?

Do the parents say they have no time for each other, are child- or work-centered, or seem disengaged from each other in the room?

Are the children kind to each other or do they bicker or jockey for parent attention?

Does one parent and the children gang up against the other parent?

Is there one child who is driving the session process and the parents seem unable to contain her?

How "Adult" Are the Adults?

If the structural model provides us with a means of assessing a family's health, Bowen's concept of differentiation provides us with a means of assessing the relationship and individual health of the adults (Bowen, 1993).

What does it mean to be a differentiated adult? Some guidelines (Gilbert, 1992; Taibbi, 2013) follow:

- Being able to take responsibility for one's emotions, behaviors, and problems, rather than blaming others, or being dependent on others to relieve one's distress.
- Being able to be assertive rather than aggressive or passive when problems arise.
- Being able to be emotionally supportive of others without being controlling or overresponsible.
- Being able to be emotionally calm; not reacting in kind to anger or anxiety of others.
- Being able to view others as anxious or fearful (rather than malicious or manipulative) in conflict.
- Being able to be calm, thoughtful, and proactive in decision making.

In law, there is a concept known as the "reasonable man" defense, that is, asking the question of what would we expect a reasonable person to do in a given situation and using it as a point of comparison and contrast. In therapy, Bowen's differentiated self, as Gilbert (1992) notes, becomes the reasonable man, and once again you compare and contrast: What's missing?; What do these adults struggle to do?; Is there a gap between what they present and what we would expect an emotionally healthy, responsible adult to be like in these situations? When you hear blaming rather than self-responsibility, blasting anger rather than assertiveness, being overwhelmed and dependent on others rather than being independent and self-controlled, you already have a good idea of what needs to change: Allen, for example, needs support to be more assertive rather than critical or angry; or Terry needs ways of managing her anxiety when she is alone with the boys; or both of them need to have ways of tackling problems as they emerge, rather than ignoring them until they build up and explode.

What Are the Family's Expectations about Therapy?

I've met parents who drop their 8- or 10-year-old child off at the front door of the agency for a first appointment. When I ask the child where the parents are, she says that they are sitting out in the car listening to the radio, or they needed to go to the grocery store and will be out front in an hour, to pick up the child. Similarly, I've met husbands who imagine that you will excuse them after a few minutes and have an intimate "girl talk" with their wives to help them to be less nervous about sex, mothers who ask if you can hypnotize their daughters so they will be less obsessed about their boyfriends, or parents who expect that by the end of the first session you'll write a letter to the school principal recommending that their daughter be readmitted back into school.

Some family's expectations are realistic (they will need to come a few times together as a family; you'll help them communicate better), but others are not (you'll have a talk with the IP, whether it is the acting-out kid, the drinking dad, or the don't-care teen, and straighten him out; you'll tell the couple whether or not they should go ahead and get divorced). Finding out specifically what expectations the family had in mind—"How did you hope I could help you?; What do you think counseling will be like?"—and either giving them what they expect, or explaining why you can't or won't is essential.

Underneath the family's expectations lie their own theories about the presenting problem. Every family has a theory about the cause of the problem they face, even when they say at first that they have no idea: it's biological ("He had a lot of high fevers when he was a baby and I think it caused brain damage") or genetic ("He's just like my uncle who acted the same way"); it's because someone else doesn't like them ("The school's got it in for our family"); it's the result of some past trauma ("Our house burned down last year"), past karma or God's punishment ("I'm being punished for having an abortion when I was a teenager"), poor parenting ("She lived with her father who never had any rules"), or something else. We all instinctively create some explanation for our problems rather than live with the uncertainty of having none.

Finding out in the first session the family's theory or theories for the problem is important because they tell you where the family believes the solutions lie. Terry's believing that the boys are doing poorly in school because the teachers don't like them is a very different focus than if she thinks it is because she doesn't spend enough time helping them with their homework or if she feels they have an undiagnosed learning disability. From your perspective as a family therapist your challenge is to expand the definition of the problem to include the involvement of the entire family, offer new ideas in order to reshape their theory, and experientially connect the problem as they see it to the patterns within the family. Knowing their theory gives you the starting point linking their ideas with your own.

Finally, we can combine the concepts of family structure and expectations to describe some of the most common family presentations. Here they are, along with their characteristics, expectations, your clinical goals, and, in order to be effective, traps you ought to avoid (what not to do) in order not to replicate the dysfunctional patterns:

THE "FIX MY CHILD" PARENTS

Characteristics: Parents present a united picture of the identified child as the cause and solution of his or her own and the family's problems.

Expectations: To work with the child individually and "fix" her.

Goals: Engage with parents by initially talking to them in the language of the child's problem (for example, "What do you do when Frank gives you a *hard time*?"); assess the child; help parents see the child's behavior in a new light (for example, educate them about ADHD) or as the outcome of a larger family process; empower parents to be change agents within the family.

What not to do: Do only individual therapy with the child beyond the initial assessment.

THE ENMESHED VERSUS DISENGAGED PARENTS

Characteristics: In these families one parent, often the mother, is overly involved with the children, is supportive, and has difficulty setting structure or limits—that is, the parent is enmeshed. The other parent, often the father, seems distant and aloof, may be a heavy-handed disciplinarian, and struggles to be supportive— that is, this parent is disengaged and distant, and parents are often polarized.

Expectations: If the enmeshed parent comes in without the partner, he wants your help managing the children when the other parent is not there or uninvolved. If they come in together, they argue, the enmeshed parent wanting you to convince the other to be less strict, the distant parent wanting you to tell the other to be more firm.

Goals: Bring both parents into the therapy process. Help parents see how it's not the other parent who is the problem, but their differences and polarization. Work toward improving their relationship and creating a united front. Help the distant parent support the other in setting boundaries, freeing and encouraging the strict parent to be more nurturing.

What not to do: Re-create the structure in therapy—that is, ignore the distant parent, re-create the disciplinarian's role in the session as the limit setter of the children and leave the other parent unempowered, or side with one parent rather than helping them both work together as a team.

THE OVERWHELMED SINGLE PARENT

Characteristics: Chaotic family, little structure or consistency, often parent has a history of abuse.

Expectations: Look to you to create structure, enforce rules, reduce chaos.

Goals: Rather than taking over, empower the parent through skill building, support. Divide problems into more manageable segments and help reduce environmental stressors so parent is less overwhelmed.

What not to do: Take over and rescue parent; create unreasonable dependency upon you; become overwhelmed yourself.

THE TRANSITIONAL FAMILY

Characteristics: Essentially a combination of the dynamics of the enmeshed/disengaged parents and the overwhelmed single parent. The disciplinarian leaves the family; the remaining parent is unable to set structure; one of the children steps up to replace the missing parent, then feels entitled and may even be abusive toward the remaining parent.

Expectations: Have you rein in the entitled child.

Goals: Develop limit-setting and structure-setting skills in parent so she can take charge and the entitled child can step down; facilitate grief over lost parent; help entitled child find a new, healthier role within the family.

What not to do: Replace the missing parent's role in disciplining the children.

THE CRISIS FAMILY

Characteristics: Family easily feels victimized by life events, takes a reactive stance to problems, often has an "us versus the world" mind-set.

Expectations: Help them manage the current crisis.

Goals: Build trust by initially encouraging family to contact you when in crisis; help family move from the black-and-white perspective ("Either we're in a crisis or we have no problem") by recognizing early signs of problems and taking action.

What not to do: Work harder than the family; create too strong a dependency by maintaining the on-call rescuer role for crises; be reactive in your own behavior and wind up feeling in crisis yourself.

THE REFERRED/NO-PROBLEM FAMILY

Characteristics: Another agency defines the problem, mandates therapy; the family is openly angry or passive–aggressive.

Expectations: To agree with them that the problem isn't a problem and therapy is not necessary.

Goals: Be clear about role; have referral source clarify concerns; explore treatment options and consequences; find a problem/goal that the family is willing to work on.

What not to do: Be the enforcer for the referring agency.

Obviously you will find some variations on these common structures, and we talk about some of them later in more detail. The theme running through all of them is the expectation that you will fill in some hole in the structure, or take charge and manage a problem—do what they cannot—rather than your helping them learn how to do this themselves. By quickly defining the family's expectations, reshaping them, and being aware of what you need to do to avoid replicating the problem, you can then support the family members in learning the skills they need to be more successful in running their lives and families.

What Is the Family's Emotional Range?

This is another case of looking for what's missing. The ability to express a wide range of emotions is like having a full scale of notes upon which we create the melodies of our lives. For many of us, however, our range is limited, and some of us are truly one-note johnnies (for example, I'm sad, I get angry; I'm frustrated, I get angry; I feel lonely, I get angry). Our emotional flexibility is shaped by social and cultural norms (men don't cry, women aren't supposed to get angry), and by the models we absorbed in our childhoods within the family. Often emotions are suppressed or distorted through drugs or alcohol, acted out (for example, spending too much money, having affairs), or shrouded in an ever-present cloud of anxiety. Having a limited emotional range, like a limited verbal vocabulary, can cause others to misinterpret you or not really understand what your inner world is like.

In a family session you may see emotional range spread out among the various family members—for example, Dad only gets mad, Mom always cries, Jake is disruptive in class, or Emily gets depressed—where each relies on his or her own comfortable emotion and only together is the family able to complete the emotional scale. Often one person's designated emotion serves as a vicarious outlet for one or more of the others: Mom's easy tears express vicariously for Dad his own inexpressible deep sadness, Jake's open hostility toward his father allows Mom to vicariously express her own rage toward Dad as well, or the children's intense sibling rivalry dramatizes the parents' more subtle marital tensions. The need for and dependence on these indirect emotional outlets can be strong and difficult to give up. Even when the consequences are negative (Jake and his father have an awful relationship), the person needing the emotional outlet will subtly reinforce them, locking the family members into unhealthy patterns.

Simply asking who feels what or observing the process will tell you what's missing in each person's emotional life, and in what ways the emotional range of each individual needs to expand. Your next step may then be to close off the vicarious outlets (Jake and Dad avoid fighting) in order to enable the others to experience and label their emotions directly.

All this wading into new emotions can raise everyone's anxiety, including your own. As new emotions begin to bubble up, the family's reaction will be to ignore, criticize, or analyze them to death. What these new emotional sprouts need most are recognition, space, and nurturance by you. Let the others know that it's okay, that they don't need to be afraid of Mom's outburst or Dad's tears.

Model good listening, waiting, compassion, and positive feedback for taking the risk; allow the process to unfold. By once again demonstrating the simple courage of moving against your own grain, you help the family see what new experiences can emerge.

What Is the Family's Reaction to You?

The reaction of the different family members to you tells you what you need to do to establish rapport. If Dad is angry and silent, your goal is to calm him down and get him talking. Generally all you need to do is explicitly say that you understand and accept his feeling angry. If Mom seems intimidated, your goal would be to get her to relax. You may want to talk about your own frustrations as a parent, or try joking with her a bit to help her see more of your humanity, rather than just your authority.

Their reaction also tells you about your perceived power and influence and suggests ways you can use these effectively. If the parents, for example, seem extremely attentive to what you say, if they look to you as the expert or as having some magical ability to fix their child, you might wonder not only how this stance may be part of the problem (Do they lack confidence as parents and see the solution as completely outside themselves?), but also whether you can use their respect for your abilities to create change more quickly. Are they more likely, for example, to try and use a behavioral chart at home as you suggested in that session? Can you be more directive and they more receptive to the notion that there may be a link between their child's behavior and their tense marital relationship?

On the other hand, if your power is perceived as minimal, if you are quickly dismissed by the key members of the family, and if they start off by challenging what you say or shaking their heads, look for ways to increase your power, such as the following:

- Taking more time to build rapport between you and the members of the family.
- Clarifying their expectations about therapy and your role and specifically address them.
- Letting them know about your qualifications and successes demonstrating your expertise by providing helpful information about the problem.

- Defining your authority, for example, by your ability to write a recommendation letter to the court or the mandate to notify social services.
- Make sure they are behind you before attempting to move ahead into new challenges and changes. You don't want to march ahead only to discover later that they've hung back and you're marching ahead alone.

These eight questions are some of the key areas you can explore in that first session; other questions or variations may come from your own theoretical approach. Taken all together they form a foundation for developing and confirming your own initial hypothesis and setting treatment goals. While this may seem like a lot to gather, much of the information about these questions will come from simple observation and listening; what is left, you can ask about directly. What you want to avoid is getting swallowed up by the family's content and for that you need both a frame for viewing the dynamics and leadership in shaping the process. With practice and growing confidence your ability to cover this ground will become easier.

Change the Emotional Climate in the Room

Building rapport sets a foundation of safety; creating deeper conversations and asking specific assessment questions begins the treatment process by providing the family members with new information about one another and the therapy process, and in turn changes their own perspectives and moods. But it is useful to see changing the emotional climate—that is, helping the family feel differently when they walk out from when they walked in—as a goal in itself. Not only will having this as a goal help you stay alert to opportunities to create an experience, it is this emotional shift that will linger and most strongly help connect the family to both you and the therapy process.

Here are some of the common climate-changing techniques you can proactively use within the session.

Tapping into Softer Emotions through Content

One of the simplest ways of changing the climate in the room is by uncovering new, and often, softer emotions. We're saying soft emotions because anger and frustration are easy—they are often what the family presents first. You want to give voice to these emotions of worry, fear, and sadness that you suspect lie below the surface by asking questions that lead to them, and tracking them until they are revealed. For example, Allen mentions that his father died last year. You may quietly ask Daniel if he misses his grandfather; move toward specificity and ask him what he remembers most about him; ask what they said to each other the last time they met. The content details are not important in themselves, rather it is using the details to stir and define his grief.

Similarly, you may gently ask Terry, who always seems to be yelling at Daniel, to say what she is most afraid of for Daniel if he continues to struggle, or to describe how she felt when Daniel was born, or how she felt when her mother used to scold her—questions that lead Terry to express that softer side of herself that in turn changes the emotions of others there in the room. When this type of probing is successful and new emotions come to the surface that are rarely expressed by that person or within the family, it catches everyone by surprise and creates a powerful shared experience.

Tapping into Softer Emotions through Nonverbal Cues

Rather than changing the content you also tap into these softer emotions by looking for the nonverbal cues: Allen's looking teary though he sounds angry about the last argument, Brian's deep sigh when his mother snaps at him to stop wiggling in his chair. You gently ask Allen what just happened, he's looking sad; you reach over and touch Brian's knee and ask him how he just felt when his mom snapped at him.

The key here to tapping into these emotions is being conscious of how you use your voice. Again, think ideal parent or partner. You want to talk gently and softly to lower the client's defenses. If the client responds by becoming defensive or shuts down, either you are sounding too demanding or harsh, or the client's anxiety is rising because of the question itself. This is where you make an explanatory statement—"I'm asking you about this Terry, because . . . "—again, in a gentle tone. Move back and forth between questions and statements to regulate the family member's anxiety.

Ideal Voice

Another way of tapping into soft emotions and changing the climate is by you saying what the ideal parent or partner may say: the ideal voice. Here you say to Daniel, for example, "Daniel, suppose your mom came to you and said: 'I'm really sorry I got so angry and yelled so much at you last night about breaking into the neighbor's house. But I was so surprised. It makes me so worried. You seem unhappy so much lately, and I don't know why and I wish there was a way for you to feel better.' What would you say, Daniel, if your mom said that?" Now if you say all this in a gentle concerned voice, Daniel is likely to lower his defenses and say something new: that he has been sad, or he's sorry about the break-in. And even if for some reason he doesn't make a shift, you're modeling for the parents how to talk differently—to translate anger into worry, frustration into fear—softer emotions that others can hear better.

Uncovering these emotions through these approaches can quickly change the climate, so be prepared for someone in the room to try and undermine what is happening. Daniel's brother may start picking on him, or Daniel may act up then and there—knock over the garbage can when Terry tears up—or Allen may make a joke about Terry's mother all in an effort to pull Daniel and Terry away from these new emotions. What is happening is that you have broken the pattern and by doing so raised everyone's anxiety to varying degrees. The rule of thumb is that the first thing others will do when a pattern is broken is try to reinstate the pattern. When that happens, gently point it out, stop the dysfunctional behavior, and refocus on the soft emotions again.

Enactments

In order to be successful, enactments require some staging. Focus on a specific topic that two family members have had trouble discussing, and that both have something to gain by talking about. Ask Dad and Brian, for example, to talk right there and then about Brian's push for a larger allowance—what he wants, and what Dad expects, if anything, in the way of responsibilities. Have the two brothers see if they can come up with a plan for sharing game time on the computer. Be clear about what they should try and accomplish, and interrupt only to keep the conversation going, not to preach. You'll know by their awkwardness and hesitation whether everyone is going against their emotional and behavioral grain. The outcome not only tells you about their ability to try something new but unlocks new emotions as the behaviors holding them are broken.

Family Sculpture

If the family seems open and engaged, you can also stage an experiential event: a family sculpture. Have everyone stand up, and ask the IP (or have several family numbers take turns) to create a sculpture of the family as he sees it, without using words. Place everyone in a physical position that represents how he seems to be most of the time (Mom is scowling and shaking her finger, Dad is off in the corner reading the paper), located where each one most often seems to be (Mom is next to sis, Dad is way off in the corner by himself), making sure the sculptor is included. Ask them to change the sculpture to create their view of the ideal family (Mom and Dad are holding hands, with the kids in between). By working the image ("Dad, how does it feel out there all by yourself?"; "Mom, what facial expression do you see yourself having most of the time?") you create images that you can manipulate and work with later. Emotionally, these can be powerful.

Interpretation and Insight

Finally, you can create experience through interpretation and insight: Talk to Dad, for example, about his own childhood, and point out how his own reaction to Daniel's behavior is exactly what he just said he hated in his own father. Mention to the couple how the patterns of their own arguments so well mimic those of the boys, or how the boys' struggles over the computer are similar to their own tensions about individual versus couple time; help Brian acknowledge that though he really wants his dad's attention, his misbehavior doesn't work, and actually only makes matters worse. The insight is always in the eyes of the beholder; it is an insight not because it seems clever to you or is accurate in content, but because of the emotional impact it has on the listener.

Education

While lacking the emotional punch of the other techniques, new information has the power of helping the family see problems in a new light: ADHD as a brain disorder, not a bad kid; the common dissociation that comes with posttraumatic stress; the regression in children that often accompanies a move or the birth of a sibling; the agitation in young children as a symptom of depression, not anger. The problem is seen through a new lens. This is what the family doctor does when reassuring you it isn't the horrible disease you imagined but something more benign and treatable. The new explanation replaces the old and reduces anxiety; tying it then to a treatment plan offers hope.

Creating an experience and changing the emotional climate, however it is achieved, gives the family a fuller sense of what therapy is like, increases intimacy and rapport, and enhances your credibility and their motivation, as well as gives you information about the family members and which approaches (for example, enactments versus education) work.

Offer a New View of the Problem and a Preliminary Treatment Plan

We now reach our last goal for this first session: to present a new view of the problem and a preliminary treatment plan. This is where you pull all that has happened throughout the session together. This is your family doctor's finale where she links together your description of symptoms, the information gathered by his or her questions or tests, and offers a diagnosis and course of action. So you do the same. Here are some examples of summary statements.

> "So you are both worried about your daughter having trouble falling asleep at night. Because of your changing work schedules, it also sounds as if you both are handling bedtimes differently. One of the things that is really helpful for children your daughter's age is to have a set bedtime routine. The structure of it and the inclusion of winding-down activities like reading books can help her relax. I'd like you to both think about a bedtime routine that you think you both could manage and we can map it out together next week. How does that sound?"

"I know you are worried about Sara's struggle with school-work, and Sara, you said you have a hard time paying attention and understanding what the teacher is saying. I think it would be good to talk to the teacher about this, and ask if the school psychologist could do some testing to see if there are some attention problems. I'd be happy to help by talking to the teacher or psychologist. What do you both think about that idea?"

"You all did a great job describing how you feel and though a lot of the problems seem to be between Dad and Jake, it affects you all. We can use our sessions to work on these problems, but I'm most worried about how quickly the arguments between you two escalate. The first step is stopping these arguments. What I'd like you to do is agree not to argue this week, and when things come up that bother you, write them down and we'll talk about them here next week. Are you both willing to do that?"

"You both said that Thomas has not been wanting to go to school since you became ill, and Thomas, you said that you worry about something bad happening to your mom when you're at school. This is separation anxiety and is not unusual in situations like this. Thomas, I'd like you and me to talk and play together next time—Is that okay?—and then I'd like to see you both alone as a couple the following week so we can map out ways to help Thomas feel less anxious. Does that sound like a good idea?"

What we are doing in each of these scenarios is linking the presenting concern with our impressions developed in the session from information we gathered (correlation between school refusal and mother's illness, lack of bedtime routines and inability to go to sleep) and the process we observed (escalation in room between Dad and Jake, tension the boys exhibited when the parents started talking about their own problems) and next steps (see parents alone, develop bedtime routine, discuss week's problems in the next session, contact school about testing). Even if we need more information—from doing play therapy with Thomas or by seeing if Dad and Jake are each able to rein in their anger—the family is left with a sense that you understand the problem, you have a clear idea of what needs to happen next, and through the session process there is a new view of the problem and relief that change can happen.

You can then assign the family homework. Homework is a way of putting the treatment plan into immediate operation and is invaluable for several reasons. It lets the family know that therapy isn't just talking about things for an hour in a room but making changes in their daily lives as well. It keeps the momentum created in the session going. Most important, it gives you a test, by their follow through, of the family's motivation in regard to both your direction and their willingness to make changes at home. It shows you what works and doesn't work (for example, the behavioral chart was too complicated), and where in specific ways the change process breaks down (Mom gives in if the child has a tantrum in a public place). Describe the homework to the family not as a solution to the problem but rather as an experiment to try and see what happens. When they come back next time, you can all use it as a starting point for beginning the session.

But homework, especially in the first session, needn't be elaborate. Often it can be simple observation: the parents noticing when the boys get along, or Terry simply tracking her irritability over the course of a day. It can be concrete, such as assigning the parents to come up with a list of questions they want to discuss next week, asking a mother and daughter to have a 5-minute discussion on what was good during the day, or suggesting that the father try and resist the temptation to leave the house when he starts to get mad. All it needs to be is something that helps the family link the session process with their real lives, and in your judgment, moves family members even slightly outside their normal patterns and comfort zones.

What we have here is a foundation for the first session, the weaving of assessment and treatment, facts and emotions, and creating safety while pushing the family out of their comfort zone. Think about your own way of looking at first sessions, the integration of these ideas with your own style and theoretical approach. In the next chapter we talk about putting these concepts in motion and walk through the details of actually running the session.

Looking Within: Chapter 4 Exercises

1. Practice rapport-building techniques by mirroring body posture, language, perceptual system, and voice tone in conversations with friends and family.

2. If you have had personal experience with therapy, try and remember your own expectations, particularly of those first couple of sessions. If you have not, what would you look for most?

3. What is your own emotional range? What emotions do you have difficulty recognizing in yourself? Are there certain emotions that you depend on others to express for you? Practice increasing your awareness of those less familiar emotions.

4. Some people naturally talk more or less than others. In order to increase your own verbal flexibility, try experimenting in personal conversations with going against your own grain—talking more if you tend to be more quiet, listening more if you tend to lead the conversation—and see what happens.

5. Cracks in the family system: How would you assess your own family of origin? What changes would you have wanted your parents to make?

chapter 5

In the Beginning

Running the Sessions

Unfortunately there's no set script to follow for a first session; what unfolds will obviously depend upon the people, the problem, and your own style. As we discussed in Chapter 4, there are goals and a way of thinking about the first session that can make it not only manageable but foundational. A good first session is like a symphony or a well-written essay in three parts—an opening with a statement of the theme or problem; a section of exploration and assessment; and a return to the opening theme, your feedback and recommendations based on your assessment, and closure—with each part connected to the one before.

In this chapter we look at the process of the first-session flow, and then move on to the subsequent sessions that make up the beginning stages of treatment.

THE PREVIEW

First the preview. This is the information you get prior to the initial session. It may be the intake staff's three-sentence note based on a phone contact with one of the family members that states the problem and its history, along with a demographic checklist form, or it may be your own phone conversation with a family. Whatever the source, this information is generally minimal, often blaming, but usually enough to get your wheels turning and give you ideas for developing an initial hypothesis.

Suppose, for example, you received the intake sheet for the Adamsons of our previous chapter: "Boys fighting a lot; doing poorly in school; Daniel recently caught breaking into a house. Parents self-referred." Treatment planning begins now. Even with this minimum of information you can begin to brainstorm areas for exploration: the ways the parents discipline the children, whether the parents are on the same page, whether the boys are copying or reacting to marital tensions, whether there have been any precipitating factors, the way anger is handled within the family, or practical issues such as whether the courts are involved, and so on. The self-referral could be taken as a strength that they are motivated to make changes.

If you work in a setting where you directly get a phone message from a potential new client, you need to respond. What to do? Call back as soon as possible and if you don't have time to talk on the phone—you're in-between meetings—call and leave a message that you received her call and that you will try back at a certain time or that she should leave a message with questions and more information. This is part of rapport building and your quick response goes a long way, giving the potential client a sense that you are professional, considerate, and reliable.

When you finally get the caller on the phone he undoubtedly talks about the immediate problems facing the family: "My son is having trouble going to sleep"; "My wife and I are getting a divorce and we don't know what to say to the children"; "My parents are elderly and my sister and I are worried that my mother is drinking too much and is depressed." Here you ask about what services they had in mind: "That you give us ideas for helping my child go to sleep"; "That we come in with our children and we all talk about the divorce"; "That my other siblings come in as well and we stage an intervention." What is the gap between their expectation and what you do?

Perhaps none: "Yes, come in with your husband and we can talk about techniques for helping your child go to sleep"; "Yes, come in with your children and we can have a safe forum for talking with them about your upcoming divorce." Or their expectations are far removed from what you can offer: "No, I think it would be best to bring you child in with you so I can understand better about why sleep is a problem" or "No, I'm not a specialist in alcoholism, but I can refer you to someone who is experienced in providing exactly what you are looking for." Whatever you say, you again are building rapport literally as you speak, by being an active listener and empathizing with what she feels.

What you don't want to do is to turn the phone conversation into a mini individual therapy session. Why? Because it unbalances the larger system. Rather than starting with an even playing field where parents are seeing you as the neutral professional, the family session starts with one parent already sharing his side of the story and the other worrying about what's been disclosed and that you are now biased. So keep it short. What you want to get out of this initial encounter is preliminary information about the presenting problem, an ability to answer client questions about services, clarify expectations, explain your approach, and help you begin to formulate ideas about the problems, treatment, and format.

Whom to See

Because family therapy is a way of thinking about families, not squeezing eight people into a room, you can decide whom you want to see at that first session. Some clinicians in cases like the Adamsons prefer to see the parents alone first. This gives them an opportunity to gather all the background information they need and allows them to explore the couple's ability to form a united front, as well as assess the marital relationship, bond with them, and talk about strategies they can begin to implement right away.

The downsides are that you are only seeing the problems through the parents' eyes—they may not be good reporters of the interactional patterns, or their concerns about "looking good" to you may severely slant their point of view—and preteens or adolescents entering a second session often feel mistrustful. They worry that unfair things have been said about them behind their backs (and often they have), that the adults are plotting behind their backs, and that you have taken their parents' point of view. You'll have to work harder to gain their trust by showing your openness, or by spending enough individual time with them that they feel you understand their point of view.

Seeing the entire family can sidestep these issues, but for new family therapists this can seem overwhelming at first. If so, consider dividing the initial session into smaller, more manageable groups or work with a cotherapist who can lend support and perspective. Other times, the parents have strong preferences ("I think it would be good for me and my husband to give you some background"), suggestions about what they feel may work the best ("Yes, I think Sue might feel ganged up on and say nothing if it's just the three of us and you; I can bring in the other kids"), or logistics ("My oldest daughter is out of town and wouldn't be able to come till next month; could we start without her?").

All of these are clinical decisions on your side: questions of style, skill, and clinical approaches. While it's a good idea to welcome the entire family to come in if they so choose, and be willing to accommodate their preferences, if asked by parents who should come to the first session, insert your own preferences. If the children are young, many clinicians will ask to see the parents by themselves. Why? There are two reasons: Unless your style is to do a play therapy assessment in the first session, or have a room that is well laid out to keep young children occupied, the younger children can be a distraction ("Our marriage? . . . hmmm, well, I . . . Ben! Put that down!"). The bigger reason is that young children are sensitive to changes in parenting and often simple changes you may suggest in routine or reaction by parents is sufficient to improve behaviors. In these cases you are the sideline coach who helps empower the parents to be the therapists.

Similarly, if there are clear parenting issues (for example, a new stepfamily with parents disagreeing about how to manage the children), having the parents come in alone to resolve their differences, rather than replaying their divisions in front of the family, seems to be a good initial approach. Older children and teens—who are able to verbally express how they feel—and younger children who can benefit by having the support of older siblings in the room are obviously good candidates for coming in with parents. From there you can decide on the next steps: some modified play therapy for tweens, individual teen therapy, meeting with the sibling group alone, or other combinations. Be clinically deliberate; choose what best fits your comfort and style with parent expectations.

THE OPENING: RAPPORT BUILDING,
DEFINING PRESENTING PROBLEMS

Armed with your preliminary information and ideas, you're ready to see the family. Ideally the paperwork has not been too time-consuming or it has been sent ahead with pertinent information—HIPPA, confidentiality, exceptions to confidentiality (child/elder abuse, suicidality), billing, cancellation policy—so you don't have to do a formal presentation of these areas and can hit the ground running. You meet them in the waiting room, lead them to your office, and make sure everyone has a seat. A brief introduction of yourself, or the agency if they have never been there before, is helpful. Even if you talked to one of the parents on the phone, don't assume that any information was passed along. How formal or descriptive your introduction depends on your own style, but needs to match the style and culture of the family. This is a good time to ask if any of them have been in counseling or therapy before. Here the Adamsons say they went one time to see someone and never went back, or Allen says that he had individual therapy in college for depression, or that one of the boys has been talking with the guidance counselor at school, or that no, this is their first experience.

You want to note what they say but this is not a time to go into the details of their clinical history. Their response, however, does give you an opportunity to talk about your own or the agency's approach: that you do brief or time-limited therapy, or longer-term psychodynamic work, or focus on families, work with a psychiatrist, and so on. This is about shaping expectations, and for families new to therapy, helping them understand what to expect, which may be very different from what they imagined.

Shift to small talk: "Allen, where do you work?"; "Terry, what's it like to teach third grade?"; "Brian, do you play soccer?"; "Daniel, do you like the new gym teacher at your school?" Or, to a small child: "What's your best friend's name?" This beginning can involve one question per person, or a brief chat with each one. This is connecting—part of building rapport, part of assessing the anxiety of each person as well as his ability and willingness to talk, to participate spontaneously and stray beyond your question, to express his attitude toward you. Here you can mirror body posture and voice tone to build rapport. By asking questions you are taking charge, but more important, you are helping the family to hear and get used to your voice, allowing them to settle down and become oriented before they have to talk about themselves.

There's a fine line here, of course, between establishing rapport and calming everyone down, and procrastinating in order to avoid your own anxiety; make small talk too long and they'll begin to feel like you are wasting their time. Once everyone seems settled, move on.

Watch the Clock

They say in sports that whoever controls the ball controls the clock, and in family therapy you control the ball . . . and the clock. You need to watch the time, not only so that you'll be on time for your next appointment but because in the initial session you have a lot to accomplish in a relatively short amount of time and pacing is important. What you don't want to do is have Terry start the conversation and never stop, or worse yet, have Terry start, then break down and cry, and leave you with little time to help her calm down or talk to anyone else in the family. Allen will feel upset that you have only heard Terry's side of the story and everyone will feel emotionally overwhelmed; without your leadership or feedback they will feel that little was gained from the session. You can use the clock to pace yourself through the stages of the session and to help you gauge whether you have enough time to pursue strong emotional avenues. This opening should only take you a few minutes.

"Tell Me Why You're Here"

Time to go to work. "Did all of you talk about coming here today?" or "Terry, you and I talked on the phone, but I'm wondering if all of you talked together about coming today." Often they haven't, and one or all of the children will shake their heads or shrug. Turning to the parents you ask, "Why don't you tell the children why all of you are here?" Notice who speaks up and whether the parents are in agreement or contradict each other; you're beginning to map the family structure. If they have discussed this at home, ask if someone can summarize what was said. While older children know about counselors from school, young children may not, and if the parents use the word *doctor*, you may need to reassure them that you don't give shots—instead tell them that you help people with worries. What you want from this opening is a clear definition of the problem and an understanding by everyone of why they are there.

All this becomes the start for a larger exploration and discussion of problems and process in the family: "What do you think about what your mom just said?"; "Allen, do you feel as worried about this as your wife?"; "Terry, what are you most worried will happen if things keep going the way they have?" Ask the hard questions in order to move toward deeper conversations. Check in with everyone about their view of what's going on and what's not working, and don't leave anyone out. Daniel, for example, may tell his version of the break-in, or the boys may start to argue right there in the room, demonstrating the problem the parents are describing. Watch what the parents do, but don't let it go on and on; remember, you don't want to replicate the problem too long.

And if everyone talks in vague and general terms ("He gets in trouble"; "The boys just don't mind us"), get the speaker to be more specific ("How does Brian get in trouble?"; "What do they do when you ask the boys to do something?"). Specificity not only helps you begin to map out patterns and gives everyone else a better picture of the behaviors involved, but helps to draw out the emotions that are masked by murky language.

Be careful you don't overcontrol the flow of the conversation. This first session and the several to follow are a balancing act between assessment and treatment, content and process, the most dominant person in the family and the others present—and also between your leading and following. You want to gather the information you need to confirm your hypothesis, stop the dysfunctional patterns, and point the family in a new direction. You want to take charge, but not so much that you train the family to be passive. They shouldn't expect that you will always ask the questions, have the answers, and run the show.

Rather than seeing yourself as driving the car, think of yourself as the driving instructor in the passenger seat. In the beginning you have to instruct more—setting down rules, clarifying expectations, showing them what buttons to push, what controls to use. But once everything is under way and rolling, once they gain experience in driving the family process, you can begin to sit back. Your job is to help the family stay on the road, caution them when they are swerving too far into a power struggle or into the ditch of passivity, encourage them to look ahead and anticipate the dangers. Occasionally you may be forced to step in and use your own brake to slow things down to avert a collision, but never grab the steering wheel out of their hands and drive them yourself. Over time the sessions become more and more their own. Your list of questions gets shorter, the sermonettes more rare. Your focus shifts from their fundamental ability to control the car toward more advanced skills of performance driving. You point out the turns that lead them out of their familiar psychological neighborhoods onto less familiar paths toward their anxiety, change, and growth.

In order to get to that point, you want the therapy to move as quickly as possible toward what it will realistically become, to give the family in those first few sessions a good taste of what therapy's like beyond the gathering of histories and the filling out of forms. If you are too controlling, bombarding the family with question after question, feeling responsible for coming up with ideas about what to talk about, always initiating, always being the one to have the answers rather than helping the family figure them out for themselves, you'll quickly feel overwhelmed and eventually run out of steam. And the family, not knowing anything else, will never have learned to drive themselves.

What usually propels all this overregulation is your fear of the family's disapproval, losing control, and chaos breaking out if you sit back and stop watching the road, causing the process to drive over a cliff. Learning to take a looser grip on the steering wheel begins with a basic trust in the family, and in yourself: a trust that the family will not only learn, but also take responsibility for their lives; trust that therapy is an effective partnership that develops over time; trust that in the worst-case scenario your courage and honesty will in themselves be enough to manage whatever may come up. The next step is in taking the risk, stopping your own pattern of control (holding back on all the questions, letting the family members talk) and discovering what happens to yourself as well as them when you do. Once you find out that your worst fears don't come true—the family doesn't hate you, the marital explosion isn't all that explosive, the stomping-out teenager comes back within a few minutes—you become less afraid, freer to experiment with your power and skills, more confident and flexible in what you do; not surprisingly, the family begins to learn to do the same.

So the process goal in this first session is to get everyone talking, and talking more openly about things that are difficult. Be careful of setting up a pattern of asking questions and everyone giving one-word answers (children, especially, will mimic their parents) or waiting for you to ask the next one. You want to encourage interaction as long as it isn't destructive, and can generally do so by looking down and not interrupting when interactions are productive and healthy. You may need to pull in the silent ones or gently restrain the domineering ones. This gives everyone a sense that you are in charge and able to control what is happening so that it is safe enough for everyone to speak.

Going Deeper: Theories

After you understand the presenting problems, the next shift is to explore the family's theory. "So, Allen and Terry, why do you think the boys have been fighting so much?" or "Why do you think Daniel broke into the house with the other boys?" Again, listen for agreement or dissension between the parents, listen to what the boys have to say, see how useful their theories are in approaching the problem: For example, "Daniel is just an angry boy [implied: like his father] who always starts the fight and gets into trouble" (possible scapegoat theory with Daniel needing to be fixed), versus "We think the boys act up when there's tension between us" (parents thinking systemically with willingness to deal with marital relationship), versus "This seemed to have started when their grandfather died" or " . . . since Daniel started hanging out with that group of kids from the high school" (unresolved family loss, influence of peers that parents feel little control over). From the theory comes what the family members have done to try solving the problem: time-outs, ignored, yelled, tried to work on the marital relationship, tried to be nice, and so on. Look for strengths and patterns: parental consistency, agreement, what works, who enacts, and who enforces.

Use your questions to track where the solution breaks down: What keeps the family from solving the problems on their own? Often family members are on the right track but give up too quickly or don't know when to back off; if their solution has the potential to work (and is not illegal), you can build on it and their strengths. For example, "What do you do when he won't go to his room?" Get a clear sense of the pattern—"I yell; he refuses; I call Allen; he pushes Brian into the room; Brian runs out; we give up"—and what's behind it (in this case the giving up). You're looking for the problem under the problem.

Finally, you can ask here about expectations: how they see therapy helping with their concerns. Listen for the differences between their expectations and your own style and thinking. The family's ideas may include that you will fix Daniel and not need to see the parents, or that you will write a letter to the court asking them to drop the charges, or that Terry will be the one coming because Allen is "so busy" with work. If there is a difference with your expectations, note it, continue with your assessment, and circle back to it when you give your feedback.

EXPLORATION AND ASSESSMENT

By this point you should be roughly a third through the session time. Hopefully through this first part of the session you have begun your assessment by noticing the patterns of communication, emotional range of different members, strengths, patterns, adult responsibility and differentiation, and everyone's reactions to you. Look for rapport and relationship problems that may remain. If Allen, for example, still seems a bit withdrawn, try and draw him out or gently comment on what you notice: "Allen, you've been quiet, and I'm wondering how you are feeling." This is all part of closely tracking the process, attempting to keep the family in lockstep with you, making the process more explicit.

The focus of this middle section is about assessment. This is where the family doctor shifts from what's wrong to asking you questions to help form her diagnosis: what you've eaten, where you've been, your previous history, and so on. You're doing the same in this first session. Once you have mapped out the ground around the presenting problem, you want to gather the information you need to build or confirm your hypothesis based on your theory and develop a preliminary treatment plan. If you imagine the presenting problem as a large stone or wall sitting in the middle of a field, what you're doing now is walking around the field, exploring all of the surrounding area. So you may ask Allen and Terry how they go about making decisions in general, or about their own childhoods and upbringing; you may ask everyone about the death of the grandfather a year ago.

While you listen to their answers you're studying the process—the family's ability to communicate, the ability of the couple to give and take, when and with whom the children take sides. As you raise questions about a broader range of topics beyond the presenting problem (for example, the past, death, anger), you're expanding the boundaries of therapy beyond the family's initial expectations. Even if some of the questions or topics may seem irrelevant to them at this time, you're doing something important in letting everyone know that all of these subjects are comfortable enough for you and are open to future discussion. What's more, you and they begin to realize that their lives are more complicated than the fraction they talk about, maybe even more than the fraction they think about.

What you're looking for is where the energy, and with it the motivation, most easily goes. Explore their emotions and emotional range. What does each person do when he gets angry? When he feels hurt? (Often anger masks hurt; hurt can mask anger; a "don't care" stance can mask both.) Ask about loneliness, depression, what one person misunderstands most about another. Ask about their biggest worry, what they are most afraid of. Ask each of the children if they could change anything about their family what would they want changed (or ask young children what they would wish for if they had three wishes). Most people will easily respond to such questions. You're stirring the pot, uncovering places where the family secrets and treasures are buried, and beginning to establish therapeutic contracts about what they each want changed with the different family members. You are showing how two people can feel the same—Allen and Terry are both equally worried about the children, but Allen becomes irritable and controlling, and Terry gets depressed and withdraws.

You are also discovering through this process how well the family can follow your lead. Do they make the effort to honestly answer your questions, or do they provide only a vague answer and drift back to their own comfort zone of topics and focus? You want to continue to build rapport, yet you want to continue to move them toward their anxiety. Use questions, like a spade, to cut into new ground and raise anxiety; use comments, like a rake, to support, smooth over, and reduce it. Create a balance between the two, as well as between your talking and their talking. If you feel like you are getting stuck or pulling teeth, go back to the process in the room and talk about getting stuck or pulling teeth.

Create an Experience, Change the Climate

In the best of all possible first sessions your exploration, as well as your stopping the dysfunctional patterns, will likely give the family an opportunity to experience their process in a dramatically different way and create deeper conversations, which in turn will change the climate in the room. However, if this really hasn't taken hold and the family has stayed polite or intellectual and abstract and you decide to try and change the climate in a deliberate way, this is the time to do it. You don't want to wait toward the end of the session to do the family sculpture or ask about the grandfather's funeral, leaving you with no time for explanation and closure.

So look for opportunities and weave them into your exploration: Ask Daniel if he misses his grandfather when the grandfather is mentioned, ask Terry about her hopes for Daniel after she expresses yet again her frustration with him, create an enactment with both boys about a plan for sharing a video game after the parents complain how much they fight about it, and do a family sculpture with Brian in charge when he seems withdrawn and struggles to say what he would like to be different in his family. You'll know by their awkwardness and hesitation whether everyone is going against their emotional and behavioral grain.

Once you do this you need to then ground any emotions that you have stirred up—Daniel's sadness over his grandfather, Terry's hopes, Brian's sculpture—with an explanation: "I asked you, Daniel, about your grandfather because people your age often feel sad inside but don't know how to express it"; "Behind your frustration, Terry, are hopes and dreams that your sons don't know about"; "Thank you for doing the sculpture, Brian . . . I'm worried that your parents haven't understood how lonely you feel."

If you don't do this it may leave everyone upset, making some family members fearful of the therapy process and of you as the therapist, while others will feel anxious and unsafe simply because they don't know where this is all leading. Again, you need to keep an eye on the clock to make sure you build time in the first session for this process.

If you get stuck any place along the way in this section (for example, feel overwhelmed, lose your sense of direction) remember to go back to the other basics of blocking patterns, looking for what's missing, tracking the process, being honest, and refocusing on the problem. If they or you are truly overwhelmed (for example, the parents are breaking into a full-blown argument, the teen is completely shut down), then take charge. Separate the parents, send the children to the waiting room, ask the parents to leave so you can have a few minutes to talk with the teen. Don't recreate the problem; take leadership and do what you need to do to retain control.

RETURN AND CLOSURE

Now we are at the last third of the session, the return and closure. You've defined the problem, explored and assessed the area around it, tracking not only the process but tracking down the information you need to form your own preliminary hypotheses.

Make Your Pitch

As mentioned in Chapter 4, this is the time to bring the symmetry of the session all together. You go back to the opening theme, link the family's concerns with what has emerged in the process and content in the session, and present what you see and can offer. Here you lay out your hypothesis for the family: "I know you both think that the house break-in has something to do with the boys Daniel was playing with, but, Daniel, it seems like you are still pretty sad about your grandfather; it's not unusual for grief to turn into 'acting-out' behavior." Or, "Terry, it seems like it's easy for you to get angry, and the boys have been doing a pretty good job of keeping you stirred up, but I also think, as you expressed a few minutes ago, that underneath this anger is a lot of worry, concern, and caring that the boys rarely get to see." Or, "Allen, it seems like you have been doing your best over the years not to be abusive toward your children like your father was with you. But it seems that even though you are able to ignore the boys' behavior for long periods of time, it only makes matters worse; eventually you blow up, scaring the boys and confirming the fear that you were trying to avoid."

Again, you're giving the family a new theory to replace the old one, showing them how the presenting problems are poor solutions, giving them a new perspective, and with that a new energy and a new way of tackling the problem. Daniel isn't a bad kid, but a kid who is unable to express his grief; Allen isn't screwing up, he's struggling to overcome the modeling he received from his own father; Terry isn't a mean witch, but someone who has developed a tough side and is having difficulty letting others know what she really feels or what she needs.

Having said that, you stop and watch and listen for what happens next. Do not plow ahead. This is crucial. This is tracking the process like a bloodhound. You need to know whether your ideas resonate, especially with those who hold the most power in the family. Ask each one for his reaction. Look for the subtle shaking of the head, the quiet but clear "yes, but," the tacit agreement with little enthusiasm. It's important that your ideas become their own; if not fully on board, they won't be motivated to follow you further. Unless Allen makes the connection among the boys, himself, and his own father; unless Terry can agree that her more comfortable anger is blocking her expression of concern and distorting her relationship with her sons; and unless both of them and Daniel believe that there truly is a link between the grief and his acting out, you have no foundation on which to build a therapeutic contract.

But if the rapport is there, if they feel as though you listened and understood their concern, and if the experience was powerful enough to shake up their assumptions without overwhelming them, they will agree with your point of view. If there is resistance to your ideas, fix the problem in the room, confront them, and talk about the process: "Terry, you're shaking your head; it seems like you don't see it the same way I am; what are you thinking?" Listen carefully to what the client says, see where the snags are, and use education to help connect the dots.

Set Goals, Describe Your Plan

If everyone is on the same page, move ahead. Suggest the next steps: "I'd like to spend some time with you by yourself next time, Daniel, if you and your parents don't mind, to talk some more about how you've been feeling." Or "Maybe it would be good if you both could try and switch roles; maybe you, Allen, could take over the disciplining so that Terry can have a chance to get out of being the bad guy. Why don't you both come by yourselves next time and we can talk about it?"

Fortify the link between problem and solution by being deliberate in your use of language. If, for example, a father's stated problem

40 minutes ago was needing help "straightening his son out," make sure you talk about how whatever you are proposing—them spending more quality time together, using a reward chart, seeing the parents separately to define the family rules—is going to help "straighten his son out." Similarly, if a parent is most worried about school performance or her own parenting skills, tie whatever you propose to those concerns in the language that she uses (for example, "improving school performance").

Again, if you still need more information, and if you need to spend more time getting to know one of the family members better, just say so. Be honest about what you are thinking and where you stand: "I'm wondering how much this is all connected to the recent loss of your grandfather. Would you be willing to meet and talk more about this next week?"; "I know I've been talking a lot to your parents today; could I talk to you guys by yourselves next time?"; "I think I can help you with setting up clearer rules at home, but I'd like to do some psychological testing first." Being clear and specific about both what you need and how you'd like to go about getting it reduces the family's anxiety and gives them a sense of movement and direction.

Here you can also clarify expectations: "I know you had mentioned earlier that you thought I would be seeing Daniel by himself, but I think it is important that we meet together as a family. Let me tell you why." Or "I remember you mentioned my writing a letter to the court. That is something that I can't do. Let me explain why." Or "Terry, I understand that you are busy at your work, but you also said you are worried about your relationship with your sons. I appreciate your coming today, but I think the only way we can really work on your relationship with them is by having you here. Does that make sense to you?"

And again, link your proposal to their language of the problem and then wait and see what happens next. Don't move forward unless you feel there is solid agreement about the plan and priorities.

That said, you need not be dictatorial. Your goal is to develop a collaborative relationship with you and the family working as a team on their problems. While some families welcome the clear direction and leadership, others may not. If parents, for example, come with a "fix my child" expectation that you are unable to change in the first session, you may make the clinical decision to set aside a session or two to assess the child, present your "findings," and then move toward what you may have initially thought: to focus on parenting skills or the marital relationship. Make this a clinical decision because it not only gives you more information, but more important, this is a necessary step to gain more credibility in the eyes of the parents and win them over to your point of view.

Think of this as continuing to build rapport and safety; since building trust is always the first priority, these actions help remove the roadblocks that are getting in the way of forming a solid therapeutic relationship. In their minds, you have taken the time to truly understand their child; you show them pictures the child has drawn and interpret them, connecting them to your concerns; they relax and are better able to listen to what you have to suggest.

Give Homework

If everyone is on board, you move ahead to homework. You might ask Terry, for example, to track those times when she begins to feel angry by sitting down for a minute and asking herself what she's worried about. You could ask Allen what his father remembers about Allen's childhood or about his father's own childhood. You could ask the boys to try the plan they created for using the video game for a few days and then sit down with their parents in the middle of the week to possibly fine-tune it.

Close the Session

You set the next appointment, shift back to small talk wishing Brian good luck in his soccer game, shaking hands once again, thanking them for coming, and walking them out. Use behaviors that provide a symmetry to the session and help ease the transition back to the outside world.

Once again, all these suggestions are not a blueprint for what you have to do, but a way of describing the overall session structure, flow, and balance. If you keep this in mind together with the basics, the session will move in the direction you want it to go.

FIRST-SESSION DISASTER

Okay, so none of this goes as you hoped. The mom or the teen stomped out. The parents started arguing and you couldn't calm them down. You said you couldn't write the letter to the court and everyone suddenly put on their coats, thanked you, and left. You asked about setting another appointment and they said they will get back to you. What do you do?

You follow up. You don't have to chase them down the hallway—"Wait, wait, come back!"—or track them to the parking lot. You get on the phone or send them an e-mail and say what you think they are thinking. You empathize with their emotions. "Teresa, I know you were angry and felt that your parents were ganging up on you. I'm sorry. I'd like to talk to you about how we can keep this from happening." Or "I realize that was a difficult session and I sensed that you both are worried about your children. I'm wondering if you both would be willing to come back one more time so we can come up with a plan to help you." Or "I understand that the court action is something you both are really worried about and you felt frustrated when I said I couldn't write the letter. Can you give me a call so we can talk about this some more?"

The goal here is relationship repair, going back to the beginning. By reaching out, expressing what you think they may be thinking, you are doing exactly that. Often this is powerful in itself—you are showing concern that often doesn't come their way, especially when dealing with other community agencies. This is the best you can do. If you don't get a response, try one more time or mail a handwritten note. This doesn't mean you are compromising your values, approach, or style, but demonstrating to the family your desire to resolve the problems between you.

THE SECOND SESSION

Some therapists do reminder calls to families between sessions. Doctors, dentists, and even hair stylists now do this routinely, calling and leaving a message reminding the family of the time of the next appointment a day or so before. It can reduce cancellations or blank spaces in your appointment schedule, and many families have come to expect it. But it is time-consuming, especially if you have to do it yourself, and some therapists object on philosophical grounds—clients should take responsibility for their obligations, they make clear their cancellation policy at the start, and reminding clients of appointments can feel like a parent reminding their daughter that she needs to clean up her room before going to the mall.

While some clients may assume that reminders are expected as a courtesy service, decide for yourself where you stand and inform clients at the start either as a one-line statement at the beginning or end or as part of your handout material. In agencies there are usually procedures in place—that administrative support will always call clients to remind them—whereas others have a firm cancellation policy. If you or the agency's policy is not to do reminders, you may want to consider exceptions: when clients may genuinely struggle with following a schedule, such as when there are issues of intellectual challenges; or when they may be emotionally overwhelmed for a few weeks; or when you find that you've not been clear, for whatever reason, about the next appointment time. This is appropriate outreach, common courtesy, and generally rare. Think it through, and be clear about your reasons and motivations so the family understands them as well.

Whatever you decide, the second session feels different from the first. Those first-session butterflies are gone and everyone feels more settled, but the family is not yet likely to be ready to take over major responsibility for the process. You need to have specific goals and start things off. What do you need to do in this session? Here are several options.

Finish Up What's Left Over from the Last Session

Is there someone in the family you need to meet: the grandmother, the older brother who was working last time, the father who was out of town on a business trip? Is there someone you need to get to know better, someone who didn't quite connect with you: the little sister who spent the last session playing with the blocks in the corner; the father who nodded his head and said the right things but seemed to be only half listening and minimally involved; the IP, who, in spite of your efforts, may still have felt beaten up by everyone else and who needs to see that you can be an advocate for him as well? Is there additional information that you need: a better assessment of the mother's depression, a history of the father's past addiction, a clearer picture of just what it is that the parents do when the kids refuse to go to bed, a better sense of just how much the little girl is affected by all the fighting?

It's in this second session that you may wish to pull the family apart (or bring them all together if you decided to see only part of the group before). For example, you may want to see one of the parents individually if you felt she was holding back for some reason last time, do play therapy with one of the children to build rapport and get a better idea of his world, or talk to the siblings without the parents to see how they act differently. These are ways of further defining goals and establishing contact and contracts with various family members, narrowing problems, or determining where the energy and motivation most lie.

If you decide to split up the family, make sure no one feels left out or paranoid about what's going on. Hopefully, you've mentioned to the parents in the first session why you wanted to see the boys by themselves in the next session. If on further consideration you decide to change the format, take a few minutes to explain this to the parents so they don't imagine that you're suddenly going to be pumping their children to reveal the family's secrets. If you see one child, spend at least a few minutes with the others, so they don't feel excluded and you don't reinforce the notion that only that child has problems. If you see one adult alone, balance it out either by then seeing the other, or by seeing the couple together.

Avoid talking about someone behind her back. Don't be fooled into thinking that what you think you may say to one "in confidence" isn't likely to get repeated to the others. Not only does saying to a wife that it seems to you that her husband has trouble with intimacy or is depressed border on being unethical, it clinically unbalances the relationship among you, the husband, and the wife. You're treating the husband as though he were a child, and setting up a potential opportunity for the wife to use this against her husband outside the office. Similarly, telling a brother that his sister is probably jealous of him is often a surefire way to have the sister find out that you are saying what you think about her behind her back and for it to undermine your relationship with her.

Firm Up Your Diagnosis for the IP

Even family therapy purists in an agency or in private practice are required to provide a *Diagnostic and Statistical Manual of Mental Disorders* (DSM) (American Psychiatric Association, 2013) diagnosis on one member of the family for funding, charting, or managed care requirements. If you weren't able to do this after the first session, now is the time. Most often when a child or teen is identified by the parents as having the "problem," it is usually around him that the chart is built and the diagnosis assigned. What you think about diagnoses and how you use them will depend on your theory, philosophy, and style. Some therapists begin and end with viewing problems in traditional family therapy terms, with individual diagnosis as secondary and supplemental—something they just need to do for paperwork reasons, or as a statement of individual concerns that usually can be addressed in family process. Others lean toward the other pole, clinically giving more weight to diagnosis from the beginning; they build on it, and look at family therapy as the means for best addressing the behaviors and symptoms it represents.

Again, a middle ground is viewing an individual diagnosis as really a matter of balancing out individual and family process. You want to ask yourself the same questions you ask of any family: How does this behavior fit within the context of the family?; How can you give the family a new way of looking at the problem (for example, does focusing on the child's ADHD give the parents a new, more compassionate way of seeing their child or only reinforce his role as the problem)?; What is the family's expectation and motivation for family treatment?; What impact will changes within the family system have on the IP's behaviors and symptoms?; How much will individual symptoms distract from or undermine the family therapy process?

The answers to these questions will determine how the individual diagnosis will fit into the larger treatment plan. What you don't want to do is have the family look upon a diagnosis as a way of "patientizing" the family member or use it as a rationale for scapegoating, not looking at or taking responsibility for the larger family process.

Decide Whether a Family Member Needs to Be Referred for Individual Therapy

Many seemingly individual problems can clearly be handled in a family context—the oppositional defiant teen who the parents describe as having an "attitude," young children with a host of anxieties, mild forms of ADHD where organization and structure are enough to keep the individual on course—are examples that quickly come to mind. Some diagnoses (major depression, bipolar illness, psychosis, severe anxiety like panic attacks and obsessive–compulsive disorder

[OCD], eating disorders, severe ADHD, posttraumatic stress) clearly require medication and/or individual therapy to bring symptoms in control and enable family therapy to be effective.

If you decide that individual work needs to be part of the therapeutic mix, discuss this with the family and explain why family therapy alone would not be a good choice, linking it to their primary concern: "I know you both are worried about Ellen's school performance, but I'm concerned, Ellen, about what you said about how you've been feeling. It sounds to me that you are really struggling with depression, and I can imagine how that can undermine your energy and focus on school. I think it would be helpful if you talked with your doctor about possible medication, as well as someone you can talk to in private about the way you have been feeling."

Then see what they say next. All may readily agree and ask for names of therapists. The parents may agree but Ellen may balk, in which case you talk with her about her concerns, and whether she would be willing to consider or go for a consult. Ellen or the parents may ask if you could see Ellen, and your response depends on your own orientation and skill, and how you see it blending with family therapy and family issues. They may ask you what happens to family therapy and how it fits in with seeing one of the members individually.

What generally works best at this point is to make the referral, have the individual therapist do her own assessment, and then together both of you can make a recommendation to the family about when and how family and individual therapy can be combined. One option would be to see family therapy as a supportive supplement—for example, having monthly family touchdown meetings to assess progress and discuss ways the family can support Ellen, while Ellen focuses on her depression in individual therapy. Or it may make more sense for you to withdraw from the case, and leave the touchdown meetings to the individual therapist to choreograph together with Ellen.

Other times individual and family therapy can run concurrently—for example, using family therapy to focus on the underlying family issues that are, in fact, driving Ellen's depression. Yet another option is to have family therapy start only after a period of individual therapy is completed and, one hopes, Ellen is much more stable, less preoccupied, and has the focus and energy to tackle family issues.

Two individual problems that can quickly turn muddy are
those of addictions and anger. It often becomes a question of who
has the problem. Often it's another family member ("I think my
husband is alcoholic because he drinks a pint of Jack Daniels every
day"; "My wife needs anger management because she goes on rants
and throws things"), while the individual blames and deflects ("He
only drinks because of her nagging, but he's able to go to work every
day"; "She is only angry because he deliberately does things that he
knows pushes her buttons"). What unfolds in the family session is a
content battle, each stacking up facts to shore their own reality and
trying to get you to say who is right.

Here it's often best to refer out. If anger or addiction is outside your expertise, someone else more experienced needs to make
that call. But even if you have expertise in anger or addictions and
feel the individual indeed has a problem, by taking a strong stand
you're unbalancing the system, and family therapy is largely over.
The angry or addicted person is not going to hear your concern but
only that you've joined with the others and taken sides against him,
reinforcing his resistance.

The biggest reason to refer out besides sidestepping the "judge"
role, is to break the cycle of blame, defensiveness, or lack of personal responsibility that keep these behaviors in place. To say that
"I would stop drinking if you stopped nagging" or "I wouldn't get
upset if you didn't push my buttons" is at best only partly true; the
responsibility for one's behavior and individual source of anger and
addictions gets missed. By asking the individual to consider getting a consult around his addiction or anger, you are taking a clinical stand, underscoring the notion that this is indeed an individual
issue regardless of the others' behaviors. You are posing to the individual what it means to be a differentiated adult.

And if the person refuses? You do what you do with any resistance. The refusal isn't the problem but a bad solution and so you
explore and empathize with the worry underneath. You point out
that having a consult is a way of deciding whether or not there is
a problem and putting the argument to rest. You explain your concerns and clinical rationale, voice what you think the person may be
thinking or feeling, and say that most people in these situations feel
the same way.

Often it's helpful in these cases to brainstorm with your supervisor and work together on deciding about options. Realize that the

best you can do is the best you can do. Do it and then you're done. The next move is theirs.

Find Out More about What Works

This is where you ask about the homework, either in your small groups or all together. Simply asking about their experience with the homework gives the family the message that you take homework seriously and that you expect them to do it. If they didn't do the homework, ask them to explain why. Some explanations might be "I mentioned it to Adrian but he just shrugged and I didn't press it"; "John had to suddenly go out of town for 4 days"; "We started to, but realized we didn't really understand what to do." If these seem like limp excuses, probe a bit further: Were they feeling too anxious about doing it?; Were they worried about doing it wrong?; Does it reflect something about their attitude toward you, the therapy, or your initial assessment of the problem?

Pinning this down tells you where the obstacles lie and what you need to do to remove them. You may discover that you were moving too fast, asking them to do more than they could emotionally handle, or didn't do a good enough job of selling your theory, leaving one of the key people unconvinced and uncooperative. Or perhaps the family's response only replicated the way they respond to other problems, challenges, or pressure from the outside, namely, by ignoring them.

If they did the homework, you want to know what they thought about it. Sometimes the family will do exactly what you ask, and the assignment will accomplish exactly what you behaviorally hoped it would, but the results seem to have little emotional impact on the family: Sure, Dad spent more time with Brian and they had a good time, but Dad says it wasn't much different from the times he'd done it before, and he seems unimpressed. Perhaps Dad doesn't see the connection of the assignment to his concerns, doesn't understand your assessment of the problem, or isn't aligned with you and therapy and is merely going through the motions. If the assignment was tried but didn't work, that is, the family wasn't able to carry it out (Mom still got mad, Brian was still fighting), you want to track where it broke down so you can help the family fine-tune it, or rethink your hypothesis.

It's also a good idea at this session to ask what they thought about the first session. Not only may you find out what someone didn't like ("I felt you were taking Allen's side") or what made them uncomfortable ("I was surprised how hard it was to talk to Brian about his schoolwork"), but also what, of all that went on, had the largest impact on specific individuals ("What you said about my father really got me thinking"; "Having a chance to hear what Terry really thought was helpful"; "Feeling that it wasn't all my fault helped me be less critical of myself"). These can all be clues to what you may want to use again. Even if they say little in response to your question, by asking the question you are letting them know that their feedback about the therapy process is welcomed.

Help the Family Further Understand How the Therapy Process Will Work

If you ask how their week was, or what problems came up, they quickly assume that the therapy will include monitoring on a week-by-week process. If, on the other hand, you take a less directive role and ask the couple or family what they want to talk about, or continue to explore their past, the family will begin to think that this is what the meetings will be like.

Because they look to you to set the pace, be deliberate in what you're doing. Once again, the best route to take is one of creating balance between initiating and responding, the individual and the group, assessment and treatment. Back up your actions with clear communication: "I know I've been asking a lot of questions during these two sessions . . . next time I won't be. I'd like you to think about what we need to talk about and bring it up"; "We're going to complete the psychological testing during these next 2 weeks, and then I'll come back to you with the results and some suggestions." Let them know how you are thinking so they can begin to do the same.

THIRD-SESSION SHIFT, OR HOW DID I LOSE THEM?

Generally by the third session things have settled down. Your assessment is complete or nearly complete, rapport is high and the family feels comfortable with you, expectations are clear and your treatment plan has been presented to and accepted by the family, or is already under way. But not always. Sometimes the third session slides out from beneath you—the family gets ornery, maybe even quits, or everyone, including you, suddenly seems to run out of steam, all catching you off guard. Here are some of what might be going on underneath the third-session shift:

• *Families in crisis or who are crisis oriented may have calmed down.* Simply by telling their stories and hearing your suggestions, or because outside events have changed (for example, the dad found a new job, the school is not going to press charges), they don't see the need to continue and simply drop out, or they are exhausted from expending all their energy on the crisis. They may have difficulty understanding the underlying issues, or doing the preventative work that can keep the next crisis from brewing.

As mentioned earlier, if you suspect the family functions in this way, educating them about crisis reactions and the possible recurrence of the problem can be useful; help them to emotionally see the connection between the underlying issues and the surface behavior. If they are still wary, offer them an appointment to come back for a checkup in a few weeks or months to encourage a preventive, proactive stance rather than a reactive one, or ask them if they mind if you give them a call just to check and see how they are doing.

If they are set on leaving, let them do so with your support. Unless you have clear clinical reservations—the son still seems extremely depressed and potentially suicidal—let them leave feeling good about themselves, rather than with the message and guilt from you that you think they're failing to follow through. If they feel supported in leaving, they will feel supported in coming back.

• *Similarly, some families take two or more sessions to ventilate and get things off their chests, and then get anxious.* They look up and realize that you're in the room with them and panic over what they think you think; they wonder what might happen next. One way to handle this is to anticipate it: Talk about what's going to happen, give voice to their anxiety, and help them once again to feel safe.

• *After a couple of sessions countertransference and transference begin to settle in.* The parents decide that you are not as all-knowing as they originally thought, the mother realizes that she really does have a hard time talking openly with men, you begin to feel that the family is not as motivated as you initially believed. They close up or drop out; you may start acting more pushy. Talk about what you see ("It feels like we were going strong for a few weeks, but now we're slowing down"); educate them about and normalize the process ("Most families in counseling feel most enthusiastic the first few weeks, then they begin to feel that they are not making as much progress"); and help them sort through their feelings ("Terry, you seem annoyed about what I've been suggesting") to keep these emotions from replicating the family process and undermining the therapy. Talk to your supervisor to help you from overreacting.

• *If you see only a portion of the family the first time or two (for example, the mother or father isn't able to come), the missing ones may feel left out of the process, or resist coming in and sabotage it for everyone else, causing them all to drop out.* In couple therapy this often takes the form of the wife coming in first, then her telling her husband that she saw a marital therapist, who now wants to see him with her. Out of his anxiety he promises to make all the changes in the world and convinces the wife to discontinue. Seeing everyone together as soon as possible; reaching out to the missing person, even by telephone; or predicting this process for those attending and coaching them on how to respond to the other can often prevent this.

• *"Fix my child" parents are comfortable while the child is being discussed or evaluated, but may panic when you shift to larger family issues, the marriage, or themselves as individuals.* As mentioned earlier, the key in these cases is pacing—meeting their initial expectations, carefully monitoring their anxiety, and making sure that you connect these larger issues to the child's presenting problem.

• *Mandated families may come for the first couple of sessions, long enough for you to say that you saw them or for them to say that they came, then drop out basically because they don't want to be there.* Contacting the referring agency right away and deciding with them how they want things to be handled if the family doesn't continue to come, can help clarify your role and provide a united front to the family.

Except for mandated cases, the driving force behind all these third-session shifts is anxiety, created by the shift in focus from the presenting, surface, external crisis orientation to the underlying, internal, right-now process. If you move too quickly or push too hard for the family members to focus on what seems too threatening, they will drop out. Maintain openness and honesty, focus on the process and make it as representative as possible of the way therapy will be, move quickly enough for the client to feel that something is happening, but not so quickly that the family feels pushed into something they don't agree with.

Periodically reiterate the treatment contract: "I think that it's good that you came in; I think the basic problem is . . . and I think I can help; I don't think therapy needs to be a long time if we work together." Remember, you have constant feedback right there in the room. If ever you are uncertain where the family stands, ask.

When some families don't show up, therapists are often relieved. If you find all kinds of reasons not to follow up with the family, it probably says something about your own countertransference in this particular case. Write the note, make a phone call, say what you think they may be feeling, why they may be disappointed in treatment, and invite them to come back and talk about it. But even doing that, you'll find, as was said earlier, despite your good efforts, there's still much that will be beyond your control: expectations that the family simply won't reveal, individual emotional triggers, or pressures on the family's life that makes them decide that therapy with you or therapy at all is no longer needed.

The challenges of the beginning are the challenges that come with starting any joint enterprise, namely, reaching an understanding and agreement about the nature of the relationship, about the way time together will be spent and how it all will work, that is, creating a shared vision. It's a time when the rhythm of the therapy hasn't yet taken over, and you are forced to rely more on your own personal strengths. But if you can succeed in accomplishing the goals you set out for these initial sessions, most of the hard part is over. You're ready to move on to the next stage.

Looking Within: Chapter 5 Exercises

These exercises are designed to help you increase your self-awareness of the issues surrounding beginnings and to increase your observation skills by practicing them outside of therapy. Go ahead and try them over the next week.

1. Think again about your own theory, values, and personal level of anxiety. What are your greatest strengths? Who do you feel it is most important to see in the initial session? Who would you not want to

see or feel comfortable seeing (for example, small children, extended family)? What would help you most in reducing your own anxiety? See if you can develop in advance your rules of thumb for the first sessions that would work best for you and the families you work with.

2. If this initial connecting with families is awkward for you, try improving your skills (rapport) in less-pressured situations (for example, meeting someone at a party, talking to the person next to you on a bus, standing in line). Increase your risk taking and comfort in connecting with a wider range of people.

3. If you were to create a client information handout for your own practice, what would you want to include in it?

4. Think of something that someone in your family—nuclear or family of origin—does that particularly bothers you. Write it down and describe it fully. Then consider in what ways other people in the family may be involved in provoking or maintaining this problem. For example, your father may drive fast partly because your mother is timid or is always telling him to slow down. Your spouse may seem to always overreact to one of your children because you seem to her to underreact or side with your child. Next, try adopting the attitude that it is not about you at all, but the other person's way of seeing the world or way of coping with some emotion inside of her. See how these new perceptions affect your feelings.

chapter 6

The Middle Stage
Are We There Yet?

*O*nce you've crossed over the mountains of the beginning stage, you come to the broad, flat prairie land of the middle. There's a sigh of relief for making it through those initial challenges, and you look forward to the steady rolling progress that the middle stage seems to promise. Here is where the bulk of the treatment will take place, where the visions and goals created in those first few weeks are forged into something solid and permanent.

Just as the relief starts to wane you find that for every good session or week there's one that isn't quite as good. The skills that you laboriously help the family learn—communication, parenting, assertiveness—have to be constantly relearned or fine-tuned. Just when you think all the crises are behind you, one flares up without any apparent warning. The ground, you discover, is not as flat as it seemed from the distance; the ruts and bumps you didn't see before seem at times to be all around you.

All of this makes for the famous "working through" of the middle stage. The toil of working through is the grind, the feeling that you are not so much digging down deeper into the layers of the family structure and individual personalities, but rather digging a hole, filling it back up, and digging it out again. For 3 weeks in a row everyone does a good job of listening and sidestepping the destructive outbursts, but then Grandma shows up for a short visit and the tension causes everything to collapse back into chaos. Mom is able to hold firm on the bedtime routine, but then she has a hard day at work, the kids double-team her when Dad isn't home, and she caves in. Dad is snapping less at the kids but still has a hair-trigger temper around his wife.

STAGES OF FAMILY THERAPY

Before we talk further about the middle stage of family therapy, let's place it in the larger context of the overall family therapy by contrasting it with the beginning and end stages. While progress is obviously on a continuum, it's helpful to think in terms of stages, and recognize the characteristics of each one in the same way that it is helpful to think of the stages of child or adult development: You know what to look for, it gives you some standard to measure the family against, and allows you to anticipate what will unfold next. Your understanding and perspective can then be passed on to the family, pointing out to them the normal and sometimes gradual changes that you see that they may not.

Beginning-Stage Characteristics (One to Four Sessions)

We discussed this in the earlier chapters, but here is a summary of the common characteristics of the beginning stage:

- Playing courtroom: arguing over facts/content.
- Arguing over right/wrong.
- Using content to fuel emotions.
- Easily falling into power struggles.
- Using "you" statements ("I'll feel better when you change").
- Little awareness of process/patterns.

Obviously some families—those with past experience with therapy, with good insight—will begin with only a few of these characteristics or move quickly beyond them.

Middle-Stage Characteristics

This is where we are now. A quick summary follows:

- Inconsistent in applying new skills.
- Seeming worsening of problems.
- More awareness of patterns/process.
- Increased use of "I" statements.
- Arguing over means rather than consistently focusing on ends.
- Difficulty emotionally self-regulating and listening around "hot" topics.

Some explanations are in order.

Inconsistent Skills

If you think about it, this makes sense. Because skills are still new and not yet integrated into the family's everyday lives, gains are fragile, and it doesn't take much for it to all fall apart. On good days when stress is down and they can be mindful, family members are able to use the new skills. On a bad stressful day, everyone reverts back to default mode.

Means versus Ends

What this refers to is that in arguments or discussions the family gets stuck in the weeds of means—each trying to persuade the others to solve a problem in his way. As the family gets better at communicating and being aware of the process, they can tell when the conversational car is going off the road and are better able to stay focused on the ultimate goal, namely, solving the problem.

Hot Topics

The older family members in the middle stages are less reactive and better able to calm themselves and regulate their emotions. However, certain topics remain sensitive, and when these are brought up, the newly learned communication and regulation skills can go out the window.

Worsening Problems

Here is where you thought everything was going well and now the parents are bringing up old issues from the past, arguing openly in the session, or worse yet, raising issues that you have not even heard about—that one of the partners is heavily drinking or another reveals terrible childhood abuse. Or the teen who seemed to be doing well now discloses that she has been purging her lunches at school because she is afraid of getting fat, or that she thinks she is gay.

Here is where it is easy to panic: What did you miss? What is going wrong? Most likely nothing. This is, in fact, a good sign. Everyone is stepping up and talking about the secrets and problems under the problems because they now feel safe and trust you. It's not uncommon for couples to come in with relatively minor child issues that are tossed to the side on the third or fourth session as they shift the talk to their relationship. The opening sessions were an acceptable way of getting their foot in the door and checking you out. Once they are comfortable and trusting of you and your skill they're ready to move on to what their underlying agenda and biggest concerns were all along. You're doing a good job.

End-Stage Characteristics

Finally we reach the end stage. While we will be discussing this more fully in the next chapter, here is a quick summary of this stage's characteristics:

- Ability to focus on ends, not get stuck on means.
- Ability to actively listen even on difficult topics.
- Ability to emotionally self-regulate.
- Ability to compromise.
- Awareness of the process and patterns and the ability to stop them.
- More flexibility—being able to move against their grains, approach anxiety.

Obviously this is an ideal, with some families coming closer to reaching these than others. It depends on their starting point, their own expectations of therapy, their and your time, and your skill and approach. Think about cases you see now, cases you have had in the past; see how these characteristics make up your work and can help you look ahead.

GETTING STUCK

While many families in the middle stage seem to get worse, some seem to get truly stuck. While this two-steps forward, one-step back pattern is probably the most common pattern seen throughout the middle stage of therapy, there are other variations. Sometimes a family will initially make progress and then not only lose ground but be back to zero within a matter of weeks.

Teresa, for example, a single parent, comes in with her two adolescent children, Lavone, age 15, and Kenisha, age 13. The presenting problems are Kenisha refusing to go to school, Lavone staying out late. In those first couple of sessions, thanks to your rapport and education, Teresa no longer is holding on to her theory that her children are bad kids made worse by their friends. She is following through on implementing the structural and behavioral changes that you both agreed on—arranging a meeting with the school staff for herself and Kenisha to discuss Kenisha's complaints; taking a clear, strong stand at home about the need for her to attend school regularly; setting clear limits with Lavone; and contacting the juvenile court for disciplinary backup. She has moved into the ideal parenting role of nurturing and providing structure, and with court support maintaining a hierarchy between her and her children.

It works. Kenisha goes to school for 3 solid weeks, and after a stern talk with the court officer, Lavone gives up testing his mother's new resolve and is staying home at night. But then everything unravels—Kenisha stays home for a couple of days because she says she's sick, and it's the beginning of the end. Her excuses become thinner and thinner, and Teresa seems to lose her ability to get Kenisha to school. Lavone at the same time activates the other front and stays out later and later, with no consequences from Teresa. Within a month everything seems back to where it started.

What's going on here? Some of this is certainly predictable. Most families make some progress and feel great as the initial anxiety and worry are reduced. But then there's some slipup, such as Kenisha's missing a day of school, and they become afraid that the gains were illusory, their original theory was right after all, this therapy stuff really doesn't work, and that they "tried" yet again and nothing changes.

What they don't fully appreciate is that progress was made, not because they managed to show up in your office but because they were beginning to do something different. They need to understand that setbacks are inevitable not because it isn't working but simply because they are inexperienced. Even after they slide back, the same skills that helped them before will help them again.

As mentioned above, developing behavioral consistency and holding the line in spite of one's emotional state are some of the real challenges at the beginning of the middle stage. To do that Teresa needs review and reinforcement of the new goals to help her stay focused, and support to enable her to take action even when she doesn't feel like it or believe she can do it. She needs help generalizing the new skills, help recognizing when seemingly new problems are really just variations on the old, and detailed coaching on what to say and do when Kenisha says she doesn't want to go to school or when Lavone comes home 3 hours after curfew. Most of all she needs ongoing encouragement and a pat on the back when things seem to slip.

But sometimes this skill training, reinforcement, and support are not enough. Over the weeks you find the situation to be more complicated than you originally thought; you discover other dynamics at work that weren't immediately apparent during the initial assessment. Teresa's low-grade but chronic depression, for example, her poor health, or her demanding elderly mother may sap her time and energy and make it difficult for her to keep on task. Other people, who originally seemed to be at the far outskirts of the family, may now appear to be more involved and undermine her efforts.

Teresa's boyfriend, for example, who used to work evenings, is now in the home at night, and he is jealous of the increased attention the children suddenly seem to be getting. Rather than supporting Teresa's new stance, he undermines her, urging her not to be so hard on the kids, or stands up for them when she tries to impose the new rules. If Teresa is to stay on track, she'll need your help, both concretely and emotionally, addressing these new problems that are threatening to pull her off course.

In other cases there is not so much the normal backsliding of applying new skills, or the erosion by other problems and family members, but an apparent struggle to develop real traction. There may be revolving scapegoats—for example, Kenisha isn't going to school, but Lavone is doing well, and then they switch; Kenisha seems back on track, but suddenly Lavone is talking back and slipping out at night to meet his friends on the corner—each changing emotional places and taking turns being the "good child" for a while. Other times the parent's internal process remains the same, even though she seems to be saying and doing the right things. In spite of her attempts to be firmer and more consistent, for example, you notice that Teresa still frets or yells or spends all her time consumed by the children, and gives the boyfriend cause to remain on the outskirts of the family. What these variations represent are the tenacity of the family's patterns to maintain and contain the family's emotions and roles. Rather than tackling the fundamental changes in process that are needed, anxiety pushes each of the family members toward slight shifts in focus, variations on the familiar, and prevents deeper change.

So does the sense of loss. Change implies not only the learning of new skills and roles, but often the emotional and psychological giving up of what the members of the family have for so long thought of as "life." Solving problems and breaking patterns can trigger new emotions and create their own new challenges. If Teresa has, for as long as she can remember, not only worried about her children but put them first, she will find her concept of herself as a mother and an adult change if her children are less of a problem and less of her focus. She will have more mental and emotional room to think about herself, raising questions, perhaps, about who she is, not just as a parent but as a person. She may have more time and energy to focus on her relationship with her boyfriend, possibly causing her to reconsider how he fits into her life, or challenging her toward new, deeper levels of intimacy.

Such changes can create, at least for a while, a hole in her old identity. She is actively trying to rewire her brain and the new ways of feeling good may take some time to replace the old ways she was used to; she may need to grieve and ponder before she can fill it in. This transition, grief, and challenge can run like an undertow beneath the changes going on up above and contribute to the sluggish, slowing-down, plateauing feeling of the middle stage.

ANTIDOTES TO STUCKNESS

So what do you do with all this slipping, sliding, and sticking? Here are some options to consider.

Grind It Out

This is the modus operandi of the middle stage—plodding over the same ground again and again, keeping everyone committed and on track, the art of saying the same thing over and over. This can be invaluable for the family, especially those who are crisis oriented who never developed the skills of consistency and follow-through, and can quickly grow impatient or become distracted. It is your perseverance that serves as a model and ultimately seeps into their thinking. Your job is to keep everyone from giving up or going off, to focus on the details in order to fine-tune the skills and strategies, to help remove the emotional obstacles that arise (for example, Teresa's feeling that she is being a bad mother), and to help them see how each one of them copes with the stress of change in a different way.

Mix It Up

Grinding it out, however, doesn't have to feel like a forced march. The middle stage is a good time to reinforce the skills and concepts by changing formats and introducing experiential work on an irregular basis (doing it on a regular basis only flattens its potential impact). Bring in additional family members—for example, Teresa's boyfriend—see siblings together or individually, do some guided imagery, sculpt the changing family relationships. Doing these things not only helps avoid the therapeutic ruts and keeps the family interested and engaged but helps ferret out additional problems that may undermine progress.

Separate/Clarify Problems

Even though Teresa is quick to dismiss her depression as just the way she has always been, it becomes apparent to you that it is undermining her ability to follow through on the suggestions you've made. It's time for you to take the lead. A referral for a medication evaluation may be the next step needed to give her the energy to make changes and break the negative cycles, and you may need to spend some time educating and persuading her to do this. Similarly, you may feel that her relationship with her boyfriend holds the key to her acting more effectively as a parent. Your job becomes one of helping her see not only that the two problems—parenting challenges and depression—are related but that the second is actually more important. How you decide to link and prioritize this array of problems rests upon your theory and its notion of causality.

Finally, there are times when you need to decide whether a new problem is really a new problem, a variation of the old (for example, revolving scapegoats), or a distraction. Just as families not in therapy return to comfortable problems when their anxiety and stress get too high, so too will families in therapy. This is the principle of triangulation—the reducing of anxiety and conflict between two individuals by both of them focusing instead on a more neutral issue. You may notice a sudden return to old complaints, patterns, or repetition of already-told stories. As you begin to help Teresa look more closely at her relationship with her boyfriend, for example, suddenly new crises may arise at school with Kenisha or at home with Lavone, reflecting the increase in her stress that new changes are creating. If you've done a good assessment and know what the family's comfortable problems are, you won't be led astray and can help the family discuss their anxiety and stay focused.

Normalize, Label, Diversify

In the midst of this middle stage your role often shifts from that of a teacher educating the family to the workings of the process and new behaviors, to that of a guide, one more familiar than they with the terrain of change. Predicting to the family the backslides, shift in scapegoats, eruption of crises, feelings of anxiety and ambivalence, and sabotage by others in the family, then normalizing the process, helps them realize that they are not failing and keeps them from feeling discouraged. It also provides the family with a sense of control as they, too, begin to understand and can anticipate just what the process of change entails.

Labeling the process has similar positive effects. For example, labeling for Teresa the school issues as her comfortable problem, the area where much of her attention and emotions so readily goes—or an adolescent's self-cutting behaviors as her way of coping when she feels emotionally overwhelmed—helps her and the rest of the family do the same. Being able to name what is happening allows the family to gain some distance, perspective, and control when these problems and emotions arise. The family can begin to see it as you see it, as part of the larger pattern, and are more free to approach it in a new way.

Finally, you can help the family diversify their emotional outlets and expand their emotional and behavioral range by both interrupting the well-worn patterns and encouraging them to go against their own grain. For example, you can guide Teresa to confront her boyfriend, and help Kenisha talk to her teachers about problems (rather than cutting class). These are the best ways to ensure they have something to replace what they are giving up. Unless they each can develop greater emotional and behavioral flexibility, it becomes all too easy to remain dependent and caged within the roles and patterns they know.

Approach the Loss

How you handle the underlying loss that the new changes create depends both on its power as an obstacle for the family and your own clinical and personal stance. If, for example, you are doing brief, solution-based treatment, or if the problems are not deeply ingrained, these emotions will most likely remain untouched. Rather than defining and focusing on the grief, you may simply pull the family along against its undertow until they are beyond its grasp, and the new behaviors—and the emotions they bring—take hold.

If loss is a difficult issue for you, if you are in the middle of coping with changes within your personal life, you may find yourself reluctant to tackle this topic and these emotions, and will no doubt find yourself attracted to a clinical theory that supports avoiding it. On the other hand, if you are sensitive to loss in your own life, you may swing too far in the opposite direction and push the family to resolve these issues, in part, at least, because of your own needs. Supervision in these cases can be helpful in sorting out the personal from the clinical.

The simple, honest approach, of course, is to take leadership and talk about change and loss directly. Ask Teresa, now that the children seem to be doing well and needing her less, how she feels about being less on the frontline as a mother, and how she imagines her own future. This kind of talk not only keeps the family, as well as yourself, from being discouraged by a sudden stall in progress, but opens the door to exploring past changes and successful transitions. As these old emotions are stirred, rise to the surface, and are finally expressed, these past losses begin to heal and the family's emotional range has another opportunity to grow.

Take a Break

As the family improves, they can burn out on the routine of treatment itself. Just as taking planned rests from intensive physical exercise allows muscles to recover and hence grow, taking a break or reducing sessions in therapy can allow the family to integrate what they have learned, practice skills on their own away from your watchful eye, and increase their own psychological muscles.

If Teresa is pretty much holding her own, having her check in with you every other week or so may be fine. If the family seems to have reached a satisfactory plateau, consider and discuss with them your moving toward some form of case management with the option to return for more intensive work as the need arises. Rather than viewing this as abandonment, families often see this as a graduation of sorts, an endorsement of their growing capability. It also gives you an opportunity to see just how much support they really need.

Be Positive, Be Brave

Families that are doing a good job of keeping their heads down and focusing on change easily get tunnel vision, get caught in the week's ups and downs, and have forgotten or couldn't fully see how they were at the beginning. Your job is to mark their progress, to point out changes that they don't notice, however small, such as pointing out to Teresa how assertive she sounds talking to the children during a session compared with the first time you met. This encourages them to keep plodding forward.

As we said in the beginning, what is behind all of this is courage. It remains the most basic antidote to all this stuckness and backsliding—staying close to the family's and your own anxiety even as distractions arise or new skills gradually take hold, being honest and clear when ambivalence and grief begin to seep out beneath the behavioral changes, challenging both the family and yourself to resist the temptations of lapsing back into the old familiar patterns, and instead approaching anxiety. By your willingness to continue to move ahead the family is able to do the same.

Keep in mind, however, that courage itself doesn't change the basic landscape. The plodding through new problems, the reassessment, reclassification, and reeducation will remain part of this middle stage. The going, in spite of your best efforts, may at times seem slow and stretch on longer than you at first thought.

HIDDEN SABOTAGE

What makes the family's slipping, sliding, and backtracking manageable is your ability as an outsider to the system to see the process unfold. The greater danger of the middle stage occurs when these same dynamics go underground—when you and the family become emotionally intertwined and become part of a system, or when you put up your own roadblocks to just how far the family can go.

Here are some of the dangers to avoid.

Induction into the System

In the room with you are Bill and Cary and their three children. The presenting problem is 8-year-old Joey's tendency to play with matches (he was caught trying to light the living room curtains on fire one day), but this is just the latest of many crises that keep the family in turmoil. You've already decided that Bill needs to take a more active role in parenting, that Cary is overwhelmed and depressed, that communication between the parents is lousy, that 10-year-old Allison is parentified and barely keeping her head above water, and that 4-year-old Tom is likely to follow in his brother's path. You've decided that your initial goals are to pull Bill back into the family process, open and clarify communication, and begin a problem-solving process among everyone.

But as soon as you ask how their week was, a verbal free-for-all erupts. All of the kids at the same time start telling their version of the story of how a hole got knocked in the wall of the kids' room. Cary chimes in and says that she suspects that Joey did it on purpose; Bill tries to pipe in but is quickly drowned out. You play referee and try to have everyone take a turn without interruption by the others; you try to separate and make sense of the stories, but before this incident is resolved, Cary is off on another, with the kids following verbally right behind. The best you can muster is to keep everyone from talking at once.

This kind of immersion into the family process, of becoming swept up and away, is fairly common, especially among beginning therapists. Rather than leading the process, you, the clinician, are limping behind, caught in the swirl of family interactions. Whether it is due to your lack of skills, timidity, or both, the problem at home is replayed over and over again there in your office. The family does more of the same, while you are left feeling overrun, overwhelmed, and confused. Eventually, you wind up feeling just as impotent to change things as they do.

Sometimes, however, rather than becoming emotionally washed away, you step up and end up stepping into one of the family roles. You may, for example, join with Cary and actually stand in for the inactive Bill by scolding Joey, backing up Cary's rules, and putting the lid on Tom. Or you may identify with one of the children and find yourself encouraging Joey to vent his anger right there and then in the room. If there has been a family loss recently—the death of a grandparent, a divorce, and the leaving of the father—you may, with the family's silent blessing, fill those empty shoes. Once locked into the role, you no longer have to struggle as an outsider, and the family no longer has to figure out what to do with you. Sit down in that empty chair, grab a plate, have some dinner, join in. The old process remains the same; only the face has changed.

This filling of the void is a lure on both sides that, like triangulation, makes for a quick and easy reduction of anxiety all around. This is what fuels the expectations of the enmeshed versus disengaged families, the overwhelmed single parent, and the transitional family that we discussed earlier, and if you step into the appropriate role of a firm yet not harsh disciplinarian or absent nurturer, the family gets better. Much will depend on your own psychological makeup. But if the fit is right, you'll find that even though you think you're working, not much work is really going on; even though the family knows they're in therapy, it all feels strangely familiar. You're no longer pulling against the family's grain and the family is no longer threatened by questions or comments that make them feel uncomfortable.

This kind of unconscious seduction is, of course, very different from the conscious, deliberate taking of sides—for example, specifically backing up Cary as a way of modeling such behavior for Bill, or using the ideal voice and giving words to the anger that you suspect Allison may be feeling but is not saying. In situations like this you are flexible, rather than entrenched; you're clear with the family and yourself as to the what and why of your actions; and you're able and ready to pull back or move to another role as the need arises.

Parallel Process

Cary yells at Joey, Joey fights with Tom, Tom kicks the dog. The dog bites Tom, Tom hits Joey, Joey steals Allison's hairbrush, Allison runs to Mom. Off to counseling steps Mom, who now turns to you, the clinician. The emotional buck gets passed up and down the line, as the patterns of action and reaction are played out over and over again. Just as it is easy for you to get caught up in the swirl of emotions and roles, it's easy to step into line and pass the buck yourself, to your supervisor or a colleague, rather than stopping it. As soon as the session is over, you're in her office talking about your experience with the family, and sounding just as much in crisis and overwhelmed as they do.

What the good supervisor or respected colleague does at this point is recognize what's happening, does the stopping, and pushes the process back down the line. He does this by treating the overwhelmed clinician the same way he needs to respond to the overwhelmed family. He helps the clinician see the parallels, and empowers the clinician to do the same with the parent.

Unfortunately, the wave cannot only roll up from the family, but also roll over them from above. If that same supervisor is under a lot of pressure by the agency head to shorten waiting lists or increase revenues, or if the clinician, new to the job, is under probation and feels enormous performance pressure from the supervisor, it doesn't take much for all of this anxiety to work its way down and get dumped on the family. Rather than the clinician remaining cool and collected, the clinician is breathing down the parents' necks, pressuring them to shape up and get their act together or pay their bill on time, and displacing on them everything she feels. Because of the power of the clinician as a role model, it's easy then for the parents to pass this same anxiety down to the children, who then may take it out on each other, the dog, the cat, or the kids sitting next to them in class.

Needless to say, all of this can easily get the family off track and worsen their woes. Rather than therapy being a safe place to try new behaviors, it becomes instead a forum for the clinician's or agency's own emotional chaos. Making it all the worse is the clinician's inability to see the impact he is having. Few families have the courage or skill to tell the clinician to keep her projections to herself, or the self-confidence to really believe that what's happening isn't their fault. If not corrected by the clinician, they'll eventually drop out, convinced once and for all that they are hopeless or that therapy isn't worth a damn.

Countertransference

Both induction and parallel process reflect countertransference issues in that the clinician is ensnared by a family's particular dynamics and pulled into the family system without his awareness. But there is another, more generalized form of countertransference that takes the form of blind spots and roadblocks that serve to emotionally protect the clinician, but limit the family's therapeutic progress.

You may, for example, be easily intimidated by men such as Bill who have high-power jobs, are older than you, or seem controlling. Rather than dealing up front with your own anxiety, you may find rationalizations to exclude him from the therapy: "It's too bad that he has to work so late, but rather than cancel, the rest of us can go ahead and meet without him." If he is there in the room, you may simply ignore him (thereby also replicating the family process and providing a double whammy), join with Cary and gang up against him, use her to express your own anger or fear vicariously, or silence Cary and act ingratiating toward him as a way of winning his favor.

Similarly, you may have difficulty dealing with problems of

sexual or verbal abuse or depression, stemming not from lack of skill but from deeper personal reactions; rather than confronting these topics and your emotions, the topic is never raised or is minimized, even when it's clear to an outsider that it's important. Perhaps your supervisor notices a pattern across your caseload, or you may vaguely sense yourself when you look back on your work that you tend to only go so far in the course of therapy. With the help of innumerable rationalizations (the mother needs to see someone individually, the family isn't ready to deal with Dad's addiction, they aren't working, they need time to consolidate the gains that they have made), relationships are cut off just when the client becomes too dependent, too provocative, too angry, too something—which triggers your own anxiety and personal emotional bottom line. Rather than pressing forward, in self-defense, you quit.

All of this can be subtle and difficult to untangle because it is below conscious awareness and potentially filled with anxiety. It's this anxiety—not lack of skill—and the anxiety-binding behaviors it generates that are the drivers here for such widespread, across-the-board patterns of avoidance, under- or overreaction, or vicarious expression of emotion by others. The anxiety distorts what you see and hear, and turns a rationale into a rationalization that limits or undermines the family's progress.

Collusion

Finally, there is a form of sabotage that arises not out of your immersion or filling in of already established roles but from the therapy culture that you and the family together create. Basically, you all fall into a rut. Each session, for example, follows the same format, propelled by the same questions or comments: "How was your week?"; "Let's pick up where we left off last time." Then Dad complains, Mom discounts him, and you mediate and give generally the same advice, which is never fully followed. Or the mother comes in complaining about one of the children, but this is only a learned warm-up to her talking about her ex-husband, or for you to simply ask questions about her past. The content is less important than the predictable spending of time together or the pseudo-intimacy feelings.

Collusion is in place when the therapy has lost its cutting edge and everyone silently agrees not to change. While there's the appearance of movement, little is actually changing; form has super-seded function. Everyone is comfortable rather than challenged. The emotions generated within the session (the mother's feelings of closeness and intimacy, the father's feelings of resentment toward his wife, the clinician's feeling of power or indispensability) become the new comfortable emotions that fuel and maintain the therapy's roles and patterns. The therapy rolls along, sometimes for years; its only value is its stability.

This is not to say that stability can't be a legitimate goal, espe-cially for chaotic families. But it's not a legitimate goal when it helps the clinician avoid the confrontation and risk taking the family needs in order to change, when it is supported by rationalizations rather than realistic family needs. Like the other forms of sabotage, collusion is a subtle process that, if left unchecked, quickly under-mines the therapeutic process.

COUNTERING SABOTAGE

Ideally, sabotage should never go unchecked and usually it doesn't. One of the primary lines of defense is good supervision or consul-tation with a respected colleague. Because this person is further removed from the family system, he is able to see the patterns that the clinician may be blind to, can detect the parallel process roll-ing his way by the clinician's presentation of the case, and knows the clinician well enough to recognize when distorted reactions are once again surfacing.

Even if the supervisor doesn't have it all worked out but sus-pects that the clinician is more entangled than she intended or is rationalizing her behavior, by simply raising the issue ("I wonder if you are stepping in for this mother who is so passive"; "I wonder if the way you feel now as you are talking is very much the way the father felt"; "I notice you have a hard time dealing with adolescents who act like this"), the statement or question itself becomes a crow-bar for prying up what is embedded below the surface. What was hidden is now out in the open; the unconscious is made conscious and loses its power.

As the clinician, you can also do your own prying. By know-ing yourself and the individual family you can anticipate the holes, traps, and roles that can ensnare you. By being familiar with your own weaknesses, you can stay alert to the cutoffs, avoidances, and attractions; the overresponsibility; and your need for clients to express what you cannot. By being sensitive to the larger patterns of your work, you will be able to recognize and emotionally separate the rationale from the rationalization. You'll be able to tell whose needs you are most trying to meet.

Finally, you can solicit the family's help with this process as well. By making the time to reevaluate the therapeutic contract at regular intervals, they (and you) can have the opportunity to say aloud whether everything is on course: Are the goals the same?; Are the strategies working? If there has been an imbalance in the family sessions, if one member has been ignored or felt ganged up on, or if new goals need to be set, here is the chance for it to all get out in the open, rather than the family dealing with their confusion or resentment by dropping out or becoming passive. Not only are you carefully tracking the process and treatment plan, you are modeling for the family the value of periodically taking stock of one's life, asking the hard questions about whether one's life is working, and being willing to make changes to set it right. During these discussions you need to be sensitive to the nonverbal as well as verbal communication of everyone in the room. If you are willing to hear only what you want to hear, what you'll get is exactly what you want, unfortunately, at cost to the family.

The simple solution is always the most reliable. If sabotage is driven by the avoidance of anxiety, it is your ability to stay at the edge of change—in the process, in the room, in your self—that is the best antidote. When the process gets too easy, too comfortable, or too predictable for too long, this should raise the alarm that something may be going off track, that the family's needs may be compromised, and that you have lost your power as an outside agent to effect change. Even if you're not sure at that moment what the right thing to do is, return to the basics of honesty and courage. Slow down, define, and take responsibility for yourself. This will help you recenter yourself and the process on the right path, and lead you and the family to where you need to be.

FIRST AID FOR THE AWFUL SESSION

No matter how good a job you do at confronting the patterns of sabotage, induction, and collusion, at some point you are bound to have one of those absolutely awful sessions that every therapist has. These have less to do with the family's or your own dynamics and more to do with the simple fact that you're having a bad day: You were awake most of the night before because your kid threw up every 15 minutes; perhaps you had a blowout with your spouse just as you were walking out the door about the dog peeing on the carpet *again*; or your mother called last night to say that, oh, by the way, she felt a lump in her breast, and though it's probably nothing, she's scheduling a doctor's appointment for first thing in the morning, but don't you worry about it.

So you walk into work feeling groggy, irritable, or worried, and actually the last thing you want to do is to listen to more people and their problems. But you do, and then Henry makes that same smirk he always does when his wife Betty talks about the trouble Freddie gave her that week, and you feel like clobbering the guy. Of course you don't, but you do come down on him pretty hard, and naturally, all he does is glare at you while denying feeling anything, leaving you feeling even more frustrated. Or Denise starts with her whiny pleas to the boys to stop arguing, but you're so tired that you just let it go until before you know it the boys are running out the door and down the hallway. She falls apart and starts crying, but you can't help her because you're off down the hall trying to find out in which direction the kids went.

These kinds of sessions can be hard to shake off. They leave you feeling angry and guilty and worried. You kick yourself for being so mean or lazy, for getting into this stupid kind of work, for getting a dog, and for getting married, for that matter. You're mad at this family for doing the same thing over and over again in spite of your best efforts for the last six sessions to try and get them to do something different. You're worried they'll never come back, and hope to God they never do.

Slow down. It's not the end of the world. First of all, give yourself a break. Sure, you could have done a better job, but you did the best you could at the time. Mistakes are called mistakes rather than tragedies because you can correct them. Take a couple of deep breaths and figure out what you need to do next.

Did the session leave you so concerned about the impact on the family that you need to do something before the next appointment? Is Henry apt to be steaming mad and take it out on Betty or the kids all week? Will he decide not to come back? Is Denise feeling so wrecked that she's likely to collapse altogether and lose all the ground she's made? Will she get depressed and start having suicidal thoughts again?

If you feel that someone in the family will act out or may go into a tailspin, or you just feel uncomfortable about it all, do something. Phone the family later in the day to see how they're doing, say what you think they may be thinking, apologize to Henry, and reassure Denise. You don't need to spend an hour on the phone—you can talk more about what happened at the next session—but do some crisis intervention. If you can't reach them, do what you do for the families who suddenly drop out: leave a message on the answering machine asking them to call you, or simply saying that you realize that it was a tough session, you're sorry, and you're just checking in; say what you think they may be thinking or feeling; write them a brief note and mail it. Sound concerned, not angry, don't obsess or feel helpless, but do something.

If you feel that yes, they'll be back, and it's not urgent to talk to them, wait until the next session. Start this session cleaning up the last one: "Before we get started on whatever you want to cover, I'd like to talk a bit about what happened last week." Then—talk—apologize if you feel an apology is in order, talk about your feelings in the process ("I felt frustrated when . . . "), or talk about yourself ("I realize I didn't say much last week; I was preoccupied because . . . "). Then ask the family to give their impressions of the session: Denise says she felt overwhelmed; Henry didn't understand why you kept asking the same thing over and over again, and frankly it was bugging the hell out of him. Or, often following the family's established pattern, they may say nothing: "I just felt a bit overwhelmed, again," says Denise, "but I was okay"; "No," says Henry, "I don't remember anything being wrong." Only later, after their trust and assertiveness increase, may they say something about it.

Regardless of what they do or don't say, you're modeling something important—how to admit and repair mistakes, how to take responsibility, how to communicate clearly when communication has broken down, and how to repair relationships. This can be a powerful experience for families that always sweep things under the rug, never apologize or always blame, or never talk about talking. Once again, you're approaching anxiety and you're dealing with the therapeutic derailment by looking at it squarely with honesty, clarity, and empathy. It's the most and the best you can do.

With all the movement in the therapy practice brought on by

managed care and the press of brief work in recent years, the traditional image of the middle stage seems to be changing; it is less the long, flat stretch that it used to be and more a way station between the beginning and termination. But even if the stages of therapy are more compressed, the challenge to appreciate the integrity of each stage remains.

To say to a family that we have reached the middle of therapy— that this is a plateau and not the end, that repetition and relearning are the nature of this period—is to define and map the contours of the change process itself. It's shaped by your theory and at a deeper level by your own values and beliefs about your role, the purpose of therapy, and the developmental process. How you think about the flow of the therapy process, in this stage and the others, will affect what you and the family will come to expect and eventually discover.

Looking Within: Chapter 6 Exercises

Just as the exercises of Chapter 5 focused on skills and issues related to the beginning stage of treatment, these exercises focus on those of the middle stage. Once again, take the risk and give them a try.

1. Think about a couple of ongoing or past cases. How do you decide when to stop with a case and when to stick with it? How much do you believe change is occurring even when it is not evident? How do you know when you are taking too much responsibility for change within the family and getting inducted into the system?

2. Countertransference. Think again about the kind of clients who are most difficult for you to work with. How do you respond to these clients? What role do you usually take? How does this role limit your therapeutic flexibility? Does it offer any therapeutic advantages? How could your supervisor or therapist best help you understand and broaden your options?

3. What kind of problems are emotionally the most difficult for you? How do you respond to them? What is your emotional bottom line? What kind of rationalizations are you susceptible to? How do you handle loss, in yourself, and in others? Again, are these indicators of unresolved issues from your past that need your attention? Who do you feel comfortable talking to about them?

4. Increase your awareness of the parallel process by noticing it in settings

outside of clinical work. Notice in a store, for example, how a child will complain to the mother, and the mother will then turn and complain to the father; or at work the way the director's urgency over some matter will trickle down through the supervisor to the staff; or even at home when your spouse lectures or your child whines to you and you pass it along and do the same to someone else. Practice stopping the process.

chapter 7

Endings

Enough Already?

*E*ndings, in therapy—and in life—are a culmination of the process and products of all that has gone on before. Like the beginning and middle stages of treatment, they reflect your own theory, values, personality, and clinical style, but, more than that, they reflect the two-way street between client and clinician that is the therapeutic process. Good endings, just like good beginnings and middles, require that special kind of clinical sensitivity to yourself and the family's needs and patterns.

We mentioned in the last chapter the common characteristics that let you know when you're moving toward the homestretch. But where and when do you draw the line? When is enough, enough? When they stop bringing in problems? When the IP is no longer the IP? But what about the trouble the couple continues to have if they try to talk to each other for more than 5 minutes? What about the mother's occasional claim that the father drinks too much? Should you try to tackle that, even though everything else seems to be going along okay? And what about the growing dependency that you sense the family has on you? How do you get them to see that they can really manage things on their own without your cutting things off and having them fall back to zero in a week?

I know what you're thinking. In all too many cases you never really get a chance to ask yourself these questions. Half the families, it seems, never make it beyond three sessions. They decide the fee is too high, or find that the insurance won't cover your treatment after all, or that managed care has a five-session cap. Or the only one who ever makes it in is the mother, and after a few weeks of this, she decides that she isn't going to give a damn if no one else in the family does. Or after two sessions everyone in the family decides they're better—Bobby did get up and get himself to school last Monday and only had one fight (which he didn't start!), and, besides, Dad's going to be out of town for 3 weeks because of work, and we'll give you a call when he gets back. The family has quit after going less than a quarter lap around the therapy track.

KNOWING WHAT'S COMING

Sometimes it's not that way. There are times when endings do come in a planned way, when the word *termination* is actually spoken aloud and discussed, and when the good ending not only brings a psychological closure to a good therapy but completes a healing deep within. Even if the formal endings rarely come with the hug or pat on the shoulder in the doorway or the long slow walk down the office corridor for the last time, endings really are important enough that they should be part of your beginning, your assessment, your vision, and, you hope, part of the family's vision as well.

Endings should be anticipated; they rarely should come as a surprise to you. Just as your own theory tells you about the beginning and middle stages, it becomes the starting point for defining the endings as well. If you are doing brief therapy, or have a 10-session cap on treatment, the ending will be fairly clear. If you see your role as lifelong consultant—giving families a boost up to get over the latest developmental hurdle, then pulling back and waiting in the wings until the next cycle arises—you can share this vision with the family from the onset and map a course together. If you view therapy as a process of peeling away layers, going ever deeper into the family's or individual's psyche, then what others call an ending may be for you only a plateau of the middle. Your theory, whatever it may be, establishes the parameters of the work.

Endings should not be a surprise to the family either. The expected time of treatment should all be out in the open, all part of the therapeutic contract. If you work under a session limit because of your or the agency's approach, let the family know at the first session so they can narrow their focus and understand what is expected. If you only do long-term work (for example, a year or more), be up front about this and help them understand your reasons (for example, your belief in the need to resolve underlying past issues). This will help the family appreciate your process, pace, and focus. Or, they may decide this isn't what they want at all and keep you both from becoming frustrated.

If your average time with clients is somewhere in the middle, varying from a few sessions to a few months, depending upon the nature of the problem and the family, say that, or simply tell the family how often the contract will be reviewed (for example, taking a few minutes every five sessions or so to see if everything is on target). However you decide to handle the therapeutic time frame, let the family know what it is.

Your assessment of the family should include an assessment of their endings. If the family seems to live from one crisis to the next, it's a good bet that they'll be ready to leave once the current crisis is over. If they report dropping out of past therapy when the therapist starting asking questions about the marriage, which had nothing to do, they felt, with their son's problems, you can suspect that the marriage again could be the hot-button issue that gets them out the door. If the family describes a pattern of avoiding grief or intimacy by finding reasons to get angry and prematurely breaking off relationships, you can anticipate this shift with you and be prepared to try and cut them off at the pass.

Don't keep your thoughts to yourself. It's valuable to talk to the family about termination as part and parcel of their other family patterns. If the Wilson parents, for example, describe a pattern of cutting off relationships when they don't get their way (pulling their child out of private school when their son isn't given the classes they think he should have, not talking to relatives who don't take their side in a dispute over an inheritance), you may want to wonder aloud whether they might find themselves wanting to drop out of therapy if at some point you too don't seem to be going along with what they expect. Similarly, in the Taylor family, the father describes his tendency to pull away from everyone and hole up in his workshop whenever conflict arises at home. Highlighting this pattern and expressing your fear that he will stop coming to therapy if the sessions seem too volatile makes his cutoff more transparent and less likely to happen.

If you can help the family to recognize their ways of using endings to cope with difficult situations and emotions, their behavior loses some of its seductive and automatic quality. By discussing their pattern of termination well in advance, you are posing a possible new option, and your confrontation about the process seems less of a personal attack. As in other areas of their lives, you are inviting them to see and stop their own pattern; you are challenging them to go against their own grain in order to increase their ways of coping with and creating relationships.

This mapping of time frames and patterns isn't any guarantee, of course, that it will all turn out the way you think it should. With some families there seems to be a running struggle over when and who pulls the plug. Even though Mary, for example, might no longer be hanging out with that 20-year-old biker, you think it would be good for the parents to iron out some unresolved divorce issues if they are to keep the same problems from coming up with the younger children; they, however, are ready to quit. Even though Sam and Helen are talking and making better decisions, Sam's underlying depression, you feel, still keeps the relationship from becoming more intimate, yet both of them feel that all is fine.

How much of this is client reluctance to engage in further treatment, therapist's reluctance to end, or a power struggle over who runs the show depends again on your theory, your view of the problem, and the scope of therapy. Your task, and the limits of your power, lies in making the family aware of your clinical perspective, the treatment options you see, the rationale, and the possible consequences of each of them. The contract, in order to remain viable, continually needs to be clarified and renegotiated, with the endpoints clear.

ETHICS: DOING THE RIGHT THING

Then there are the ethical issues. Dependency and abandonment can be looked upon as opposite ends of a spectrum when it comes to client–therapist relationships, and both are ethical issues. Dependency can be defined as a good relationship with no change. Here the client and therapist have fallen into a comfortable relationship. The week's events are talked about, goals are mentioned and often are the same ones that were set long ago, but both parties are essentially going on autopilot and continue to meet because of comfort, habit, and intimacy. From the outside it's easy to see that little change is going on; both are treading water.

These dependency relationships are different from those where client and clinician continue to meet as a means of helping the client remain stable. Jack may check in with his therapist every week at the mental health center, and though in terms of content little seems to change ("How was your week?"; "I saw my brother over the weekend"; "Did you take your meds?"), it is the regular checking in and ongoing relationship that, in fact, keeps Jack stable. Without it he would go off his meds, or hole himself up and never go outside his house. No change in this case is a good sign of progress.

Obviously it's easy to confuse the two—meeting to maintain accountability, crisis prevention and stability, or meeting out of inertia and habit. Here is where you need to have a critical eye to your own work, where you pay attention to and update treatment goals and plans and regularly address them with the client. And finally, this is where you often need supervision to help you sort out when and if changes need to be made.

The other ethical pole is abandonment. You've seen Kate four times and it is clear to you that you are in over your head and don't have the skills to provide what she needs or is asking for. Or you have been seeing the Wilson family but the father got laid off from his job, has lost his health insurance, and they can't afford your fee. You certainly are not required to continue with the family if they can't afford to pay you, but ethically you can't terminate suddenly if they are in crisis or unstable. If the dad is severely depressed and potentially suicidal, and the daughter is beginning to decompensate, you are ethically responsible to maintain services until an appropriate transfer to another clinician can be arranged. You can't leave a psychologically vulnerable client high and dry. When in doubt, talk it over with a supervisor or respected colleague.

QUITTING TIME

No matter how and where you envision the end, there are plenty of signs to tell you when a family is ready to quit. One of the best signs, of course, is that everything is better. The presenting problem is resolved, as are the underlying factors responsible for its creation.

You'll notice a relaxation, even boredom in the sessions—the edgy overreaction and crisis mentality have dissipated. Conversations fall to small talk, clients start forgetting some of their appointments or find reasons to spread them out, and you find yourself wondering what you should do next. The sense of purpose and direction seem unclear.

Share with clients what you have been thinking and feeling: that things are better and have been steady for a while, and that you're wondering what they want to do. Generally at this point the family members start nodding their heads and give a sigh of relief because they finally have permission to say what they also have been thinking for the past month. Once you broach the subject of termination they're ready to make a beeline for the door.

If, however, you put this discussion off for too long, some families will just drop out. Even though they're doing better, they may not have the courage to tell you they want to leave: they may be worried about how you would react, or they may have too many mixed feelings about it themselves. Rather than approach this anxiety, it's easier for them to simply stop coming.

This awkward, unsettled ending can dissuade some families from calling you in the future, even if they would like to return, and the longer the time, the greater the awkwardness and anxiety. Three years later you'll meet them in the checkout line at the supermarket, and if they don't look away or head for a different aisle, they'll casually mention how well everyone is doing. To finish this unfinished business and give them permission to come back, it's a good idea to always do some form of follow-up with families that drop out.

Obviously, not every family leaves because they're all better. Some are a little better and that is enough for them, or not much better at all, but problems on the job, financial pressures, or illness take over and push therapy to the bottom of their to-do list. Again, while dropping therapy can often be seen as another example of a family's crisis mentality and difficulty with setting priorities, it can also be a realistic response to the events in their life. The loss of a job, a serious illness, the sudden death of a parent—all life transitions that may possibly benefit from therapy support—can be so overwhelming and emotionally demanding that these events themselves monopolize the family's energy and resources. Therapy, rather than being a source of support, feels like another obligation to worry about, at a time when additional worries are the last things they need. While some families will make the effort to describe all of this to you in a last session, a majority of others will not. Instead, they will fail to show up or cancel a series of appointments, or leave several garbled voicemail messages, saying they will call back when they can. Again, a follow-up from you will encourage them to return when they are ready.

Finally, there are those who are ready to end because things, as they see it, aren't better, or may be even worse, than when they first started—Vinny was having some trouble going to school, but now Andrea is talking about how depressed she is and the parents are fighting like never before. They may blame you for stirring up trouble, or feel invaded by your seemingly constant prodding. Or they have already spent $500 and you're still asking questions, not giving them enough advice, or making anything better. A few clients might be angry enough to tell you how they feel, but most will just call and cancel because of car trouble. They never call back.

Sometimes you have to agree with them. The therapy actually hasn't been going well. You were hoping things would get rolling in that next session when Grandma and Grandpa were scheduled to show up and talk about their own marital woes, or after you got the results of the psychological testing on Vinny. Other times the problem is one of expectations or timing. Somehow their vision of the process and your own were never clarified or reconciled. They expected you to see Vinny by himself and fix him in two sessions, and here you are bringing in everybody and asking a lot of stupid questions about their childhoods or how they feel after a fight. Or perhaps you spent three sessions doing an assessment, and in the fourth you're turning up the heat on Mom and pushing her to make decisions that she has never had to struggle with before. Their anxiety goes through the roof, they don't understand the rationale for it all, and they decide to leave their trauma making at home.

The problem, often seen in hindsight, is that you weren't tracking the process closely enough, didn't see or acknowledge Mom's anxiety, or didn't do a good enough job of describing the treatment plan and time frames—the waiting on Vinny's test results. It's hard not to feel angry with yourself if a family pulls out after a bad session, and even harder if you thought things were going fine. The therapy may have been more important to you than to them, or in spite of gains they still felt they weren't getting what they wanted. Feeling rejected as a clinician is no small thing, especially if your self-confidence is shaky or if a lot of your own identity is caught up in your work and how well you do it.

It's unrealistic to expect there will always to be a perfect balance in the therapeutic relationship. You're a person first, therapist second, and there are always some families that you like more than others, some you may like more than they like you. If they suddenly leave, it's easy for all those little-kid feelings of being bad, wanting a second chance, and making things right to be stirred up within you. You have the urge to call them, see what's wrong, and have a chance to explain what you did and what you meant to encourage them to come back.

At first glance such thoughts and fantasies may not seem to you like bad ideas, and on some level they may not be, but realize as well that they are being amplified by your own countertransference feelings of loss. Go talk to your supervisor first to help you sort out your sense of rejection and loss from the family's real clinical needs. If this seems to be happening frequently, if your commitment to the family always seems to be greater than theirs, this is a sign that some old issue for you is being stirred up. It's probably compromising your ability to do your work effectively; it's time to consider some therapy for yourself.

As mentioned earlier when we talked about awful sessions and third-session dropout, some follow-up is important, and how you decide to do it depends on your own individual style and relationship with the family. You can call and for some families with your active listening and concern, they may say what they have been feeling—that treatment is going at a slower pace, or that the last session was too upsetting. Here you have an opportunity to repair. Other families feel this is invasive, that your calling feels like you're tracking them down and putting them on the spot. It only encourages them to make up all kinds of transparent excuses and promises that they'll come in next time. Leaving a planned phone message (for example, calling their home when you know they are at work) provides the intimacy of your voice without putting them on the spot.

Others like to send a follow-up note: "Sorry you couldn't make our last appointment, give me a call so we can schedule another." or "I've wondered if you feel that the therapy hasn't been helping as much as you hoped it would. Perhaps it would be worthwhile for us to talk about this, to help me understand better what you're needing, and what I could do differently." Whatever you say, let them know that they are welcome to give you a call should the need come up in the future.

Like other actions you take with a family, your response is never neutral, and your decisions should be driven by clinical concerns and knowledge of the family, rather than your own awkwardness or convenience. You are still serving as a model of good communication. In effect, you are providing in written or verbal form your half of the dialogue that would ideally happen if the client came into the office. If you haven't heard anything after a few weeks, follow up with whatever your normal procedure is: for example, simply close the case and document your actions in their chart, or send a letter telling the family that you are closing their case.

CLOSING YOUR DOOR

Of course, there are times when you're the one who wants to terminate. You feel like this family is not getting anywhere or your supervisor tells you the waiting list is 3 miles long and you need to make room for the new clients. Perhaps they never really follow through with your suggestions, or the people have rubbed you the wrong way since you first met them in the waiting room, or you feel they are setting you up to testify in an ugly court battle. Or maybe it's a matter of skill; while you know pretty much what to do, you're clearly outside your comfort zone and white-knuckling it through most sessions.

So you literally jump for joy or give a sigh of relief when it snows or they call to cancel because of the flu. You put off returning their phone calls, or call back, let the phone ring once and hang up or you seem a little bit too enthusiastic when they suggest having the school psychologist work with Susie at school instead of spending the money to see you. Short of paying them not to come back, or quitting your job and leaving town, you'll do just about anything not to have to go on.

Or perhaps your considering termination is not about relationship chemistry or skill at all, but an honest reevaluation of the family's needs. The father needs inpatient drug treatment before any progress can be made in family therapy; the mother needs social services in order to get environmentally stable before any therapy can be effective; the son is becoming psychotic and needs hospitalization for evaluation, medication, and stabilization; the family is too chaotic to effectively use or even get into outpatient services—home-based services would better fit their needs. Your role changes from a family therapist to a referral source.

Whatever the reason for the change—skill, chemistry, or referral—it's time for some supervisory consultation. If the family needs a shift in services for clinical reasons, your supervisor needs to be aware of your thinking and plan. If the urge to escape from some of your clients is part of a larger pattern for you, you may decide that you need to work it out in your own therapy while you continue to see the family. If you lack particular skills, you may decide that with enough supervisory support and skill coaching, you can work through certain issues with a family. If you and your supervisor agree that your reactions are interfering with your ability to work with them, or that you are clinically in over your head, you may need to pull out.

Of course, there will usually come the day when you really do need to leave, not just the family, but the work—you're leaving the job—going back to school to study 13th-century English literature or septic tank repair or you're getting married and moving to Oklahoma. These are easier to explain to the family in some ways, but often only a bit less so than leaving for other reasons, as discussed above. Many families already have old issues around abandonment, and your leaving only stirs up these feelings. You need to give the family as much notice as possible, help them sort through these feelings, give them permission to get angry at you for pulling out (that is, ask "Are you angry about my leaving?"), or angry at you for having the flexibility to do with your life what they feel they cannot. When handled well, these kinds of endings can be invaluable experiences for mending old wounds.

Whatever the scenario, whatever your reason to end services, honesty rules once again. While it's tempting to attempt to drive those difficult families away with your neglect, or, worse perhaps, your rationalization that they really don't need to come in any more, it's dishonest and destructive. Instead, you need to use all your good communication skills: the "I" statements; talking about yourself, not them; and talking about feelings, as well as facts. Explain why other services or another therapist would serve them better, and then listen. Make sure they don't misunderstand what you are saying and blame themselves for your giving up on them.

Consider easing the transition to another therapist, or to a hospital, by personally going with them the first time. This gives you a chance to describe in front of the family member your summary of the work and the problem, or gives the client the opportunity to sort through her feelings and describe your relationship and work together to the new clinician. This not only provides some closure but helps the new person be aware of and sensitive to the loss issues that may arise as he begins. The more the family has invested in the process and the relationship, the more important all of these steps are.

GOOD ENDINGS

Regardless of the circumstances surrounding any case, what you are always ideally shooting for are good terminations. They are like any other good death—they leave enough time and space around them for everything that needs to get done and said to actually get done and said. The basic elements include everything you've read about in all those textbooks: give the family notice, set an ending date, and explore the feelings about the leaving. Expect testing, crises, and everything seeming to fall apart; better yet, predict the crises for the family so that they realize it is all part of the ending process; review all the skills learned and progress made. Help the family see that their own feelings of loss and abandonment don't take away from their ability to go forward on their own.

Most clinicians use one of two basic ending formats, and if you're a seasoned therapist you undoubtedly worked out your own style long ago. One is the decisive "Do it and leave" approach: set an ending date several weeks or months in the future, meet at the same regular pace (weekly, biweekly), and stick with the plan no matter what. The date is negotiated with the family and may be built around another convenient marker: summer vacations, start of the school year, and the like. The other approach is the "fade away": spacing out sessions over increasingly longer periods of time, for example, weekly, then monthly for a couple of months, then again in 3 months, and then in 6 months if needed.

What you choose depends on your own preference and the needs of the family. The "Do it and leave" has a counting-down effect that's clear and definitive for the family, but can raise anxiety, which in turn can promote crises as the count gets shorter—that's not a reason not to do it, but a reason to be prepared. The "fade away" reduces some of the anxiety by giving the family an opportunity to see for themselves that they can really handle things on their own. But it also can give the impression that the ending is less defined, more open-ended; in their anxiety it's easy to go into denial and pretend that it's never going to happen. Potentially, you could wind up stretching things out so long that other developmental life events pop up ("Would you believe it, Jane just got pregnant!"), fueling the need to continue monitoring or to crank treatment back up. Most often you can simply give the family a choice of formats, map out together what it means in concrete terms, and then enforce the plan.

Enforcement can seem easier said than done when and if termination crises start to mount. The best approach should the family fall into crisis mode is to be matter-of-fact: Reassure them that they know what to do; coach them through problem solving the situation, intervening in as minimal a way as possible; and predict and interpret the crisis in light of the upcoming termination. Generally, with your steady presence, positive coaching, and reassurance, their confidence will increase and the crises will rapidly diminish.

This doesn't mean that you may not have doubts—that maybe they need more time, more support, or that maybe you're throwing them out the door and they're not ready. Talk it over with your supervisor or colleague. Try to sort out what the family's need is for accountability and support and once again what is your own separation anxiety, your own loss, your own sense of inflated importance. Take the time to separate out your reactions from theirs as best you can.

The pragmatic nature of therapy means that you think and prepare and then do, and then see what happens next. But you may face a scenario where the family can't pull out of the crisis even with some minimal support. New problems, though seeming to you to be manageable with the family's new skills, seem to them to be foreign and overwhelming. They need some time to regroup before trying once again to go on their own. As always, you talk about the process of being stuck, help them to see the bigger landscape, build on their strengths, and work together to give them the final push they need.

WRAPPING IT UP

It's often good to have some form of a closing ritual with the family. This is especially true for families with whom you have worked intensely—home-based cases, cases you've had for a long period of time—or where there are young children who do not fully understand the ending process. Drawing a picture all together, doing a formalized recitation of the changes each has made, sharing a meal (this is easy and usually quite appropriate with home-based work), and doing a closing experiential exercise (a guided fantasy about the future or about giving each other symbolic gifts) all have a way of bringing together and acknowledging the mixture of emotions that endings bring.

It's always useful to have some kind of joint review of what the clients have learned. This allows both you and them to actually articulate the progress made and, more important, helps them recognize the skills learned. These skills are what they can draw on when similar problems arise in the future; you can underscore them in the discussion.

As you have done all along, you once again set the pace, modeling the way to do it. You're the one who needs to talk about the mixed feelings that both you and they have. You're the one who keeps everyone and everything on task so that distractions don't derail this part of the process any more than any of the others. You're the one who, with honesty and caring, shows the family how people can leave and continue on with their lives.

The door is always left open, for a quick phone consult or another round of work, for problem solving, or for a brief consultation as the family moves through new stages of development and old issues once again raise their head. Some families, of course, never return. Others make the out-of-the-blue phone call on some Thursday afternoon, sometimes seeking useful information, offering good news, sometimes just seeing if you're still there. Some come back 1, 2, or 5 years later for a few sessions or for a few months. And once again you start, hoping to pick up where you both left off, but, not surprisingly, finding out that you both have changed. There's a new beginning with new expectations.

Again, the reality of practice makes these good endings rarer than they should be, but when they come they are invaluable for what they offer—the sense of groundedness, completion, and defin-itiveness. At that last session there's that wonderful sigh and sense that something important has happened.

We have finished our trilogy of the beginning, middle, and end, ideally covering all the basic parameters of family therapy practice. We're now ready to look at the family therapy with specific cases over the course of the developmental cycle.

Looking Within: Chapter 7 Exercises

1. Take a few moments and think back over endings in your own life, those clearly marked: the graduation from high school or college, your marriage or divorce, the death of a parent. Or look at those numerous unmarked ones: the way you and your childhood best friend just drifted away, the gradual ending to your relationship with an old boyfriend or girlfriend, the way your father one day called you for your advice.

    Try to remember how you felt, the feelings that led you to the ending, the way you handled those emotions, how free you felt in showing them to others, and how you behaviorally coped in the days and months that followed. See if any of those patterns affect your expectations of termination with clients, or affect your own emotional bottom lines in your work.

2. As you did with middles, take the time to think about your notion of termination, your role, your stopping point according to your theory. Are there times when termination has met your needs more than those of the family? How can you increase your awareness of these countertransference reactions when they come up in your work?

3. How do you personally handle rejection? For what types of families and under what circumstances would their leaving be particularly hurtful to you? Imagine talking to one such family, saying how and why you felt the way you did. What personal issues, if any, does this stir up for you?

4. Take the time to think once again about your own needs from doing family therapy, your own needs issues of loss and separation that may affect your practice, and your own ways of avoiding families you do not like.

5. What kind of cases or problems would you automatically consider transferring out because you feel your skills and knowledge are limited? How could you increase those skills?

6. Develop termination rituals that reflect your own personality.

chapter 8

Billy Has a Problem

Kids in the Family

*B*illy sits quietly, scanning the toys on the shelf, his arm tucked under the arm of his grandmother, as she describes why they've come to see you. Although he's 7 years old, Billy looks 5 because he's short and skinny. His blue eyes are clear and bright, but he avoids eye contact with you. He's seems a little bored.

Billy has been with her now for about 2 months, says Ms. Williams, and she is having a hard time getting him to mind. She always feels like he's pushing her, and thrusts out her big hand to emphasize how she feels. "More often than not he'll throw a fit if he doesn't get his own way," and, she admits somewhat sheepishly, she sometimes gives in just to settle him down. But settling down isn't what he does too often; he's always doing something. In fact, the only time he's quiet is when he's sitting in front of the TV or sleeping. He's doing well in school, though. No problems there; he likes it, has friends, and seems smart. The grandmother turns her head and smiles at Billy. She looks exhausted.

The grandmother had already supplied some history when she called: Billy had come to her following a 3-month stay in a foster home. He had been living with his mother and her boyfriend, Tom, and his 3-year-old half-brother until the night the boyfriend beat the brother to death. The details are unclear; Billy was in the home at the time, but no one knows just how much he saw. His mother told him that his brother had choked to death on a toy. The boyfriend was arrested and convicted of murder and is now serving 15 years in prison. Although present when it happened, Billy's mother was not charged, but Social Services removed Billy from the home. The mother continues to live in the same town she had been, some 200 miles away, and hasn't seen Billy for 5 months. Ms. Williams is angry at Billy's mother and father—who is her son Edward and who divorced Billy's mother when Billy was 2—for both ignoring Billy. She's worried about the effects of the death on him and about his reluctance to talk about it.

Living with the grandmother is her husband, Ray, who, like her, is in his late 50s, and is out of town several days a week as a truck driver. Also in the home is her middle son, John, who is in his late 20s; he's recently divorced and the father of a 3-year-old son whom he rarely sees. Grandmother's youngest son, Ben, is stationed in Thailand in the Air Force. In addition to caring for all these men, she also looks after her own elderly parents and runs errands for them daily. No wonder she looks exhausted.

The start of each new case is like standing at the edge of a dense forest. All we can see before us are the faint markings of paths among the trees. As we take the first steps into the wood—gather our impressions and begin to organize them around the client's personality, priorities, and motivation, as well as our theory, personality, and interests—we discover that the forest is actually crisscrossed with numerous paths. While we usually assume that there is only one path that takes us where we want to go, we see that there are, in fact, several possibilities.

Together with the family we make choices, trusting our intuitions, following the most pressing needs, pragmatically closing off one treatment option, trying another, coming back to the first, trying still a third. While our knowledge and experience can give us some idea of what we may expect, it's only by actually working with the family over time, seeing the consequences of our choices, and setting and resetting our priorities based on environmental and psychological changes that we can actually know how close we are to coming out on the other side of the forest.

In the previous chapters we have laid down a broad foundation of concepts, strategies, and techniques common to family therapy. In this chapter and the next we shift gears and follow the story of Billy as it actually unfolded in the course of his therapy, and look at the everyday, pragmatic nature of therapy. As we reach decision points along the way we'll stop to consider some of the options that were available. As we do, consider how you might decide to proceed in a similar situation.

FIRST IMPRESSIONS

Let's start by giving you a couple of minutes to develop your own impressions so far:

- If you were seeing this family, what, according to your own theory, would you want to know?
- What is your tentative hypothesis about the cause of Billy's misbehavior?
- What are Billy's and the family's strengths?
- What parenting skills do the grandparents need to effectively manage him?
- What's missing in the family process?
- Where would you focus first?
- How would you make contact with Billy?
- How do you envision the course of therapy?

Okay, time's up. Here's my short list of brainstormed ideas; compare them against your own:

- *Presenting problem.* Billy is testing limits at home and his grandmother is having difficulty managing his behavior. She's also concerned about Billy's reaction to his loss and trauma.

- *Possible family concerns.* It's unclear why Ms. Williams has difficulty setting limits with Billy: Is it a learning problem (a weakness in her parenting skills?) or a problem about learning where her emotions (feelings of anxiety and guilt) are interfering with putting those skills into action? What about her high level of stress and possible depression? Can her husband, Ray, and her son John help her with parenting and become more involved with Billy?

What about the family structure and Billy's role within it? Are the grandmother and grandfather able to work together as a team? Is Ray feeling left out of the grandmother–Billy relationship? Has Billy learned to only get negative attention? Is the hierarchy weak and Billy feels entitled, knowing that he can wear his grandmother down and get what he wants? What is the marital relationship between the grandparents like? Who holds the power in the relationship?

How has John coped with his own sense of loss surrounding his divorce and son, and what impact has that had on the family? What role can or should Billy's parents play in his recovery?

• *Possible concerns for Billy.* Obviously, Billy is struggling with grief and the loss of his mother, father, and brother. He may feel guilty about his brother's death and the boyfriend's imprisonment, or feel responsible for his parents' abandoning of him. He may be suffering not only from posttraumatic stress from his brother's death, but from other violence toward his mother and him that we, as yet, don't know about.

Is he identifying with the aggressive boyfriend, or does his behavior reflect a typical testing of limits in a home with new rules and structure? Is he clearly depressed, or does he have ADHD or an attachment disorder?

• *Strengths.* Billy's grandmother clearly cares and seems committed to him. The home environment, although stressful, overall seems stable. Ms. Williams is willing to seek professional help. Billy, in spite of all the trauma and change, is doing well—he does not appear to be severely depressed, can make friends, does well in the school structure, and seems to be fairly bright.

• *Therapeutic options.* Begin family therapy with Grandmother, Grandfather, Billy, and John to improve communication, define clear rules and roles, reduce stress, strengthen the hierarchy, explore loss, and develop support and nurturance for each of them. What about including Billy's mother and father in the family therapy to focus on loss, roles, support, and coparenting? Or seeing Ms. Williams individually or together with her husband to order to work on parenting skills and help them manage Billy?

Perhaps supportive individual therapy with Ms. Williams would help her to reduce her stress and be better able to act more consistently with Billy. Psychological testing for Billy could be considered; it may serve as a quick way of assessing his personality and coping skills and isolating underlying emotional conflicts. Individual play therapy with Billy could help him work through his past trauma and grief, provide ongoing support, help him learn better ways of coping with his emotions, and provide him with a positive male role model to offset the negative ones he has seen. Maybe consider some combination of all of the preceding.

• *Therapeutic don'ts.* We need to be sensitive to issues of abuse or abandonment with Billy. The overwhelmed grandmother needs not to be further overwhelmed by therapy; we need to be consistent and structured with the grandmother.

• *Therapeutic dangers/countertransference issues.* These include feeling angry or frustrated with Billy or his grandmother, as well as being overwhelmed or wanting to quit the case. We need to watch out for feeling overresponsible for the family, and having the urge to step into a parenting role.

These last two points need some explanation. As mentioned earlier, the presenting problems and symptoms become broad working metaphors that can tell us what to avoid and where to be careful in our approach in order to prevent ourselves from becoming emotionally snarled within the system. Given Billy's history, we clearly know that he is sensitive to anger and aggression, from his experience with his mother's boyfriend, and may have abandonment issues (from the loss of his parents). We need to keep these things in mind as we interact with him and plan his treatment.

Similarly, because the grandmother is already feeling overwhelmed, we want to be careful that we don't do anything to make her feelings worse. Because she is struggling with inconsistency and lack of structure, we need to model consistency and structure for her. If we don't and replicate her own behavior, she will become confused and probably more inconsistent than she already is.

Being aware of what to avoid based on the client's experience is only half the equation. Recognizing the subtlety and power of the dynamics means acknowledging that we too may be inducted into the system, that we may be capable of feeling like the other adults in Billy's life who get angry, frustrated, or are insensitive to endings or breaks in contact. We may find reasons to send him off for individual therapy, or decide that the case and family are simply unworkable. Similarly, there is the danger that we may end up feeling like the grandmother—overwhelmed and willing to give in, or feel that we have to fill in the slack, be overresponsible, and wind up exhausted.

By acknowledging the therapeutic dangers inherent in a

particular case we are acknowledging the family and individual dynamics that can pull us like an undertow toward the replication of the family's problems, behavior, and emotions. Only by looking out for them, looking in, and sensing when we are becoming emotionally ensnared, can we step back and regroup.

Again, at this point, we don't know how much of this will come to pass, and we need to assess Billy and his grandmother further. But through our brainstorming we have defined both our therapeutic possibilities and our limits. We have a clearer view of the therapeutic space we can work within.

OPENING MOVES

Some clinicians feel awkward about including children in family therapy. Two cultures, two different worlds, those of the children and those of adults, both need to be explored and understood, yet it's difficult. Parents feel they have to be careful about what they say around the children; children, especially if they are young, often feel intimidated by the office, the questions, and the seriousness of all the talk they don't understand. Like Billy, many children sense that they are in an adult place and grow quiet unless welcomed in some way. How you bring together these different worlds once again depends on your theory and style, and as mentioned earlier, you can always choose to meet with the parents alone first.

At whatever point you decide to include a young child into the sessions, it is always a good idea to see parents and young children together first. Start the session by having the parents describe why they came, clarify your role with the child—that you are a worry doctor, that you don't give shots—and get enough background to know what you want to explore with the child individually. As you talk together with the parents and child, the child will come to feel more comfortable with you, will get used to the sound of your voice, and can learn from watching the parents' reactions that you are a safe person. Then when you ask the parents to leave, the child will be less anxious and feel more comfortable staying with you. If the child balks at the idea of being alone with you, throwing him- or herself around a departing parent's ankle, don't force it; the goal of therapy is to reduce trauma, not create it. Let the parents stay for a while when you begin to interact and play with the child.

This is what we did with Billy, seen together with his grand-mother (the grandfather was out of town); it was a middle ground between a parents-only session and a whole-family session. It demonstrated a bit of the parent–child interaction, and helped him feel more comfortable with me. The next step is seeing him individually.

WORKING WITH PLAY

If fitting children into the family therapy process seems hard for some clinicians, the notion of play can seem even harder. Some clinicians simply don't feel comfortable with play as a therapeutic medium; they prefer words to crayons or blocks, and the direct language of problem solving rather than the symbolic language of fantastical worlds within sand trays or playhouses. Others just don't feel comfortable around children—they don't have little ones of their own, or struggle tapping into their childhood memories— and will choose either not to treat them at all, or to work through the parents. Still for others, the problem is largely one of their limited skill and experience; they simply haven't been trained in play therapy, are uncertain about the effectiveness, and aren't sure about how to go about doing it.

If this is the case for you, if you are untrained or uncertain about ways of using play therapy, it would be helpful for you to take some time to explore and become educated. Talk with colleagues who do play therapy, or better yet, see if you can observe a session. Read books, look for training videos, attend a play therapy conference. These methods map out the play therapy terrain, teach you skills, and increase your confidence, but more important, your exploration can help you better define your own theory and values regarding the treatment of children and their role in a family therapy context. This exploration will help you discern for yourself whether you see this type of therapy as a tool for assessment, treatment, or both; whether you view it as a potential healing process in itself, or more as an effective backdrop for talk therapy. You'll begin to define when it is better to do individual play therapy than work with the parents, when to see the child together with the parents, or when play therapy may be contraindicated. And undoubtedly, through exploration, discover what about play therapy you personally like or dislike.

Play, at its most basic level, is, of course, the medium of expression for children in the same way that words are for adults. Because they lack the vocabulary of an adult and a brain capable of creating the concepts and analogies that the adult mind can, children's words are often only flimsily attached to their thoughts and emotions. Rather than using language to express fantasies ("I'm looking forward to the big date on Saturday night"), wishes ("I wish my roommate was less critical"), and images ("I could see myself exploding and quitting right there on the spot"), the child is able to do the same through play. The family living in the playhouse always fights, and here comes the police officer to tell them to stop; the lion puppet tries to eat the mouse puppet, and the mouse runs and gets help from the zebra; the clay turns into a snake that slithers along around the outside of the bedroom and scares the little girl; the picture of the family leaves out the little brother, or he is merely a tiny speck squashed between the two angry parents.

When 5-year-old Jamie, sounding just like her mother, yells at the doll for not going to bed, she is expressing her needs and conflicts just as clearly, though more symbolically, as the adult who complains about the way her boss dumped on her once again. Your asking Jamie why she is so mad is no different than asking the adult why she feels like her boss is being so tough on her—all that is different are the media in which each relates.

What do you need, practically speaking, to do play therapy? Not much. Crayons, paints, drawing paper, clay. Some blocks, a playhouse, people figures to live in the house, some cars, trucks, an ambulance perhaps. Puppets, animal figures, toy soldiers, some Legos: toys that stimulate imaginative play. Board games: for younger children Uno, Candy Land, and Chutes and Ladders; for older ones checkers, Battleship, Risk, and Sorry can be used to build rapport and as background for talking. (Electronic/video games are usually too intensive and stimulating, and it's too easy for the game itself to become the focus.) Get a deck of cards, hook up a mini basketball net over your office door, and use a Nerf ball for the basketball. Most of what you need to get started can be found in Walmart, at garage sales, or from friends whose kids have outgrown their toys. Set them out in your office where the children can see and choose from them.

Apart from these larger issues of play therapy theory and techniques, and your own values and style, are the practical questions of using play therapy within the context of a particular family. Will the parents of this family, for example, support the play therapy process? Are they able to see it as a form of treatment rather than just play ("All my son said you did last week was play Candy Land with him for an hour"), or would focusing on their parental skills better meet their expectations and increase the chance for success? Are they, and you, willing to take the time needed to engage in what may be a slower process? Is there any danger of the child's IP status being reinforced through individual focus? Is the child a good candidate for play therapy?

If you identify yourself as a play therapist and view play therapy as a best-practice model for treating children, this last question may seem foolish. While there are different theoretical approaches to play therapy, just as there are to adult therapy, there is no right way to play in play therapy, just as there is no right way to talk in adult therapy. You may be directive, for example, and offer specific games or toys to use, or suggest various scenes to play out. You then watch what unfolds, make reflective comments, label the child's emotions, and perhaps encourage problem solving. If your style is nondirective, you may let the child choose whatever toys or games she wishes, observe the play, and occasionally say what you see the child doing and expressing.

Whatever the child does is information and grist for the mill. If the child refuses to play or plays in a seemingly closed and unproductive way (for example, plays checkers for the whole session for 10 weeks), you still have clues as to how the child relates to adults or follows rules, approaches emotions or new situations, or competes against others or is able to be assertive, just as adults who seem sensitive to your comments, try and fill the space with small talk, or only occasionally grunt information about their interactional style.

While all this may be true, there remains the question of whether play therapy is a good match for a particular child and family. Just as some adults use one form of therapy more effectively than another, so too do children. Most children, for example, starting at age 10 or 11 on up, see any forms of imaginative play (the playhouse variety) as babyish. They would much prefer to talk, or use some structured play (for example, board games, cards, basketball) as a background activity, a way of containing their anxiety while they answer questions or initiate conversation. Others do not want to play so much as hear their parents talk and have their questions answered, or, with your support, get things off their chests and solve problems at home or school. Still others are so reluctant or anxious about seeing you that the most effective and efficient course may be to work with the parents and effect changes at home through them.

What you actually wind up doing with children, then, is—as with adults, somewhere between the ideal and pragmatic—a blend of your comfortable media, needs, and style with theirs. For some children you may decide to use play therapy only as an assessment tool, a way of gathering information about the child that can then be passed on to the parents to help them view their child in a different light, or to help you develop behavioral strategies that the parents can implement at home. If, for example, you learn through his play that Bobby is worried about his parents divorcing, feels that he has to take care of his depressed father, or feels guilty about his younger sister's cerebral palsy, this information can help the parents be more supportive of Bobby or motivate them to talk to him about what has happened.

In another case it may be clear to you that play therapy may be the best not only for assessment but treatment as well. Only through the play process, for example, may the child be able to express many of the emotions that cannot be talked about directly. For example, Todd expresses his anger at his father by drawing a picture of him and then scribbling over and over it with a black crayon: anger that he is not able to express at home. For another child, what you do together doesn't really matter—playing the card game rummy this week, drawing pictures next week—but by playing together with you the therapeutic relationship becomes the support that allows the child to talk about his fears and worries. Just as you encourage adults to move against their grain and take risks, you do the same with the child in play. As the child becomes less anxious, more open, and more confident, you may decide to intersperse whole-family sessions, involve other siblings in the play process, or work concurrently with the parents.

It's important to remember, however, that the therapeutic contract is not only between you and the child, it's also between you and the parents. While some parents are too content to have you take over their child and treat her, often dangerously replicating their already ingrained hands-off stance, other parents can seem anxious or annoyed by what seems like a dark hole of individual play therapy. How you ultimately choose to work must reflect the parents' concerns and priorities as well.

If, as mentioned earlier, they are particularly disturbed by the behavior of one of the children, spending a few sessions in the beginning in individual play therapy with that child, rather than pushing for family therapy, not only builds your own rapport with the child, but addresses the parents' immediate concerns and their confidence in you. It gives you a stronger basis for recommending family therapy when you do—after all, you have evaluated the child, and have your own sense of what the child needs most. If, on the other hand, the family is in crisis, it may be better to begin with whole-family sessions, calming the emotional fires at home so they are less of a distraction before you shift to individual work with the child.

The bottom line here is that play therapy with children is another approach, another modality, another clinical choice. You can flexibly integrate it into your family therapy models and adapt to your own style and strengths, as well as the needs of the particular child and family.

THE MORE THE MERRIER?:
THE QUESTION OF MULTIPLE THERAPISTS

In sorting through treatment options, there is one final option to consider, namely, whether it's useful to divide a case and family among more than one therapist. The classic family therapy approach is just to go ahead and see everyone. The traditional child-study model favors this approach: A child specialist works with the child individually while another clinician works with the family.

Probably the worst basis for deciding this approach is convenience and logistics: you don't have time to see both the child and the family in the same week so you rope in a colleague to help out. This dismisses the clinical needs of the family. Some clinicians bring in another therapist as a way of offsetting their limited skills—rather than fumbling through play therapy, farm that individual work out to a specialist and turn your attention toward your strengths in family therapy—but this approach has to be weighed against the impact of multiple therapists on the family.

Often it's better to do it all and increase the supervisory support and coaching. In other cases rapport or the lack of it is a deciding factor: the adolescent female, for example, could significantly benefit by some individual therapy to supplement the family therapy, but she has a strong negative transference to a male therapist. In that case, bringing in the female therapist to see her and having both of you work together with the family may be the most prudent option.

Those clinicians who are uncomfortable with family work and think psychodynamically rather than systemically often seem to fall into a one problem–one therapist approach, with Mom, Dad, and the IP seeing separate individual therapists, then all coming together with a separate family therapist. There are significant downsides to this approach. Coordination among the therapists, which is essential, becomes difficult. There's the danger not only of confusion for the family members over how to integrate their different therapies or how to set priorities regarding goals, but also of clients splitting therapists—disclosing some information with one, some with another, deciding one is nurturing, the other cold and mean.

In the worst-case scenario, all of the therapists wind up replicating the family dynamics with confusion over who's in charge, fragmented focus, and squabbles over the treatment plan itself. To have this type of treatment work requires all the treatment team members to work together like a functional family. My own preference is to do as much of the work myself as possible—not for control, but for consistency and coordination of the elements of the treatment plan. The family and I can cobble out one vision together that incorporates the overall needs of the family, rather than juggling several.

If you decide to go this route, you'll still find a few exceptions described earlier: for example, asking a school or private psychologist to do psychological testing, but being clear that her role stops at the assessment. Or if you believe a child may benefit from a medication evaluation, refer the family to a physician or psychiatrist, and coordinate so she is aware of your therapy goals and progress, and you can remain updated about the medication. If you are struggling to build rapport with one of the key family members, you may consider bringing in a cotherapist to help out; for example, have a female therapist come in to support a mom who is the sole female in a family.

Once again, the bottom-line criteria become moving toward what is missing and being careful not to replicate dysfunctional patterns. As with all the other clinical options, consider your own style and strengths and make your decision clinically based and intentional.

BREAKING GROUND:
FIRST SESSIONS WITH THE CHILD

When a child remains quiet in the first session or two with parents, it's important to make the extra effort to connect with him. Because Billy was reserved when I saw him together with his grandmother, I decided to meet with him for a few sessions alone to build rapport, get to know him, and discover how he would use play therapy. Surprisingly, Billy was eager to be seen alone.

After glancing around the room, Billy makes a beeline for the Legos. He matter-of-factly tells me that he wants to build one of the models pictured in the instructions. It is clear that he can read well for his age, and has good spatial perception and coordination; he is much better at figuring out how to create a model than I am. He quickly begins to gather the pieces he needs and enlists my help in finding some of them, all with an air of seriousness and intensity. When I try to ask him about his coming to the agency, about living with his grandmother, about his father, and his mother, he ignores the questions, says he doesn't want to talk about it, or says he doesn't know. He keeps all of his focus on the Legos and all of his communication limited to directing my help. At the end of the session, Billy hasn't finished his model, and he asks me to save it for next time. He wants to know when he is coming back.

The next several individual sessions aren't much different. Billy still talks little, though when asked he mentions without much enthusiasm that he saw his father over one weekend, and describes in a few sentences his school and teacher. When asked to draw his family he says that he doesn't draw people well, and when asked to draw anything else says he doesn't like to draw much. He does play Candy Land and tries to cheat when it appears he is going to lose. When I say that he isn't following the rules, he seems upset and reluctantly gives in. In the second game, Billy makes up new rules as he goes along so that it always works to his advantage. Again his mood is fairly solemn, but he mentions several times that he likes to come and wants to know when he is coming back.

Impressions? What seems most striking is Billy's need for control of the session: directing me, controlling the conversation, and controlling the outcome of games. What don't we see? What's missing? Obviously no strong emotions, like anger; no discussion about his past or the trauma; no aspect of his inner world, his fantasies; none of his misbehavior that his grandmother is reporting in the home. Billy isn't replicating his problems in the office. Why?

His behavior isn't surprising. Many children who have been traumatized have learned to cope by controlling themselves and others. They're both protecting themselves from other inner and outer dangerous emotions, and, on some level, replicating the control they experienced from powerful adults. Billy has learned that it's more important (and safer) to be in control than to be who he is. The only place he shows his emotions is at home with his grandmother. He probably trusts her enough to let down his guard, but he also may replicate with her the emotionality that he saw between his mother and father.

Is Billy a good candidate for play therapy? The answer lies in your orientation. As mentioned earlier, from a psychodynamic, more nondirective perspective it's a ridiculous question. If clients show up, they're working in therapy, even if the working is both of you slogging through all the defenses and layers of resistance. Billy is clearly showing up; in fact, he enjoys coming and likes me. At a minimum, the relationship has the potential to give him an opportunity to be with a man who isn't abusing or rejecting, offsetting the male images he has within him.

The better question that a more directive therapist may ask is whether Billy is using the play therapy process effectively. The answer would probably be no. Compared with other children who start re-creating their inner and outer worlds from the start, Billy is not using the play as a medium for portraying his emotions and conflicts. Instead he's only showing his defenses, either because he's terribly closed to his inner life, still frightened of me, or both. What he's not doing is being resistant to the therapy process itself. Some children clearly don't want to be in the room, not because they are anxious about the process but more because they are angry with their parents who made them come. They refuse to play or do so passive–aggressively. Billy is not like this; he is playing out his life. It's just going to take a while to reach the deeper layers of it.

What would you do? Would you see him in play therapy, maybe have someone else see him individually, or stick to family or parenting work? It might be good to see his grandmother before making any decision.

THE REST OF THE STORY: ASSESSING THE GRANDMOTHER

Ms. Williams comes in alone. Despite my efforts to reach her husband, Ray, he is driving all over the state delivering supplies for a hardware store and is unavailable. Although it's just 11 in the morning, she already has that dog-tired look. After she got Billy off to school, she needed to stop by her parents' house to take them to the grocery store for a few things. After lunch she's going back to help her mother clean the house.

Ms. Williams talks easily. Billy seems to have settled down some in the past couple of weeks, but he still gives her a fit at times, especially in the past few days that Ray has been away. Although John, her son, is usually home in the late afternoon, he does little with Billy and does even less when she's having a hard time with him. She's not sure how much longer John will be staying with them; he keeps talking about moving out. She knows she ought to be more consistent with Billy, but his tantrums wear her out, and then she starts feeling sorry for him. She finds herself making bargains with him all the time—bribing him with TV, treats from the store, desserts—if he'll clean up his room, finish his homework, not pester her in the grocery store. Sometimes it works and sometimes it doesn't.

Ms. Williams can easily talk about Billy's mother, about how she didn't like her from the start, how the mother dumped Ms. Williams's son Ed, Billy's father, for that lowlife who killed his own child. But she sounds more sad than angry. She also has mixed feelings about Ed: Maybe he's just having a hard time right now, she muses, maybe he will eventually take custody of Billy; 2 minutes later she says that she also knows that he really doesn't show any interest in the boy, that she ought just to realize that Billy will stay with her.

The overwhelming feeling in the room, however, is that she's overwhelmed. She is the caretaker of her immediate family and her family of origin. There's a history of depression in the family, and even though she shows no vegetative signs, it's easy to believe that she may get pretty depressed at times. She clearly seems committed to Billy and overall is doing fairly well, especially considering the fact that she is doing it all alone.

When asked what she wants, Ms. Williams says she needs help learning to be more consistent. She feels that it's good for Billy to see someone himself; she is still very worried about the effects of his brother's murder on him. She doubts that her husband will ever be able to come in and questions whether it would make any difference, since he is away from home so much.

Once again, impressions? An overworked grandmother with a good heart. A soft touch who has a hard time setting limits for both Billy and herself. She's motivated to work on her parenting, and that's certainly needed. She supports individual therapy for Billy, and it already seems to have a somewhat positive effect. What to do about Ray? Try harder to bring him in? Is it realistic if he really is away so much?

What about her son John? If he is really going to move out, would it be better to help Ms. Williams be able to handle Billy on her own? What about Ed—is it possible to get him involved?

Could Ms. Williams manage better if she were able to set limits in other areas of her life, such as with her parents, and reduce her stress?

We are at the first fork on the path. What to do? In situations like this it's helpful to look first at what the family is willing to do and weigh that against the possible results of pushing them to do something different. This family's motivation is for play therapy and individual help with parenting. In spite of Billy's control in the sessions, they seem, from his grandmother's report, to have a positive effect on his behavior at home. This may have to do with the process and therapeutic relationship, or with Ms. Williams's own decrease in anxiety now that someone is there to help her or help Billy deal with his past, or both. In the long run, of course, the play therapy ideally could become a flexible medium for unlocking Billy's emotions, and the consistency of a positive relationship may counter the negativity and loss of the past men in his life.

However, I feel that only doing play therapy would not be a

good idea. Rather than bringing in the grandmother and other parental figures in Billy's life and helping them learn to relate better to him, there's the danger that I, as the individual play therapist, will, in effect, displace them, making what's already occurring worse. When beginning play therapy with a child like Billy, who has had so much loss, I need to be clear and certain about the family's commitment and availability, especially if the process and progress will be slow. If I become too impatient, I'll wind up replicating the problem and become another abandoning adult in Billy's life.

Working with Ms. Williams alone, as she suggests, may help her set the structure Billy needs, reduce her anxiety, and increase her self-confidence. But like the play therapy, there are questions. Is it practical or foolhardy to believe that she can continue to carry the load of the family alone? Would individual work with her on parenting only maintain a potentially dysfunctional system? We may have to try and see. Sessions with Billy and his grandmother together at this early stage wouldn't seem promising—I could imagine sessions filled with complaints of the week, a lot of questions, silence from Billy, and to him only a milder form of verbal abuse. As he feels more secure and settled and begins to open up more, this format may become a positive option.

Your own theories may suggest other options: exploring with Ms. Williams her own depression, past losses, or the dynamics underlying her sense of overresponsibility; a parents' support group for Ms. Williams, or a psychiatric evaluation for her depression; the use of a play therapy group or a battery of psychological testing for Billy. How about moving the therapy out to the home? A home-based therapist could see Billy and his grandmother there where the problems were occurring, give Ms. Williams hands-on demonstrations of parenting skills, have her observe and participate in the play therapy, and perhaps have greater success in pulling in Billy's uncle or grandfather. All of these are possibilities.

What was finally decided was the combination of individual play therapy with Billy and parenting education and support for Ms. Williams, a decision reflecting my own skills, interest, and orientations, the availability of services (home-based services, for example, had a huge waiting list), and the family's motivation and immediate needs. This plan was presented to both Ms. Williams and Billy, and they seemed satisfied.

PUTTING THE PLAN INTO OPERATION

Over the next few months I saw Billy individually each week in play therapy, and saw his grandmother, either in individual sessions or for a few minutes at the start of Billy's session about every other week, to discuss parenting problems. Billy continued to need to control the session and resisted suggestions to engage in drawing, painting, storytelling, sand tray, clay, talking games, and other more expressive media.

The offering of play suggestions was, I felt, an important part of the process. Just as it's valuable to give adults a clear sense of the range of topics and forms that therapy may take, so is it important when working with children to help them see the range of what play therapy offers, and to find the medium that best suits the individual child. Some children, for example, love drawing or painting, but hate playhouses or board games. Others don't seem to care what the activity is. Many active children like to play outside, others seem attracted to the containment or regularity that the office session provides. It's up to you to introduce the choices and help the child discover the forms that allow him to best express his inner self.

Billy rejected all of these less-structured forms because they created too much anxiety. He was able, however, gradually to express violent themes through playing with cars and trucks (creating gigantic crashes), toy soldiers where battles always ended with his army defeating mine, and—surprisingly—with wrestling with me.

Billy was a big fan of professional wrestling, and knew a lot about the different characters, their strengths and weaknesses, and, most important, whether they were good or bad guys. In a typical session he would move the furniture in the room to the corners, we would block the sharper corners of the furniture with cushions for safety, and Billy would assign me to be a particular "bad" wrestler— The Black Knight, Sergeant Destruction, Lowthar the Crusher— while he would always be the week's current world champion. We negotiated rules (for example, where the ropes were, whether it was a tag team, how you were pinned, how long the match was) and they were restated and clarified at each session. Although Billy only weighed about 60 pounds, it was here that he became most animated and most aggressive, and where he always had to win. And he did; I made sure of it.

What's going on here, is this therapeutic? Doesn't this rough play only replicate the physical aggression he had already seen? Certainly—and that was the therapeutic rationale for doing it. Through the wrestling matches Billy was able to play out the anger that was being bottled up or dumped on his grandmother. He also was fighting with a big strong adult man, on some level not much different from the one who terrorized him. But now he had the opportunity to win. In his imagination he became powerful and able to overcome his enemies, rather than a helpless victim. He also had to learn to express aggression with constraint; the rules of the play included clear restrictions on aggression (you can't punch) and having to stop and let the other one up if either one of us felt hurt, tired, or uncomfortable. These rules taught Billy the beginnings of self-expression and self-control. Finally, this play provided Billy with a way of making physical contact with a man who, in reality, was not aggressive, but more nurturing. While he was pretending to pin me to the mat, he was, in actuality, getting hugged back.

All of this raises the larger question of touch in therapy. As therapists we all have greater awareness of clients' possible past physical and sexual abuse than we may have had in the past; we know and are sensitive to the potential ethical dangers that physical contact can pose. Some therapists have moved toward feeling that any physical contact with clients is out of bounds. I tend not to be so austere. While we are thankfully way beyond the touchy-feely times of the past when everyone got a big hug or we justified clients sitting on our laps as part of a reparenting process, there are times when a pat on the back as a client walks out the door after a difficult session can physically give to a client what he can't yet psychologically give to himself, when a gentle tap on the knee can be an effective nonverbal signal to a family member that he is once again getting hooked into a dysfunctional pattern and needs to resist the temptation.

Our ethical codes define clear bottom lines regarding physical contact, and our sensitivity to the client's history, experience, and reactions in the moment should serve as guides as to what we can or should not do when it comes to issues of touch. We should be clear about our clinical rationale based on the client's goals and needs, be wary of rationalization, and be open to supervisory input when in doubt. But we should not, I believe, automatically dismiss the use of touch as a potential adjunct to talk therapy.

If I had initiated wrestling with Billy because I thought it was a good idea, rather than following his lead, he most likely would have simply gone along. But emotionally this would have been potentially injurious to him because we would have succeeded in replicating his powerlessness, as well as potentially triggering old emotional and physical reactions. If I had failed to set rules and literal boundaries, or had not ensured that he was safe, or had ignored his own limits, I would have once again repeated in minor form the neglect that he had previously experienced. But I was following his lead, working within his metaphors, and the wrestling became an outlet for his emotions, an opportunity for self-mastery and self-regulation, and a chance for him to literally rewire the meaning of touch.

MAKING PROGRESS?

Billy settled down more and more at home and, with support from me, Ms. Williams was able to set clearer limits. She used time-outs and taking away of privileges, along with verbal positive reinforcement, to shape Billy's behavior at home. Within 5 months the presenting problem—Billy's testing of limits at home—had waned considerably.

Here and there, however, were periods of a week or two where things would slip at home: The grandmother was less consistent with the rules, the structure began to collapse, and Billy started pushing and the grandmother gave in, setting off a self-feeding cycle. From the grandmother's point of view it was Billy who started the backsliding process—for some reason he had a hard day or week and would test her. From where I stood it was Ms. Williams who actually started the cycle. Some additional outside stress would stretch her psychological resources, and she was unable to maintain her consistent focus on Billy.

Within the 5 months several environmental disruptions and emotional crises had occurred: Ray was unemployed for several weeks before he found another job; John was having problems with his ex-wife and getting depressed; and Ms. Williams was worried about her father, who was having pain in his hip and needed to go to the doctor. As the stress increased and Ms. Williams became more worried, upset, and depressed, she let things go, opening the door for Billy to return to his older behaviors, and further increasing her own stress. As the problems resolved—for example, when Ray found a job—the structure returned.

What sense do you make of this dynamic? Do the new parenting skills collapse in the face of stress because they are still fragile and not well integrated? Does Ms. Williams's chronic depression grind her to a halt when the stress is high enough? Does Billy become defiant as a way of getting his grandmother's attention when she seems preoccupied and he starts to feel abandoned? Or is he trying to save his grandmother, attempting to pull her out of her depression by his negative behavior? Is he "needed" as a problem at these times because he also provides an outlet for his grandmother's or the family's frustration and anger? Has he learned to sacrifice himself as the scapegoat?

All of these are possible ways of looking at the pattern, and they're important only in the way they help you proceed. Once again, consider the options and your own inclinations. Would you support Ms. Williams in staying on track with the parenting, perhaps interpret to her Billy's behavior and role in the family based on his past experience? Would you advise her about how to solve the problems at home, realize the limits of her own responsibility, offer support or specific skills (for example, teach relaxation exercises) to help relieve her anxiety, and refer her for medication? Would you bring in Ray or John, or both, to get to the sources of the stress, and use the crises as an opportunity to get them involved in the family therapy process? Would you do something different with Billy perhaps, increasing the frequency of his sessions, or working to help him express his anxiety verbally rather than behaviorally?

All of these are workable. Pragmatically you could try one of these, several, something altogether different, or decide that these changes are, for right now at least, merely a blip and do nothing different at all.

I decided to do something altogether different. In situations like this it's often useful to go back and look at what's working and to find ways to support those processes. Overall, the current approach of doing play therapy with Billy and focusing on parent education and support with Ms. Williams was creating stability at home and improvement in Billy's behavior. It didn't work when the stress became too great for Billy's grandmother. If there was a way of reducing her overall level of stress, then crises, when they arose, would debilitate her less, and, I reasoned, she would be able to continue to maintain the structure that Billy needed. Pulling in Ray or John, or helping Ms. Williams find ways to reduce the responsibilities she had with her parents all theoretically have the same impact, but practically speaking, weren't, in her view or mine at the time, good options. Trying to make such changes would be enormously difficult (so who would help the parents?) and would undoubtedly create even more stress, only compounding the problem.

I supported Ms. Williams in maintaining the behavioral structure as much as possible (the redoing and reinforcing that is part of the middle stage), and emotionally by simply listening to her. I also arranged respite care for Billy a few days a week after school and on alternate weekends, an idea that both Billy and his grandmother thought was great. Here he would spend time with another family, one that was part of the community respite program. This program arose out of the community need to help overloaded parents of physically and mentally disadvantaged children, as well as families like Billy's, by giving them a break from a few hours to a couple of days at a time, on a regular basis.

As it turned out, the respite family that was assigned to Billy had two boys around Billy's age. The family did a lot of activities (soccer, camping) that Billy didn't get to do at home, and the parents in the family were both supportive and good at limit setting, exactly what Billy needed. Ms. Williams appreciated the break, and Billy not only enjoyed the time there but found that he could separate from his grandmother and she and he would be all right.

It helped. As the crises came and went, both Billy and his grandmother were able to step outside of them a bit better. More important, Ms. Williams was better able to see the connection between her stress and Billy's reaction, and could even anticipate the start of the negative cycle; his behavior was less and less seen as arbitrary or instigating. All the pieces seemed to be coming together.

Looking Within: Chapter 8 Exercises

1. In considering the initial assessment of Billy and his family, what most strikes you as important to focus upon? What therapeutic options would you choose based on your style and theory?

2. What are your own feelings and thoughts about the use of touch in therapy?

3. All children engage in play as a means of understanding and coping with the stresses of their world. When you look back on your own childhood, what type of play was most prevalent? What themes continued to run through your play even as you grew older? What do you think they may say about your stresses and needs?

4. This became a fairly long-term case. What would you do if you were restricted to a shorter time frame or were unable to commit to working with Billy so intensively?

chapter 9

Billy

The Story Continues—
In the Middle of the Middle

As we discussed in Chapter 6, the middle stages of treatment are a time of developing skills and reinforcing changes (in infinite variations, it seems) over and over again until they can be permanently integrated into the family's patterns. The middle stage can also be a time when the focus of treatment will shift. Once the child problem is settled, the marital issues come to the surface; now there is time and trust in the therapeutic relationship to explore a parent's individual concerns, such as her own past history of abuse, depression, or problems with sex or drugs. After a quick start, individual sessions with the child may seem to level off and show little movement, but crises may break out elsewhere in the family as the still-active dysfunctional patterns are pushed in new directions. A shift to parent sessions to firm up skills may be more productive, or if the child has become stronger and articulate through individual work, it may be a good time to focus on family sessions.

Billy slowly progressed during this middle time. While he stayed relatively closed to his past, he did begin to let go of his need to be in charge. In sessions he no longer needed to direct me. My relationship with him, based on being absolutely predictable and reliable, increased his sense of trust. He was able to compromise, he was more sensitive to my feelings, and his play themes became less violent. Wrestling, once so intense, became more of an occasional thing. At home Ms. Williams was by and large able to maintain the structure that Billy needed, and with the help of regular respite, things generally went smoothly. But then everything became unsettled once again—the parents came back into the picture.

Although Billy's mother hadn't seen Billy for 2 years and had no contact beyond a couple of letters, she now started writing, telling him that she wanted to come visit. Ms. Williams would come into sessions waving letters, wondering what to do and how to respond to Billy and to his mother. She had fantasies of his mother taking Billy away, of her filling his head with something (she didn't know what) about the past, and causing him to regress back to where he started. Why couldn't she, the grandmother wondered aloud, just leave him alone?

The grandmother's reaction wasn't unusual. Anytime an absent parent comes back into a child's life—for both the child and the caregiver—it creates anxiety that can disrupt the system. For Ms. Williams the mother became a threat: Even though the grandmother had legal custody, the mother was his mother, and could, it seemed, take him back if she wanted to. Making it all the worse, of course, was Billy's reaction. He idealized his mother and was excited about the prospect of seeing her again.

Ms. Williams realized she couldn't stop the visits without court action, but she decided that there needed to be some supervision, and so she drafted a few additional relatives to be around when the mother came. I asked about Billy's mother coming to a session—this would not only provide a safe forum for meeting and talking but would give me an opportunity to see this other important person of Billy's life up close—but no, the grandmother replied, his mother was planning on coming on Sunday only for a few hours.

The mother didn't come. No phone call. No letter, nothing. Fortunately, the grandmother and I had discussed this possibility. Ms. Williams was both relieved and angry. Billy said little. Ms. Williams was tempted to use this incident as an example to show Billy just what kind of person his mother was, but I tried to help her see that this was her agenda, her emotions, which were very separate from Billy's own. He needed the opportunity to deal with his grief himself and to come to terms with his mother and their relationship without the grandmother injecting her own feelings. I tried to talk to Billy about it and made interpretative comments about how he might feel—angry and sad, that she really didn't care, that there was something wrong with him—and offered to help him write a letter to his mom. In typical Billy style, he remained closed and quiet.

On the heels of this incident reentered Billy's father, Ed. A shadowy and sporadic presence, he too suddenly expressed an interest in seeing Billy more, and even talked to Ms. Williams about taking custody. Why all the renewed interest wasn't clear; Ms. Williams suspected that it had something to do with Ed's stable relationship with his girlfriend. Because it was her own son, she felt less threatened, but only slightly. She quickly made clear to Ed that Billy (and she) could not handle any fickle or quick changes. If he was serious about custody, he could prove it by visiting regularly, and everyone would see how things went over the course of a year.

Billy was less excited about his dad's visits. Because his parents had divorced when Billy was 2 years old, his memories of his father were nonexistent, and his experience with him since he had been with his grandmother had been disappointing. Again, I invited the father into a session, but he said he worked long hours and couldn't get the time off. The father began weekend visits, but after a month started to find reasons not to come. Within 2 months he had stopped seeing Billy altogether.

This kind of sporadic involvement can be devastating for a child. The child has no stable relationship on which to lean; he literally becomes afraid to open his heart. The rejections are a narcissistic injury, proving that he is unlovable, which can cause depression and rage. It also can be infuriating for you as a therapist. It's difficult not to identify with the child, and like the grandmother, be angry at the parent and project your reactions onto the child. But while your own countertransference can give you a clue as to how the child may be feeling, your focus is on helping the child sort through his own grief reaction.

Billy remained stable for a few months in spite of these rejections, but then the stronger emotions began to surface. His mother wrote another letter, and Billy refused to look at it. When Ms. Williams pressed it on him, he tore it up. He started having tantrums again at home when he couldn't get his way with his grandmother, and often refused to go into a time-out when he misbehaved. Finally, there was an incident at school where a child pushed him on the playground and he attacked the child with such ferocity that it took three teachers to pull him off. He kicked one of the teachers so hard that he cracked her leg bone.

The deterioration didn't stop there. His classroom behavior became increasingly oppositional, culminating 2 weeks later in another outburst where he turned over all the desks in the classroom. Now not only was Ms. Williams in a panic, so was the school administration.

In individual sessions Billy said little and behaved no differently, but in a joint session with Billy and his grandmother, she repeated what Billy had told her: that the boy on the playground reminded him of Tom, the mother's boyfriend. This is a classic posttraumatic stress trigger, and what eventually came out of the session, with questions and prodding by both the grandmother and me as Billy sat on the floor near my chair, were Billy's memories of his brother's death: his hearing the commotion in his brother's room, his own fear about what was happening, the screams of alarm by the mother, and the police. Most of all he remembered Tom blaming him for his brother's death.

The memories and the emotions were finally breaking loose. It may have been triggered by the reappearance and subsequent reabandonment by the parents, the lowering of his own defenses through therapy, the increased sense of safety by the grandmother's consistent presence and structure, the passage of time, a combination of all of them, or none of the above—it's difficult to really know. But what was clear was that Billy was beginning to process his trauma, and the emotions surrounding it were coming to the surface. What he needed most was support to verbalize these feelings, adequate channels for expressing them, and help understanding what was true and what was not.

What was not true, of course, was that Billy was responsible for his brother's death. As happens for many abused children, words heard in the moment became indelibly linked to the traumatic experience itself.

Tom's accusation had stayed with and had haunted Billy for all those years.

It's tempting as the clinician to jump in and simply say to Billy that Tom was wrong and that he wasn't to blame. While intuitively this seems to make sense and, in cognitive-behavioral terms, corrects the cognitive distortion, this kind of response can feel like a too-quick, flip dismissal that has little absolving effect. Unless Billy had the opportunity to say why *he felt* he was to blame, that feeling and the idea would continue to stay within him. By our questions and listening, his grandmother and I needed to let him know that we understood how he felt.

I asked if he sometimes felt that Tom was right, that it was his fault. He nodded. Did he think he should have done something different? Slowly, in half sentences and mumbles, he said that he felt that he should have somehow stopped Tom. How? I asked. He shouldn't have listened to his mother—he should have left his room, hit Tom maybe, tried to pick up his brother and run away into the back woods. Something. He teared up. He said he felt mad at himself for not doing anything.

As he spoke we both listened and restated and sympathized with his feelings. His grandmother held him. We then both reassured him as other adults who knew him and cared about him (in contrast to Tom, who didn't) that it truly wasn't his fault. This seemed to calm Billy. As we were walking back down the hall after the session the grandmother said that now that this lid seemed to be off the box, so to speak, she worried that Billy would continue talking about this at home and that she wouldn't know the right thing to say. I told her that she just needed to let him know that it was all right to talk about all of this as he needed and wanted to and that she only had to listen.

Billy did not talk any more about this at home, and it seemed as though a breakthrough had been made. As clinicians we look for these important moments when weeks or months of therapy all come together and we feel that the client is finally on a different course. But breakthroughs are in the eye of the beholder and are not always clear. Later that week Billy had another, seemingly unprovoked, outburst at school. The school principal arranged a meeting of all the people working with Billy.

COORDINATION WITH SCHOOLS

School behavior and performance are an important part of your assessment of a child or adolescent. The perspective of teachers, guidance counselors, and the principal can help you gauge how widespread particular problem behaviors may be, and how the child responds in a setting different from home. Billy, for example, traditionally did well at school, as well as at camp and the respite home, environments where the structure remained consistent. School, in fact, for Billy and many other children, often becomes a place of important regularity and emotional security.

It also is possible for home and school to become emotional dumping grounds for each other. Some children are quiet and well mannered at school, but belligerent at home. The home may be a safer, more secure place for the child to be him- or herself, and a place where the trials and traumas of school life (being teased or picked on by other children, feeling criticized or castigated by a teacher, feeling embarrassed or shy) get acted out. Such children often expend a lot of energy "holding it together" at school and emotionally collapse once they hit the door.

For some, the pattern is reversed. The child who is perfect at home may be a holy terror in the classroom. Sometimes this reflects the home's low expectations of behavior—the child can essentially do whatever he wants at home, and rebels under the rules and regulations of the classroom—but more often it's the case that the home is not a safe place to show anger. The child copes at home by stifling strong emotions and uses school as an arena for releasing them. A positive change at one site may or may not create positive changes at the other. It's good to check and see whether a child is truly integrating changes and improving across settings.

It also is important to see if the home and school are working together. Often they are not. While the school personnel are ideally concerned about the welfare of the whole child, in more pragmatic terms they're most concerned about the child as a learner. If the child is a good student, completes the work, and keeps her hands to herself, underlying emotional issues can be easily ignored. When the child refuses or stops learning, bothers other children, or becomes a distraction in the class, as Billy did, the school sees a major problem, and at this point may refer the child for counseling. The school is essentially having a problem that the parents or child may or may not see.

This was the case now with Billy. The school teacher and administration were frightened by this 60-pound boy, by his rage and his unpredictability. While recently schools have developed protocols for crises (due to shootings) and violent student behavior, this school at the time had no protocols for handling children like this, and no organized response to such behavioral or emotional outbursts. Instead, they reacted differently each time, and often, in their seeming panic, overreacted. One time as Billy flung desks around the room the teacher cleared all the other children out and watched through the window in the door until uniformed police finally arrived; their response unknowingly re-created Billy's past.

In large multidisciplinary meetings with school personnel the therapist has several tasks, depending on the particular child and circumstances. Sometimes his job is simply to be present as an advocate or support to the parent who has clear ideas of what he wants for the child, but who feels intimidated by all the heavyweight professionals sitting around a table. At other times the school wants input from the therapist about the counseling and insights the therapist may offer in formulating a plan for the child at school. The therapist is often in a unique position to serve as a bridge among home, school, and office, providing a unified point of view for managing the child. What the school personnel generally don't want is the therapist criticizing their efforts, or telling them, unless they ask, what they should do. Their goals and needs for the child may be very different than those of the therapist, and like the therapist and the parents, they too feel they are doing the best they can.

So what could I say about Billy? At the start of therapy I had secured signed releases from the grandmother and Billy to talk with the staff at the school, and had already spoken to Billy's teacher, guidance counselor, and principal several times in past months. At the meeting, with the grandmother present (Billy occupied himself in the nearby computer lab), I reviewed the history of my work with Billy: how he had responded to play therapy over the course of almost a year; about his need for control and the gradual easing up of these defenses; and of the grandmother's work in providing a more structured environment at home, which Billy needed to feel safe. I also told them, with Ms. Williams adding details along the way, about Billy's recent experience with his parents, and the disclosure of his memories about both his brother and the abusing boyfriend. Finally, I said that I thought Billy was actually getting better and beginning to heal. His recent behavior, though disruptive, was possibly and hopefully linked to the release of anger and grief that Billy had kept such a tight hold on for years.

While this last point was initially hard for some of the school staff to accept, when heard in the light of Billy's history and with my interpretations, they were able to agree. Framing these changes as positive gave the school personnel a new perspective, as well as helped them be more sympathetic to Billy's situation. Hearing this summary helped the grandmother realize just how far Billy had come.

Do you agree with my interpretation? If you were working with a child who presented with minor behavior problems, had been traumatized early in life but expressed little about his experience in therapy, and now began to have emotional outbursts and destructive behavior, would you think he was really making progress (things have to get worse before they get better approach) or would you think, based upon your theory and perspective, that he is really beginning to fall apart? What recommendation would you make to the school?

Regardless of the way Billy's new, aggressive behavior may be interpreted, it clearly could not be ignored. A different response and plan of action was required. We are at another fork on the path. Some questions and options to consider:

• Is it true that the school environment is no longer able to support him? Given the structure of the classroom and the demands on the teachers, would school become in reality only an arena for his negatively reinforced destructive behavior and deteriorating social relationships and self-esteem?

• What specific changes could and should the school make that might make a difference?

• Would he do better in a school setting that was more structured or geared for children with emotional problems, or would he, in fact, do worse because of the stress of the change and the influence of potentially more negative role models?

• Would such a placement be premature? Would it represent a falling into the trap anticipated at the start, namely, a replication of the multiple abandonments he experienced with his parents?

• Should I, as the therapist, do more: increase sessions, take a more directive approach, secure some sort of evaluation or consultation? Should medication, in spite of his young age, be considered?

These are difficult choices. Success, it seemed, depended on what the school could tolerate and provide in the way of a positive response and services; on Billy's ability to verbalize, rather than act out his anger and sadness; and the length of time it might take for him to work through his grief and anger and become less explosive.

What was finally decided at the meeting was that the school staff would try and put more emphasis on prevention. They were not comfortable using any form of restraint, but they would more closely monitor Billy's behavior over the course of the day and offer support—the teacher would check in with him and see how he was feeling, especially when he seemed irritable; she would take time to help him talk about and solve his problems with other children. Because he seemed to have the most difficulty in the afternoon, Billy would be given supervised individual computer time both as a way of reducing his afternoon stress and as a reward for good behavior. Finally, the school psychologist agreed to meet with Billy weekly for half an hour to further shore up problem solving and support within the school.

It seemed like a good plan and everyone around the table felt optimistic. It seemed to dovetail well with the home and therapy goals—developing consistent supportive but structured environments, helping Billy verbalize rather than act out his emotions—while I would continue to address the underlying grief and anger in play therapy. After the meeting, Billy's teacher, his grandmother, and I met with him to explain the school changes, and I followed up when I saw him at the next therapy session. Billy seemed fine with the plan.

The changes didn't hold. After a honeymoon period of a few weeks, Billy exploded one morning when the teacher wouldn't let him get up to sharpen his pencil. The school administration once again panicked, and this time suspended him. They refused to allow him back into school until further evaluation could be done. I made arrangements for Billy to spend 2 weeks on the children's ward of the local private hospital.

NEW EYES, NEW IDEAS

While it's hard not to see a sudden hospitalization in the middle of therapy as cause for disappointment, I thought the school's idea to get a thorough evaluation done was a good one. The old dynamics were beginning to be played out: the emotional explosions on both sides, the cutoffs, the potential abandonment. Two weeks would give everyone a respite, a chance for regrouping and recharging. Through the workup some new information and recommendations might come out. Having someone with new eyes see a client, whether it be on an outpatient or inpatient basis, can be invaluable for overcoming the blind spots that can develop over time, for reaffirming what you know, or for providing a new perspective that can generate new ideas.

As could be predicted, Billy did well in the hospital. Once again the tight structure decreased his negative behavior, and group therapy with other children his age helped him to be more verbally open about his feelings overall. While he didn't talk much about his brother, father, or mother, he willingly participated in all the activities, kept a journal, and was able to make brief comments about his past to various staff. Both the grandmother and I made separate visits to see Billy at the hospital, in an effort not only to see how he was doing but to maintain the reliability and predictability of his relationships, and reduce the sense of abandonment.

Some useful information and changes did come out of Billy's stay in the hospital. Thorough psychological testing confirmed a diagnosis of posttraumatic stress disorder and depression. The evaluators agreed that his recent explosive behavior was a result of a relaxation of his defenses through therapy and a relatively more stable home life; they suggested that the therapy continue as it was. Billy was placed on imipramine to relieve his depression and clonidine to reduce his aggression. But it was the formal reporting of the findings by the hospital psychologist and psychiatrist to the family—grandmother, grandfather, and John, Billy's at-home uncle—that had the most impact, especially upon both the men.

Consultations are often valuable not only for what they offer in terms of information, but also for who delivers it and how. In this case the clout of the psychologist and psychiatrist in their white coats in a wood-paneled office carried authority that I as the therapist could never match. The evaluation, testing, and medication sent a clear message to these men that Billy truly had serious problems and needed their help. (Of course, in a different setting with a different family this could backfire—the medication becomes proof that the child is the only one with the problem, and reinforces her role of scapegoat.) With my prompting, the psychologist and psychiatrist strongly encouraged the men of the family to become more involved and back up Ms. Williams as much as possible.

The confrontation had an effect. When Billy went home a few days later there was renewed energy in the family. John, in particular, not only supported his mother when she set limits with Billy, he started taking a more active interest in him, playing catch in the evening, helping Billy with his homework, and stepping into a paternal role. Although the school administration kept their fingers crossed, knowing Billy was now on medication, they took him back in. His teacher reported that he seemed calmer, steadier in his mood, and better able to do his work.

Often there's a honeymoon effect after a hospital stay. With the respite, new information, or change in treatment, and the fact that the child is discharged (and therefore medically certified as better), it's easy for everyone to have renewed optimism. The problem is, of course, that all this optimism can wear off in a matter of days and, now that the "hospital solution" has become a solution, it's tempting for parents to bounce the child right back if things start to slide downhill.

Such transition problems become even more difficult when a child has been in the hospital for several weeks or months. Like the family of the sailor or soldier who may be out of the home for months at a time, the family with the hospitalized child learns to reshape itself around the hole created by the child's absence. The parents have forgotten just how time-consuming the child really is, or how quickly tension and triangles can build, or another child has been able to slip in to take up a lot of Dad's attention that used to go to the hospitalized child. Faced with the challenge of the returning child and the need for the family to create a new role for the child, unfortunately, it's often easier for everyone to just let her fall back into the old role.

CALLING IN REINFORCEMENTS

Such falling back happened to Billy, but not for lack of trying. Crises once again began to brew—Ms. Williams's father fell down and hurt his leg, her husband was laid off again from his job at the hardware company, and John's 5-year-old son came to stay for a few weeks while his mother was in the process of moving.

Everything fell apart. Now that John was spending free time with his son, Billy resented the cousin and all the attention he was receiving. Even though the grandfather was now around the house more, the noise and commotion created by the additional grandson, as well as his own depression around his job loss, made him irritable and withdrawn. And Ms. Williams, who had been doing much better with the support she was receiving, once again became overwhelmed, anxious, and depressed. Billy once again became more demanding, and his grandmother once again caved in and gave in. The structure began to collapse.

The deterioration at home spilled over to school. Although there were no explosions, Billy began to act up. He talked back to his teacher, argued with other children, and didn't complete his work. The school went back to Plan A with the weekly meetings with the psychologist and afternoon computer time. This seemed to take the edge off, and gave the school some sense of control. In therapy Billy was able to talk about his jealousy and resentment of his cousin—a remarkable achievement for this silent child. I supported the grandmother and grandfather and worked with them to solve problems and stop the backslide, but neither one could really get mobilized. In order to avoid another hospitalization, I decided to call in reinforcements.

Home-based services were started to supplement the office-based therapy. Twice a week, for 2 hours at a time, a female therapist went out to the home to help the grandmother and grandfather (when he was around) manage Billy in specific situations. It was hands-on, primarily coaching the grandmother on the setting of limits and the implementing of time-outs. She also met with John and encouraged him to keep up his relationship with Billy, as well as back up his mother. Finally, the home-based worker served as a support for Ms. Williams, providing her with an opportunity to talk to someone about the stresses and strains she was experiencing. Although the family was cool at first about having this stranger in their home, they quickly warmed up to her. To provide even more support to Billy and the family, social services arranged for Billy to be placed in respite care with another family on a regular basis.

It wasn't enough. Even though Billy continued to use his individual sessions productively—both playing out and talking about his anger at the cousin, the abandonment by the uncle, his worries about his grandmother—and actually behaved well for a day or two after a session, he couldn't maintain it for more than that. Neither could the rest of the family. Within a few hours after the home-based therapist left, Ms. Williams or the grandfather would undo everything the clinician tried to reinforce. Even when John's son returned home to his mother and some of the stress was reduced, the structure in the home remained weak.

Billy had another explosion at school that came seemingly out of the blue. He punched a boy and bloodied his nose, slipped out of the teacher's grip when she tried to stop him, kicked her, and then ran out of the school and hid in some bushes off the school property. The police were called, and it was they who found him.

Billy was expelled. The school administration would provide home tutoring for the remaining 3 months of the school year. Now that he was home all the time, his grandmother was frantic. Both Ray and John were working temporarily at full-time jobs, and she was stuck home with Billy all day long. He pushed at her, and she invariably gave in just to get some peace.

Another crossroads. Once again several therapeutic options open up. Should individual therapy for Billy, for Ms. Williams, or home-based services be increased? Send him back to the hospital, have his medication reevaluated? Maybe just wait it out?

Again, it depends on how you see the problem. How much did the presence of the other grandson re-create and refuel Billy's own dormant feelings about his younger brother? (I tried to pursue this with him but got nowhere.) Is the chaos and abandonment, this time by the school, increasing Billy's anxiety and fears? How much of Billy's behavior is the product of the family dynamics, where Billy is so entrenched in his role, where the grandmother is so overwhelmed and her potential supports so unavailable?

All the professionals who were involved with Billy—me, the home-based therapist, school principal, special education coordinator, school psychologist, respite care coordinator—met with the grandparents to consider these questions and options. The consensus was that we had probably reached the limits of what outpatient services could do. We recommended placing Billy in a specialized residential treatment center for at least 6 months. Here he could attend school in a setting that could appropriately respond to his behavior (small classes, token economy, use of time-outs and restraints if needed). He would get individual and group counseling, and ideally have a chance to focus and work more intensively on his past trauma and loss, develop his social skills, and learn more effective ways of handling his emotions. The center we had in mind was close enough that the family could visit as his earned privileges would allow, and the overall plan was to gradually increase visitation stays as the time of discharge became closer.

We also thought it would be best for the home-based therapist to continue to come once a week to do family therapy. Both she and I felt that the environmental and emotional problems within the family, if not alleviated, would undermine the structure Billy would need even after discharge. Ms. Williams's depression needed to be addressed, probably through medication, perhaps with individual therapy or marital therapy as well, and the men in the family needed to change their role and become consistently involved in parenting if Billy was going to be able to grow up in their home. Finally, as a way of maintaining our relationship, keeping a check on his progress, and offsetting his sense of abandonment, Billy would continue to see me two times a month. In order to facilitate coordination and treatment planning, everyone was to meet with the facility staff on a regular basis.

The family and I felt both failure and relief at this decision. On one hand the initial goal of not abandoning Billy seemed betrayed: the boy was to be sent away, replicating another loss, yet another desertion by the adults in his life. On the other hand, time was running out. The next year or two would, in my mind, be crucial in Billy's development. Unless he was able to grieve his losses, heal the trauma he experienced, and find healthier ways to express his emotions, his current behavioral patterns could solidify, increasing the risk that he could, like his mother's boyfriend, become dangerously violent. The grandparents, too, looked ahead with anxiety. Unless Billy could learn to manage his emotions and behavior or they could learn to better handle him, he would, as an adolescent, easily spin out of control.

Of course, Billy had his own mixed feelings. The grandparents and myself told him that the move wasn't because he was bad or being punished, but because we were having trouble giving him all the help that he needed. We wanted him to be able to go to school (something he wanted very much), rather than stay at home, and this seemed the best way to do it. We told him the plan for visits with the grandparents and me. He seemed excited about all the activities that the center provided, and knowing that he would be seeing and talking to everyone on a regular basis seemed to reduce much of his anxiety.

Although Billy had a difficult adjustment at first, he settled in within a couple of months and quickly moved up their level system. Although he did not talk much in individual therapy, he did open up in group—there were a couple of other children who had lost parents through death or divorce, and this helped him talk about his own feelings. When he came home on weekend visits, he seemed to the grandparents to be better behaved and more open. When he came to see me, we primarily spent the time catching up and playing games—more relationship maintenance than any therapeutic exploration.

The family procrastinated on seeing the home-based therapist, and this contributed to an extension of Billy's stay at the center by an additional 5 months. Part of this procrastination came from the family's need to have a break from focusing on problems. Part was probably due to their difficulty in understanding how talking about parenting would be helpful if Billy wasn't there to create problems, and a good part was their own anxiety about stirring the family pot and talking about family problems that weren't specifically tied to Billy.

Like most families that have focused their attention on the problems of one child, Billy's absence made them more acutely aware of what else was wrong in the family. Without the ability to use Billy as a familiar distraction, they became more aware of the tensions and problems, and their first reaction was to ignore the whole thing.

The home-based therapist persisted. Just as the family members needed to learn how to interact with one another without Billy being in the center of them all, they needed to learn how to interact and trust the home-based therapist without exclusively focusing on Billy and his problems. It took a lot of reassuring by the therapist, a lot of interpreting and normalizing of how they might be feeling, and a lot of explaining over and over again the connection between Billy's long-term improvement (and coming home) and their ability to change the way the family operated.

It took Ms. Williams almost 4 months to go to the doctor and start on the Prozac that the doctor prescribed. It took more than 5 months before the couple consistently would meet for couple therapy. Family sessions with John were eventually included when the marital issues spilled over or when there was a need to talk about parenting issues.

When Billy finally returned to public school, he did well. He continued to check in with me once a month or so, and because of the skills he learned at the center and the fact that he's getting older, we could talk more and play less. He still had no contact with his parents, but he is more able to look at those relationships as a reflection of them and not himself. Although he put much of his past behind him, losses (the death of his dog, his uncle moving away for a few months) sparked his defiance and irritability, tested his grandparents' ability to maintain their limits, and stirred memories of his brother's death.

While presently stable, the risks for the future were obviously still there. His grandparents had trouble in adolescence with all their children, and while their awareness and parenting skills had increased, the danger of sliding back into those patterns remained. It was made all the worse by the simple fact that the grandparents were getting older. They would physically find it more and more difficult to keep up with a growing adolescent.

The normal ups and downs of adolescence were right around the corner for Billy. As is typical for teenagers who have been abandoned by their parents, Billy's feelings about his parents—anger at their neglect, curiosity about what they are like—will undoubtedly come to the surface. These feelings in turn will drag up the unresolved past all over again: his wondering what's wrong with him, his guilt over his brother's death perhaps, and his anger that things have turned out the way they have. Without emotional support from the adults around him, I could imagine him becoming depressed, acting up, and potentially getting into trouble with the law, or being at risk for drug abuse. We can't live in the future, but by anticipating these dangers, we hope they may be prevented. That may be the most that we can do.

LOOKING BACK

Partially successful cases like this one are a familiar experience to anyone who has ever worked with troubled families. What this case has in common with many of them is the overwhelming impact of environment. For many of the families that are seen in clinic or agency settings, the difficulty lies not with motivation or ability to learn skills, but the multiple problems that seem to constantly badger the family—unemployment, poverty, illness—that keep the family in a crisis mode, and like this family, make it difficult to maintain a positive momentum. Even with all the family work and residential treatment available, these environmental forces may still drag them down. Ideally, through therapy they will have fewer internal distractions and acquire greater family resources to help them weather these emotional storms better.

What this case also illustrates is that all clinical work doesn't turn out smoothly, and even with the best of intentions and skills, treatment can become derailed. Good clinical work is pragmatic: new approaches have to be tried, and often a combination of services needs to be included until the right fit is found. This case also demonstrates the circularity of the work in the way one path eventually connects to others. Therapy, for example, could have started with the family and moved toward individual work with Billy, or started with the marriage, if the couple would have permitted it, and then tied into Billy's concerns. The initial focus could have been on the school, helping them to better accommodate his needs or carrying their more structured approaches into the home. The starting point is in a sense arbitrary, merely an entrance into the larger system and system change.

Billy's story also illustrates the boundaries and limitations of each of the systems and institutions: the family's reluctance to change its way of parenting; the school's own goals, needs, and inability to control Billy's behavior; my own scheduling limitations in seeing Billy more often; the limited resources available for respite or home-based services; and the limits of the community in responding with more expensive residential treatment only after all the other options had been tried.

Such limits are part and parcel of every community's services, and in recent years these services have been more and more strained. The mental health center where I worked is no longer able to provide long-term work, home-based services are sparse, and state budgets limit who and how long children can be treated in residential settings, in spite of the call for more children's services whenever there is a school shooting or similar tragedies.

This case was also a snapshot of the state of therapy at that time. While the core of Billy's treatment would undoubtedly remain the same—the focus on his trauma, the work with the family and its stabilization—other tools could come into play now if he were seen today. New medications now available may have helped him with his impulsiveness and outbursts, and new techniques such as EMDR (eye movement desensitization and reprocessing), which were not yet on the therapy scene, could have possibly been effective in relieving his posttraumatic stress. At any moment in our history as a therapeutic community, it is equally possible to be amazed at how far we have come while at the same time realizing how unsophisticated and limited our methods really are.

Finally, the story of Billy illustrates the resiliency of a child and family to survive trauma, and the inestimable effect that love and commitment can have. Without the family's ability to care for and see Billy for who he is and can be in the future, and without some commitment by the larger community to provide treatment services, it's easy to imagine Billy going from foster home to foster home, and in and out of the hospital, increasingly locked in a downward cycle of negative behavior and self-fulfilling prophecies. Now his future, while still uncertain, is resting upon an increasingly larger base of past and present experiences that include people who only want the best that life can give him. In the life of a child, this often is the best we as adults can do.

Looking Within: Chapter 9 Exercises

1. If you haven't done it already, write down your own assumptions about problems in children. What is the major source of the problems—within, without? What is the role of development, of family, of the past? Where do the solutions lie? What is your primary role as the therapist?

2. What type of problems with children would you have the most difficulty with—acting-out 10-year-olds, sexually abused children, hyperactive or aggressive children, children who have suffered a loss—not only in terms of your skill, but your own emotional response? How are you to handle such cases and emotions: avoiding them by farming them out, becoming controlling, minimizing the problems, becoming overwhelmed and passive, overidentifying with the child?

3. If there was something from your childhood that you most regret, what would it be? What do you wish your parent or parents did more of for you? How do you wish your relationships with your siblings were

different when you were a child? What part of this has had an impact on your work with children now? How?

4. What skills do you most need to develop in working with children: play therapy, art therapy, psychological testing, work with younger children or older ones, integrating children in the family process? How could you learn those skills?

chapter *10*

"See How She Treats Me!"

The Parent–Adolescent Struggle

"So, how was your week?"

Ms. Harris, a slight woman with graying blond hair and drooping shoulders, takes a quick glance at her 15-year-old daughter, Ellen. Although Ellen is slumped in the corner of the couch, it's easy to see that she's several inches taller and about 20 pounds heavier than her mother. Her head is turned away, and she's staring absently at the lamp.

"Okay, I guess," says Ms. Harris. She sounds tentative and glances again at Ellen. Ellen, still looking at the lamp, just breathes heavily.

"Actually, we did fine until I tried to get Ellen to clean up her room."

"I *did* clean my room!" snaps Ellen, whirling around to face her accuser. "*You* just didn't think it was good enough!" She is glaring.

"You left all those clothes all over the floor, after I asked you nicely to pick them up." Ms. Harris sounds almost angry, but she's holding back, being careful.

"I said I was going to wear them, didn't I?"

"Yes, but—"

"And then *you* wouldn't let me talk on the phone!"

"I asked you if you could call back later—"

"I told you I was almost done!"

The mother turns to the therapist. "And do you know what she did? I asked her again nicely to hurry up, and then she had a fit, and threw the phone against the wall and broke a picture!" She seems mad, but suddenly her lower lip is pouting out, and then she collapses into quiet tears. "I don't know why she needs to do things like that. I didn't raise her that way."

"Oh, you're pathetic!" sneers Ellen.

Welcome to the world of adolescence. Here in Ellen we see perhaps a larger version of what Billy potentially could become, and in some ways these families are similar. Just as Billy was dealing with the loss of his brother and parents, Ellen, and the two younger children, Marie, age 12, and Betsy, age 7, are all dealing with the death of Harry, their father and Ms. Harris's husband, of a heart attack a year and a half ago. Since then the family has struggled financially, with Ms. Harris working two jobs, and emotionally, as each family member tries to fill the holes in the family and in their lives.

It's Ellen who is the center of concern. She's the one who has gotten into fights at school, has rages, tries to boss around her younger sisters, and hits them when they don't do what she wants. She makes demands of and challenges her mother, and feels entitled. Ms. Harris, in many ways like Billy's grandmother, makes feeble efforts to assert control but, more often than not, caves in. Here at the third session it's clear that both Ms. Harris and Ellen have some major changes to make if both are to survive this adolescence.

MOVING UP

There are also significant differences between Billy and Ellen simply because of the differences in age. As we move up the developmental ladder from children to adolescents, there are dramatic shifts in the therapy process. Here's a quick list of some of the obvious ones:

• *The stakes are higher.* While an elementary school-age child like Billy may get suspended from school, or tear up his room when he is angry, teenagers like Ellen won't have much trouble taking drugs, shoplifting, getting pregnant, running away, or engaging in seriously dangerous activities that could have long-term consequences on their future.

• *Different parenting skills are needed.* Ms. Williams, under the worst conditions, could, with a little bit of help, always pick Billy up and put him in his room for a time-out. Ms. Harris can't do that with Ellen. Parenting a teen requires an entirely different skill set: having a greater sensitivity for personal boundaries and a greater reliance on compromise and negotiation; the ability to know what battles to pick and which ones to let go; and the ability to recognize the power struggles and not fuel them, to balance limit setting with nurturance. Many parents lack these skills or have trouble making the leap. They feel frustrated when what used to work no longer does or can.

• *Others outside the family have increasing influence.* Younger children are most affected by their home and school environments, environments created by adults who are in charge. Ellen, however, is not only reacting to her mother, or even internally to the loss of her father, but, like other teens, also to the wider circle of friends who pull her in various directions as she struggles to define for herself who she is. She is sensitive to how and what they think about her, and worries about how she fits in. These are the other voices that she hears in counterpoint to those of her mother.

• *Parents often under- or overreact.* Recognizing your waning influence, the risks intertwined within their decisions, and the sense that the time you have to affect your child's life is quickly running out can intensify a parent's reactions. Some, in fear and panic, overreact and overcontrol—threatening, demanding, pushing their child—to be more responsible, stay away from trouble, or, better yet, not to grow up at all. Others, swinging too far the other way, feel that it is too late to turn things around, and allow their child to have full rein over them and to make his or her own decisions. Such parents have essentially given up.

But what drives these over- and underreactions are the parents' memories of their own adolescence: a distorted still life, perhaps, filled with the painful throb of past mistakes, ongoing regret over roads not taken, an aching awareness that they and their parents failed in important ways. Such memories push parents to try to stop history from repeating itself with their own children.

• *Therapists' reactions can be more intense.* It's not only the parents who are sensitive to the risks and dynamics of adolescence; so too are therapists. When an adolescent is referred for therapy by the court—the "one last chance" before being sent off to a correction center—it's the therapist, as well as the teenager, who's under the gun. When a therapist sees destructive family dynamics souring the child's life, but faces parents too overwhelmed or impotent to change them, when a therapist wants the best for the adolescent but feels stifled by bureaucracy or limited community resources, the therapist, too, can feel that time is running out. He or she starts to believe that it is necessary to work hard and fast in order to avert dire consequences, or the therapist decides, like the parents and the community, that it isn't going to matter and stops trying.

• *The adolescent has more opportunity to fill a surrogate role.* The elementary school-age child can, of course, learn to copy and fill roles in the family. We could imagine that if Billy had stayed with his mother, for example, he would, even at his young age, absorb and act out more and more the boyfriend's control or violence, or would step in to support her emotionally.

As the adolescent moves closer to adulthood, the pull to fill such roles becomes even stronger. Here we see the oldest son working full- or part time to help support the rest of the family and giving the mother advice when she asks or even doesn't ask for it; the 16-year-old daughter who watches the kids and makes dinner while Dad is working late; or, as with Ellen, a 15-year-old who feels, as the father did perhaps, not only that she has some responsibility to direct her younger sisters but also that Ellen will get her mother to do what Ellen wants without objection.

• *The adolescent can be more verbal.* One of the main differences between child therapy and adolescent therapy is the capacity of adolescents, and some tweens, to do more "talk" therapy, rather than symbolically express themselves through play. The adolescent's vocabulary and comprehension are greater, and their world is more complex. Unlike the elementary school child, for example, whose sense of right and wrong is governed by whether or not someone punishes you, teens are slowly developing the ability to think abstractly. Their notions of personal values, ethics, and morality are emerging and now can be questioned and discussed directly.

That said, we know from research over the past years that teen brains are very different from that of adults (Giedd, 2008). The prefrontal lobes that are responsible for executive functioning—planning, problem solving—are not fully developed. Throw in hormones, peer pressure, and the availability of alcohol and drugs, and it's often surprising that many teens do as well as they do.

• *Confidentiality is more vital.* While confidentiality certainly exists between young children and therapists, it is flexible; because the children rely so exclusively on their parents to help them negotiate through the world, the parents need as much information as possible in order to help the child. As children become older, begin to both separate from the parents and see themselves as more independent, they no longer need to nor want to rely as much on their parents to help them solve problems. The boundaries between them and their parents are more firm; they can now begin to help themselves, making confidentiality more absolute and important. As the therapist, you need to work harder to both build trust and assure the adolescent that his or her confidence will be respected.

Even though child and adolescent work are clearly different, the shift from one to the other varies from family to family. There are many 13- or 14-year-olds who would rather paint than talk, just as there are some 10-year-olds who wouldn't dare play a game or touch a toy. There are adolescents who, due to intellectual or physical handicaps or limitations, are developmentally delayed and may not only play more and talk less but may need to be managed by their parents as if they were younger. While some teens can work well in the solitude of individual therapy, many others are intimidated by this intimacy, and do best in the familiar interaction of family therapy where they can bounce off parents and siblings.

The way to find out how "adolescent" an adolescent is, is to *ask* (about the teen's and the family's expectations), to *do* (talk with the adolescent alone, together with the parents, offer to play cards and see what happens), and most of all, to *listen and watch*. What helps the adolescent open up? What stimulates the most energy? What seems to have the most impact? By the end of that first session you should have a pretty good idea of just where the adolescent sits on the developmental continuum and how you can best join with him or her.

FALLING APART

Of course, there are all those families that you'll never see, the ones that manage to survive the trials and tribulations of adolescence not only intact but relatively smoothly. Why do some families struggle more than others?

Limited Parenting Skills

As suggested earlier, some parents of teens simply reach the limits of their own parenting skills and knowledge. They can't make the shift from physical–authoritarian management to a verbal–negotiating one. The father who threatens to spank his 6'2" son if he doesn't cut the grass by Friday is setting himself up to fail. But if that's all the father knows, if threatening physical punishment sums up his entire repertoire of skills, his influence over his child has effectively ended.

Teens' Limited Skills and Struggle with Transitions

Some teens have similar struggles with their own skills and transitions. Their problem-solving or decision-making skills may be weak; they may have limited social skills; and the transition from elementary to middle school, and middle school to high school feels overwhelming. They have trouble shifting into adolescence and get stuck. Even though they are separating from their parents, they have a hard time crossing over and finding a place for themselves in the often competitive but potentially supportive world of peers. They are caught between these two worlds—of childhood and adolescence, of home and peers—and in neither. These teens often feel lost, are filled with loneliness and isolation, and as many school shootings have shown, at risk of violently acting out.

Physiological Changes

Adding fuel to these struggles are the ups and downs of normal physiological changes. The spiking of hormones leads to the spiking of emotions, without the strong prefrontal lobes to help balance them out. Parents of 13-year-olds complain about the rapid shifts from explosive anger to explosive tears, and to moodiness and withdrawal; some parents weather this better than others. If a teen has low self-esteem or poor coping skills, he or she may not be able to verbalize feelings and strikes out instead; rather than seeking others who can provide help, a teen may hold in his or her feelings and questions and get depressed; rather than finding healthy ways of relieving the pressure and stress, such as through sports or creative arts, another teen may turn to drugs, sex, or acting out.

Increasing Influence of Friends

With the increasing involvement of friends, many parents of teens invariably blame their child's misbehavior on friends—it's the group of lowlifes he sees at school, it's those girls up the street who do anything they want, that crowd on the corner that are putting ideas in his head, leading her astray. And they may be. Many programs for teens—family models, court diversion programs, multisystemic therapy (MST), a widely recognized evidence-based approach to dealing with juvenile offenders—place a great deal of emphasis on improving the peer group and increasing environmental supports. When parents view peers as the primary source of their adolescent's problems, the solution it implies is that if you eliminate the friends—move, place the child under house arrest, enforce a strict curfew—the teen will be cured.

This might help, but often not for long. Somehow the child manages to find another group of scruffy characters in the new neighborhood or drifts back to the group once the curfew is eased. The problem is two-dimensional: the influence of friends and the reflection of him- or herself that the teenager sees in them. The teen needs help learning how to be more assertive, improve social skills, and increase his or her self-esteem; and as MST demonstrates, how to find and use healthy supports within the family and with new friends.

Changing or Entrenched Roles within the Family

When an adolescent, like Ellen, takes on an inappropriate role within the family system, both the parents' ability to manage the child and the child's abilities to cope are stressed. By replacing her father's role in the family, Ellen, at 15, is not only filled with a sense of over-responsibility but also entitlement and power. In our diagrams of family structures (see Chapter 4) she is the C, child, replacing the P, parent, as the one in charge, with her mother and the other children below. The mother's weak parenting skills locks the dysfunctional system in place.

Similarly, the child who has been the scapegoat and a vicarious outlet for a parent's anger or the "good child" who secures his or her place only by complementing the scapegoat's role can each over time become more and more entrenched in their roles and extreme in their behaviors. The scapegoat's behavior, once tolerable, now escalates and comes to the attention of the community, while the good child is more set on showing just how good he or she can be.

Parents' History

Running underneath all of these adolescent potholes of skills, stress, and roles are the parents' own history and the power of this history to repeat itself. Sometimes these are genetically based: the son whose father has a history of bipolar illness finds himself sliding into bouts of severe depression; or the mother with ADHD finds that her son has similar problems with inattention, impulsivity, and hyperactivity. Often, however, it's the combination of role modeling, family dynamics, and environmental forces that work together to repeat the past mistakes from one generation to the next: the mother who was pregnant at 14 finds, in spite of her constant warnings, that her daughter is pregnant at 15; the father who never went beyond the ninth grade finds himself arguing with his son who wants to quit school and work at a gas station; the mother who married an alcoholic and abuser painfully watches her own daughter endure the same fate.

What drives the replaying of these scripts is not only or even necessarily the replaying of the content, but the recycling of the underlying family and environmental dynamics. While the mother harangues her 15-year-old daughter to be careful around the boys she associates with, she isn't aware that it's also the haranguing itself and the subsequent rift in their relationship that propels the daughter into pregnancy, just as her own mother's haranguing did to her. The son who feels that what was good for his father should be good enough for him finds his father's arguments to stay in school hypocritical and dismisses them. The daughter who saw her mother abused by her father not only expects men to act this way and associates intimacy with violence, but unconsciously copies the victim role that her mother modeled.

Seeing this replication of your life in the life of your child is both painful and powerful, and often pushes the parents into counseling. It's also part of what creates the ambivalence and reluctance that such parents come to display. To look beyond their panic forces the parents to look not only at the forces affecting their child and family but also, painfully, at the forces that shaped their own past.

To talk about the life options open to a teenager and the power of history to repeat itself is to talk about the fundamental challenge of adolescence, namely, leaving home and setting a course for adulthood. Every family creates its own emotional climate, its own escape hatches, its own ultimatums that let the adolescent know how, when, and in what direction to leave. Some seem hopelessly trapped within the narrow choices they have; others work so hard not to become their parent that they don't figure out how to become themselves; and some, through the helping hand of another adult in their life, find a way to step outside the environmental and family patterns to become someone different.

What about your own experience? If you look back on your own time of leaving home, your reactions to your parents' past, and your relationships with other adults outside your family, what is the moral of the story of your own adolescence? What behaviors did you want to emulate? What was that emotional bottom line that you reached in your relationship with your parents that told you it was time to leave? What mistakes of theirs did you or they want you most to avoid? By being aware of your own personal triggers and your own unfinished business, you can better separate your clinical judgment from your personal reactions when working with parents and teens.

THERAPEUTIC GOALS: THE BIG PICTURE

Given the differences between children and adolescents, the therapeutic goals in a family context with most children is relatively straightforward. Help the parents take on the skills and structure of a healthy system and the child most often will be okay. In complex cases like Billy's, the clinical challenge is deciding how to off-load a majority of those same goals to individual therapy or the larger community when the family is unable, for whatever reason, to step up to the plate.

With adolescents the goals are more varied. Some of the common areas to focus on when treating teens and their families follow:

Education and Teaching Skills

Learning problems or problems about learning? Often both, but as with children this is often a good starting point. Talking about skills and educating parents about adolescents and their psychology are less threatening to parents; your concrete suggestions can increase their own sense of power and control. Provide them with information about adolescent development—for example, needs for privacy, adolescents' sensitivity to hypocrisy, the testing of limits, even something about brain development and limited abstract thinking—to help normalize the behaviors that seem to aggravate them so much. Coach them on how to detect the power struggles and stop them, raise sensitive topics, understand and use the power of positive feedback, give the child permission to talk about his or her anger or sadness, know when to lay down the law, or how to achieve a united front. Once parents have had the opportunity to tell their story and express their own concerns, these invaluable bits of information are always welcomed. They change the emotional climate in the room; the parents leave seeing the problems in a new way.

Other times, of course, coaching and providing information isn't enough. Parents may know the information or you provide the information but they struggle to carry it out: problems about learning. The parents fail to take a united stand; they don't emphatically say to Tyrone that he can't go out; they complain, but don't go down to the school and talk to the teacher to find out why Helen is failing. Here we're back to problems within the hierarchy, perhaps within the marital relationship, among the family roles, or unresolved issues from the parents' past. You may be creating and miss seeing that a parallel process is taking hold in which the parents are responding to your seeming direction with the same resistance with which the adolescent responds to theirs. You once again fall back to the basics: clarifying expectations, looking for what's missing, moving toward anxiety, following the process and blocking the dysfunctional patterns in the room and in the home, and looking for the problems that might underlie the poor solutions that the presenting problems really are.

Realigning the Family Structure, Increasing Positive Support

When it's clear to you that problems stem from the adolescent's inappropriate role and hierarchy within the family system, realigning the system is the obvious goal. In the session process you point out when the adolescent isn't acting like an adolescent, but as an adult. You challenge the parents to set limits, to act as parents rather than peers. You give the parents permission to assert their power (though not be abusive) that you as therapist, the courts, and the schools will all support. They need to know that teenagers, like Ellen, shouldn't be out of control or too much in control, and needs to learn to be responsible and appropriate. They need to understand that the bottom line is that the adolescent, because of his or her age, can't win, and that the community is on the parents' side.

This message is particularly valuable for single parents who feel overrun by all-too-powerful teenagers. Your saying this doesn't of course make changes quickly happen—the parents still have to confront their own anxiety about changing roles and learning new skills—but your challenge and support gives them a vote of confidence. The clinician, or more often the court, serves, in fact, as the second parent, forming a united front to the child, which becomes the starting point for realignment.

Creating a workable structure is only half a solution. Parents need to provide positive attention and nurturing in order to give adolescents something to move toward, not only away from. Nurture and control go hand in hand. Often a parent, like Ms. Harris, feels comfortable with nurturing but struggles setting limits; for other parents the opposite is the case. In two-parent families, it's easy, as mentioned earlier, for the parents to polarize, with one's firm limits serving as a counter to the other parent's seeming softness and leniency. The united front collapses, and the teen splits and tries to maneuver through the cracks. Balance is necessary: a combination of clear and age-appropriate boundaries with love and attention, and respect and appreciation. In embattled families, often the best place to start regaining control is to help parents to be more respectful and appreciative.

Managing Conflict, Stopping Violence

These are always one of your top priorities. While parents of young children need help to manage tantrums, with teens it can all quickly escalate into the territory of assault. You need to take a strong stand on this. Anything less and you are inadvertently condoning the behavior. For families that have a long history of conflict or violence, or parents who have grown up with it, their tolerance is obviously skewed. You are the voice of reality.

The starting message about heightened emotions is that once an argument starts and emotions are ramping up, the issue is no longer about the problem but about the emotions: the car is going off the road. The goal for them is to put out the fire of the emotions.

There are generally two levels to dealing with conflict and violence. One of the most useful stances parents with teens—especially those with oppositional defiant disorder (ODD)—can take is learning not to personalize their teen's behavior or verbal attacks. Instead they need to think of this as not about them, but rather a reflection of the teen's own internal struggle. When the teen gets enraged, for example, it's helpful for the parents to see this as the teen's solution, albeit a poor one, of dealing with some other emotions swirling within: he is picking a fight as a way of relieving his own internal angst. By seeing the outburst or acting out as a sign that the teen is having a hard time rather than a preemptive malicious attack on the parents, the parents are being "differentiated adults" and are better able to step back from the conflict; they may even be able to show some compassion for the teen's struggle.

First Line of Defense

Parents' first line of defense when a family member begins to escalate is to say little: anything they say at this point is like throwing gasoline on a fire. Even the most benign statement is likely to trigger a strong reaction. The best thing to do is to do little, calmly listen, and reflect back the other's feelings: "I know you are feeling upset . . . ". The parents need to be coached to avoid the temptation to get angry themselves and defend their position by stacking on more facts. Any counterattack only fuels the other's emotions and he will instinctively ramp up—barraging the parents with cuss words, and so on—to pull them back into the argument. Why? Because the pattern is broken, anxiety rises, and the other is trying to restart the pattern. But if the parents can hold steady and not feed the emotional fire, the teen will begin to settle down. Only when the teen is emotionally flat-lined—no longer emotional, which may take minutes, hours, or even the next day—can the parents then return to the discussion of the problem.

Again this is the first line of defense, but this can be difficult, especially for parents who were never nurtured themselves. They've learned to think of parenting as yelling, threatening, or slapping across the face or behind when a child gets out of hand. They worry that not counterattacking is letting the kid walk all over them, allowing him or her to be disrespectful of them, or teaching him that there are no limits. The parents need to be reassured that they can always restate and reset limits after the storm is over, even set limits at the time if necessary (for example, call the police if the teen gets too aggressive). They need to constantly be reassured that they do have the power, but can be most effective if they can avoid the power struggle.

The way to best convey this attitude is not just to tell the parents to do it, but to model it: toward the adolescent (for example, nurture Mary by saying "Your teacher told me that you have been doing wonderfully the past week at school" or by remaining calm when Mary gets upset and begins to complain) and the parents ("From what you've told me about your father, Rochelle, it sounds like you did the very best you could for you and your sister; it must have been really tough for you," or listen sympathetically when the parent voices her frustration) in the session. The starting goal for any treatment plan is empowering parents to be parents. To do that you usually need to treat them the way they need to treat the adolescent.

Second Line of Defense

If this fails and the parents struggle to control their own emotions, then the second line of defense comes into play. Here the parents need to call a halt to avoid further escalation. Here you give the parents a clear plan: "As soon as you can tell that the situation is getting out of control, and that you are getting too volatile, you need to call a halt." Here the parents say: "I'm getting upset. I need to go cool off. We need to take a break." And the parents do two things: they shut up and walk away, and they set a timer that is visible to everyone (a large kitchen timer is great for this). They set it for 30–45 minutes. They say: "I'm going to come back and try again when the timer goes off."

The idea behind this is that once one person stops the argument, the other person gets anxious that he didn't get the last word, is cut off, or that the other person won't come back. The timer reassures him that they will. At that point, once again the other person is likely to escalate to draw the parents back in. This is to be expected, you say. Then they need to do whatever they need to do not to reengage: lock themselves in the bathroom, get in the car and lock the doors. The first time they do this the parents need to expect the teen to escalate even further and you need to map out with them concretely what they might expect and how they can handle not reengaging.

After the timer goes off, they come back. They try the conversation once again. If it escalates again, they reset the timer. Only when everyone is emotionally flat-lined can they sanely try and talk about the problem. If they can't do it with repeated tries, the family needs to hold off and bring the discussion into the therapy session.

It's helpful to write these steps down and give them to the parents. In the heat of the moment they will not be able to think this through or remember what to do. If they stick the list on their refrigerator (yes, they can take it down when company comes over) they don't have to scramble or fall back into default mode; they don't have to think about it. This becomes their homework and it is important to check with them on using these strategies in the next session. Often having a plan and knowing what to exactly do helps them not reengage and can begin to stop the pattern.

Finally, though we are talking about teens, these same strategies also apply to couples/parents who escalate and are at risk of violence. The same instructions are given.

Dealing with Individual Issues of Self-Abuse, Eating Disorders, Substance Abuse, Depression, and Anxiety

While many hard-core family therapists prefer to do as much of the work in a family context as possible—coaching parents on specific skills and stances, improving communication and negotiating problems, realigning the structure—individual therapy, either in conjunction with family therapy, or as an initial primary focus, is a logical option for the teen who's depressed, overwhelmed, or has poor self-esteem and is struggling with the trials of adolescence. In chaotic or violent homes, giving the adolescent an opportunity to talk to an empathic adult, an ideal parent, not only can be a refuge but also a powerful corrective emotional experience. The teen learns that it can be safe to express yourself and take the risk of intimacy, that you can learn to separate yourself from the craziness around you, and that adults and the adult world are more varied and complex than the one-dimensional impressions they have understandably formed. And just as you coach parents on how to respond to their own emotions, you can help the individual teen to do the same.

That said, it's helpful for you to have in your clinical toolbox ready-to-go treatment maps for common emotional issues. It's not unusual for many beginning clinicians to be relatively strong on assessment skills—able to quickly diagnose and define—but weaker on treatment. Their treatment goals are vague (increase self-esteem), or they struggle translating these goals into smaller and measurable session-by-session ones. Without a clear map, it's easy to become reactive rather than proactive, to get caught in details of content like the client does rather than seeing the larger process, and to feel like you are constantly scrambling and building the train as it's going down the track.

To help you avoid all of this, here are some quick treatment maps for common adolescent and adult issues. Take what is useful and see how you might integrate them with your own theoretical orientation.

Self-Abuse

For adolescents who cope through self-abuse, such as cutting, individual therapy can help them learn the terrain of their emotional life. Cutting behavior is quickly addictive because it works: physiologically, endorphins kick in; psychologically, it is controllable and immediate. It is what you know you can do that helps you feel better . . . a seemingly much easier solution than the risk of confronting your mother when you are angry at her for scolding you, or approaching your boss when you are worried that he or she may be critical of your performance.

The goals here are several: to stop the cutting behavior itself by having other alternatives immediately on hand; reducing the critical self-talk; and most important, dealing directly with the problems stirring the emotions. Sixteen-year-old Kate, for example, started cutting after her best friend's boyfriend started tweeting messages about her smoking pot at a party. He called her a big loser, echoing what she often thought of herself. When asked about the cutting, she said that she was angry at both her friend for breaking their confidence by telling her boyfriend, and angry obviously at the boyfriend for broadcasting her behavior and his comments to so many others at school. She was afraid to go back to school, worrying that everyone would be judging her.

Cutting for Kate was a way of dealing with anger that she couldn't express directly to those who were, in effect, bullying her. The session focused on both the cutting itself and her feelings about the situation. She didn't want to cut but didn't know what else to do when she felt that distressed. Together Kate and the therapist came up with a plan to help slow her automatic response. When she felt the urge to cut, she was to journal for 10 minutes, writing down all of her feelings about the situation. The time limit was specific in order to keep her from stirring up too many emotions and feeling further overwhelmed. After that she was to do 10 minutes of aerobic exercise—walking quickly around the block, jumping jacks in her room—to increase endorphins. Finally, the third step was to do at least 10 minutes of self-care. For some this can be a hot bath. For Kate, it was sitting on her bed, snuggling with one of her childhood stuffed animals, and listening to some of her favorite music. It's important that the self-care be something that the client can do independently. Calling up a best friend may be helpful, but not a good option if the friend can't be reached.

The idea here is to take the 30 minutes to emotionally settle without the use of cutting. Having the plan in place and actually writing it down and putting it somewhere where Kate easily could read it, like the violence plan for parents, helped her not to have to scramble for options in the moment when she was so overwhelmed and the pull of cutting was so strong. This is something she would have to practice repeatedly and the plan itself would undoubtedly need to be fine-tuned. In some cases a consult for medication is in order to help reduce the anxiety and depression, as well as teaching meditation and the like, so that new behaviors are more manageable.

The other focus of the session was on the problem itself. Was

Kate willing to talk to her friends, her parents, and the school guidance counselor about her embarrassment and what this boy had done? She agreed to think about talking to the school guidance counselor and her parents, but decided to post a response on Facebook, and talk directly to her friend about how angry she was.

The goal here is helping Kate be empowered rather than victimized, assertive rather than internalizing, and self-affirming rather than self-critical. Weekly sessions focused on her ability to refrain from cutting, determining how and why she struggled at particular points, and paying careful attention to self-criticism and overall negative self-talk, as well as providing emotional support and concrete planning to help her approach her problems directly. Role playing helped her improve her communication skills, and sessions with her parents focused on both solving problems in the home, as well as defining ways the parents could concretely provide emotional support when Kate was feeling overwhelmed. The aim was to give her tools to replace cutting and handle emotions differently, support her in stepping out of her comfort zone, and through success experiences increase her self-confidence and self-image.

Eating Disorders

Eating disorders can be considered another form of self-abuse, and like cutting are about internalization—bingeing, purging, and restricting become bad solutions to underlying problems of anger, anxiety, and depression—and like cutting, are powerful because they work. Even though an adolescent may feel she cannot control much of what is happening within and outside herself, she can control food and body image.

For those watching from the sidelines—parents, partners—this can be difficult for them to comprehend. In an effort to be helpful, they encourage the client to stop or start eating. This only overwhelms the client more or sets off a power struggle. Early on, parents and partners need to be educated around the eating disorder and rather than struggling with their own devices, the client needs to say to family members what it is they can do to be helpful in a concrete way when the client is upset ("Ask me if I'm doing okay"; "Give me a hug"), rather than instinctively focusing on eating or not eating the mashed potatoes.

The overall treatment plan is similar to that of self-abuse: changing behaviors around food by being aware of triggers, monitoring emotional states, and having concrete behavioral plans for meals; challenging and changing negative self-talk and criticism that undermines assertiveness, fuels depression, anxiety, and shame; and dealing with the problems and emotions driving the eating behaviors directly and assertively. Bulimia can often be treated on an outpatient basis, with a team approach of a therapist, a nutritionist to teach healthy eating and break the bingeing–purging, yin and yang eating patterns, and a physician to monitor overall health and possibly provide medication. If the patterns seem to be too difficult to break on an outpatient basis, a short stint of residential treatment with its intensive focus may be called for.

Unlike bulimia, anorexia, unless in its very early stages, often requires residential treatment just to get the client to a healthy weight. Once a client's weight drops too low, her brain is too impaired due to starvation to make effective use of outpatient therapy or even medication. It is the mental health disorder with the highest death rates (Arcelus, Mitchell, Wales, & Nielsen, 2011), stemming from heart attacks and related electrolyte imbalances from starvation, as well as suicide. Regardless of the setting, eating disorders usually require a team approach: individual and family therapy focuses on identifying emotional triggers, assertively addressing problems, and teaching self-regulation skills; a nutritionist focuses on meal planning, healthy eating, increasing weight, and approaching "fear foods"; and finally, a physician assesses overall health, monitoring electrolytes, and providing medication for anxiety and depression.

What obviously makes eating disorders so tenacious is that unlike drug addiction where the individual can learn to avoid the addictive drug, here the individual can't. They need to be able to eat and at the same time shed the destructive emotional components that can come with it. This is a tall order that requires a long-term, multifaceted approach.

Substance Abuse

The fork in the treatment road when dealing with adolescents who use drugs and alcohol is determining where they are on the spectrum of casual user to full-blown addiction. Unless you have training in substance abuse, it's best to refer the client to a specialist for an evaluation. The truly addicted teen (or adult) needs residential treatment to break the pattern, and then intensive outpatient support (Alcoholics Anonymous/Narcotics Anonymous groups) to remain clean. Individual and family therapy are part of the plan for the same reasons therapy is indicated for cutting and eating disorders: to deal with emotions and problems directly.

Depression

Certainly you can see depression running in families and for some there is clearly a genetic component that requires medication as well as therapy. For many others who present with the signs and symptoms of depression, the source is often situational. They are depressed because they feel trapped, stuck at the bottom of a well, unable to get out. For teens who have limited coping skills, little real control over their lives, peer pressure, and psychological and physiological changes that are at times overwhelming, it is not surprising that depression comes to the fore.

From an evidence-based cognitive-behavioral approach to depression, the focus of treatment is on recognizing the depressive mind and depressive self-talk of pessimism and self-criticism; learning to counter such self-talk through more realistic and positive thinking; and most important, like the other issues, taking behavioral action. The mantra here is that if you keep doing the same thing, you will keep feeling the same way. If all the elements of your life are depressing—you are lonely, you hate your job, you have no dreams for the future—it's not surprising that you'd feel depressed.

For teens, depression often circles around the self-criticism of not fitting in or keeping up with peers, the trapped and abused feelings that come from various forms of bullying, feeling trapped in a home life that is chaotic or tense or depressing, feeling the burden of worrying about parents and their problems, or losses that come with breakups with boyfriends or girlfriends. Sessions focus again on the several fronts: actively moving against problems, being proactive in relationships, working hard to counter negative thoughts, and using family or even peer sessions to express feelings and solve problems rather than internalizing them.

Anxiety

Depression and anxiety are the underground streams flowing beneath the other issues, but like depression, there may be a clear presenting problem in the form of generalized anxiety, phobias, panic attacks, obsessive–compulsive disorder (OCD), or posttraumatic stress. If situational depression is about feeling trapped, anxiety is about living in the future. The anxious mind is constantly searching for and fabricating "what ifs": What if I don't pass probation on my job, what if my boyfriend is really disappointed with the birthday gift I gave him, what if I didn't sign my tax return in black ink and the Internal Revenue Service comes knocking on my door? There is a genetic element to anxiety, and an environmental one. Those who grow up in chaotic or abusive families, who have been traumatized in some way, become hypervigilant and hot-wired for anxiety. A coping skill that once kept you alert and alive is now running on overdrive.

A useful metaphor for anxiety is that it is like a runaway horse with the client barely holding on and having no control. What often happens is that if you let the horse run, and if you do what your anxious mind says, you will eventually feel relief. This is what happens with self-abuse and eating-disordered behaviors. In the classic OCD scenario, if you worry that you are going to get sick and die because you touched the doorknob, your anxious mind tells you that if you wash your hands 10 times, you'll be okay. So you wash your hands 10 times and then you can relax.

The trouble is that brain circuits get increasingly stronger, and the anxiety makes the world increasingly smaller. Within a few months the same person is washing his or her hands 20 times. The person who had a panic attack is now afraid to go to Walmart for fear of having a panic attack there, and within a few months is a full-blown agoraphobic and unable to step outside of his or her front door. The way out of this is pulling on the reins of the horse, and like the other issues, taking charge.

What this translates to in terms of treatment is helping clients recognize when the horse is starting to run, physiologically or cognitively, and deciding whether the what ifs are real problems or not (worrying that I may lose my job because the company is downsizing is a real problem; obsessing that a meteor may fall on my house or that coworkers noticed and are talking about whether my tie is crooked are not). If it is a real problem, action needs to be taken: encourage your client to talk to someone in the human relations department; set up a meeting with your supervisor to see where you stand in the changes. If the problems are unrealistic, focus on lowering the anxiety itself by deep breathing, mindfulness, meditation, emotional freedom technique, and so on.

Treating anxiety is about pushing back behaviorally. In classic treatment of OCD, for example, the client needs to wash his hands 9 times instead of 10. Will he be an anxious wreck if he does that? Absolutely. But if he can get through that with support, good self-talk, and medication, and discover the next morning that he did not, in fact, die, anxiety begins to loosen its grip; the disasters that the anxious mind predicts don't actually come true. The aim here, as it is with depression, anger, and other negative emotions, is for the client to run his mind and emotions, rather than his mind and emotions running him.

Finally, there is one additional goal to treatment: desensitizing oneself to anxiety in general. What this means is learning to tolerate anxiety rather than being overwhelmed by it and doing what it says. This is done by what we have been saying throughout—by stepping outside comfort zones, running toward the fear—and it does not matter where one starts or what one does as long as it is at least slightly uncomfortable. As the comfort zone gets bigger, as one has more success experiences in overriding the anxious mind, self-confidence and a sense of self-mastery increases (Taibbi, 2013).

Once again, sessions can focus on each of these components: approaching problems, recognizing and changing thought patterns, developing weekly plans for concrete action, choreographing family sessions to raise difficult issues, teaching relaxation techniques, and mapping out and following up on taking acceptable risks.

As you can see, in nearly all situations a combination of approaches is the most effective. Parents can be given guidelines on new and specific behavioral changes they can begin to make in the home in order to avoid power struggles, break the dysfunctional patterns, and provide support—coached, for example, not to struggle with their anorexic daughter about finishing her dinner, but instead asking her about her emotions; helping an anxious teen by giving sufficient notice about changes so they are not rattled by the transitions. Individual therapy with teens can focus on helping them define their internal world and choreographing in advance their upcoming discussion with parents in family therapy about their needs or their appropriate, assertive voicing of complaints. Family therapy can be the forum for learning communication skills, problem solving, demonstrating nurturing skills to parents, drawing out the hidden sides of everyone's role, or clarifying the intention behind the behavior. An adolescent group, if available, can provide further opportunities for the development of social skills in a safe environment and can help reduce isolation. Confrontation by peers can have a far greater impact than such confrontation by a therapist, and accelerate change.

Whatever way you choose to support a teen, be alert to the dangers of usurping the parents' role. For parents who blame the child, and are passive, frustrated, or tired of trying to handle problems, stepping back and letting the clinician step in becomes all too easy. For the adolescent who feels misunderstood, resentful, and hungry for intimacy with an adult, a deep dependency on the therapist becomes a real possibility. As with Billy, this doesn't mean that you should never take this approach; sometimes it is the best course to take. However, you need to make a deliberate clinical choice and be clear about your commitment to the teenager.

Influence of Parents' Pasts

Finally, when the forces of the parents' past are being replicated in the life of the adolescent, the starting point for assessment and treatment planning begins with the parents' own ability to see and understand how they have helped create the dynamics that have enabled the replication to happen. Following in one's footsteps is chalked up by some parents to fate or genetics as a given over which they have little control—for example: "My cousin had a boy just like Simon who wouldn't listen and he eventually got in big trouble with the wrong crowd."

Others who see the shadow of their own lives mirrored in their child find it too painful and retreat into minimization and denial. What the adolescent is doing—shoplifting but not breaking into houses, dating older men but not pregnant at 13—is different enough or doesn't seem quite so bad to them as their own past; the problem, they decide, isn't with them, but only with the child or with the influence of friends. For still others this replication of history is all too apparent, but only creates enormous guilt and panic and little else; the forces that create the problem or how to change it are outside of their awareness.

Your focus certainly doesn't need to be on the blame, but on helping the parents see that while their past is part of their own and their child's present, it's a present that can be changed. Parents need to know that they have to stay neither walled off by denial nor mired in guilt, but can increase their control and power by recognizing and changing the patterns and process that create and maintain the problems. The fact that the father is emotionally abandoning his son just as his own father physically abandoned him is less important than helping the father see his son succeed.

H. L. Mencken once said that most complex questions turn out to have a simple answer, but that it's usually wrong. While it's simpler to talk of adolescent problems in terms of one source/one goal, in reality problems between parents and adolescents usually stem from several sources, all intersecting at one time—poor parenting and coping skills; an overwhelmed parent and adolescent; poor communication; and inappropriate roles and misalignments born out of the family's struggles with past losses, traumas, and environmental stress. Which you choose to focus upon the most will depend on your theoretical frame, personality, and priorities.

If you are most comfortable thinking systemically, a lopsided hierarchy, such as the Harris family, is what may stand out most in the first session. If you feel comfortable in the role of teacher, or come to see many of your families as warped by unrealistic expectations for teenagers and themselves, educating the parents on normal adolescent development and appropriate skills may naturally seem the best course. If you draw from a psychodynamic orientation, your work might entail seeing the adolescent individually to unravel defenses and increase insight. All of these approaches are valid and can be effective; once again, there are many paths through the forest from which to choose.

But while your theory, comfort, and family expectations may be a starting point for your brainstorming, pragmatics and practicality need to be considered as well. If you work in an agency that has heavy caseloads, or find insurance limiting the length of treatment, you may need to think in terms of moving through problem and solution in layers, from the simplest and least interventionist to those more complex and long term. For example, if a parent comes in complaining of a child like Ellen who is running the family, your structural understanding of the family would indicate that it is important to start by reinforcing the parental hierarchy. You might focus on helping the mother tighten up her parenting and set clearer limits as a first goal. If this works and the troublesome teen settles down and starts to get attention in more positive ways, therapy can be brief indeed. If, however, the mom has a hard time implementing the structure, or if the teen's depression over her peer relationships comes to the surface once her acting out stops, a shift can be made to family or individual work. These next layers of problems are only addressed if simpler solutions fail.

WALKING THE LINE: OPENING MOVES

If it seems that as a therapist you have to do a lot of juggling—between adolescents and parents, past and present, individual work and family work—you're right. Unlike treatment of younger children, working with adolescents requires walking a finer line, carefully balancing the adolescent's needs with those of the family.

The balancing you have to do reflects the awkwardness and precarious balance that both makes up adolescence and distinguishes it from childhood. A child may be reluctant to come to therapy, but his or her parents can make the child come, and usually rapport can be quickly established through play therapy. A child may be under considerable personal stress, but his or her sensitivity to and dependency on the relationship with the parents and home environment makes it likely that the smallest of positive changes will ripple down and help the child. A child may be severely acting out, but he or she is unlikely to be involved in criminal behavior or facing decisions that can have lifelong consequences (for example, abortion or adoption versus becoming a teenage parent). The parents of a 7-year-old may be worried about what the school says, but there's a feeling that there is time to work it out.

This all changes with the adolescent. Instead of one or two adults and a child, there are one or two adults and another half adult, each side representing different cultures, with you as the bridge between them. Many therapists (especially those in their 20s and 30s, it seems) find it easy to identify with their adolescent clients and see them as the victims of rigid parents. Their efforts to get the parents to "loosen up" can quickly cause the parents to see the therapist (especially if he or she is younger than them) siding with their teen and not them. They quickly dismiss the therapist as being out of touch with the real world of parenting.

Your fate with the teen isn't much better. Because of your age, you may be seen by an adolescent client as "one of them"—simply offering to play a game of checkers won't automatically win the teen over. While your ability to build rapport and ease anxiety in a child can often easily be done by his or her seeing you create a comfortable relationship with the parent, this same move with adolescents can backfire. If you seem to be too much on the side of the parents and working too hard for their agenda, and if there is any suspicion that confidentiality will be broken, the relationship never gets off the ground.

Your place in the middle between these generations means that your opening moves are extremely important. In order to build a foundation of rapport, you need to demonstrate to the teenager across from you that you are different from his or her parents. This doesn't mean that you have to know who's on Billboard's Top Ten, talk only in this year's street slang, do card tricks, or have a tattoo the size of Montana on your forearm. It means that working with teens is like any other cross-cultural work: You need to show respect and a sincere interest in understanding the adolescent world. Ask questions ("What is school like for you?"; "What is most difficult about being your age?"; "What do you most wish you could do?") and demonstrate a patient willingness to listen.

But the parents are your customers as well. You can't leave them in the waiting room thumbing through old issues of *Time* magazine for a couple of months wondering what's going on in there and what they're paying for. Their place in the hierarchy of the family, their anxiety, and often their problems, including the behavior of their child, require you to include them.

As with the younger child, part of your assessment is figuring out just how much time you need or want to spend with each family member, which problem (parent's or child's) has the higher priority, and which treatment format (individual, couple, family) is the best approach. As with children, as one option closes—the adolescent thinks you're a jerk and never comes back—the others remain open. All is not lost.

Still, it's easy to wind up feeling like a bouncing ball if you're not careful, shuttling back and forth between the generations like a state-department diplomat. The way out of this is not to think in terms of being *between*, but *above*; your client isn't the adolescent, or the parents, or even the adolescent *and* the parents, but the family system.

Your role needs to be clear. Your job in those first few sessions is to build rapport with and trust on both sides, gather information, and develop a therapeutic contract with the parents and the adolescent regarding their goals. If possible, use your understanding of the family dynamics and the structural problems to link those goals together.

Kamesha, for example, is infuriated with her mother, who won't ever let her go out with her friends; her mother is furious with Kamesha because the only thing she seems to talk about is wanting to go out. You could help both of them see how they are having a power struggle and polarizing each other, or better yet, explore whether Kamesha's wanting to go out stems at least in part from the tension and criticism she feels when she's at home. You could help the mother talk about her own teenage experiences and how they may fuel her fears about her daughter going out, the way she feels rejected by Kamesha, or how her complaining may simply be her way of getting Kamesha to pay some attention to her. Rather than mediating how much time to spend with friends, your goals become helping mother and daughter become curious about the role of this issue in their lives, and encouraging them to find positive ways of communicating and spending time together.

Similarly, when Gabe complains that his parents are always on his back, and his parents complain that Gabe isn't doing his schoolwork and is never as conscientious as his older brother, the problem isn't schoolwork or criticism, but helping Gabe move out of a scapegoat role. The parents need to know that they can help Gabe with school by first seeing him as different from his brother, while Gabe can be challenged to get his parents off his back by finding other ways of gaining their attention and helping them see him for who he is.

Your job then is to see what the parents and adolescent may not—their blind spots—and to offer a perspective that incorporates both sides of the problems. You need to say and show from the onset that you're not working for one or the other, but both. Successful adolescence is, after all, the ability to integrate into the family grow-ing differences and needs.

While you're clear about what you'll do, you're also clear about what you won't do. Some of these limits are dictated by your theo-retical model: no, you will not only do individual therapy with the teenager to fix him or her; yes, it is important that the father attend the sessions, or that the couple come in together to work on their communication and conflicts. Then there are the legal and ethical limits of confidentiality: you will need to notify parents if there is suicidal or homicidal risk; you will need to contact protective ser-vices if abuse or neglect is suspected. It's best to clarify these ethi-cal and legal limits as soon as possible. The key here is to be clear, informative, and matter-of-fact from the beginning.

In addition to defining your role, good beginnings require that you be careful to create symmetry and balance. As mentioned ear-lier, seeing the entire family at the start of the first session has the advantage of not only helping you see how they interact right away, but reduces the paranoia that family members have at being left out of the session. If there's a need to see the parent and teenager separately—to build rapport, to see what each is like apart from the other, to educate or discuss material inappropriate for the other (parents' or teens' sex lives, marital issues, details of what the teen may do outside the home)—that's fine as long as the time is bal-anced, and you are clear in your plan so that both sides have an overall sense of what's going on. The quickest way to build para-noia in a teenager or anxiety in a parent is to leave either one of them out in the waiting room for a few sessions while the others are back in the office with you. Once you've finished your assess-ment and you have discussed and come to a consensus with every-one on the type of treatment format that will be used, the balance becomes less crucial.

ASSESSMENT: THE ADOLESCENT VARIATIONS

Many families with teenagers enter therapy in a state of war, so you need to move quickly to calm things by helping everyone have his or her say, by taking both sides and helping them see in the room how everyone bounces off of one another without even being aware of it. But once the dust has settled you need to gather the information you need to establish a treatment plan. The assessment of an adolescent and his or her family is not much different than any other family—you still want to see the patterns, the structure, define the problem, see what's missing, clarify the family's theory of the problem, and so on. However, the adolescent stage of development prompts some additional questions, especially those surrounding communication, problem solving, and rapport that you may want to ask yourself and the family members. A quick checklist broken down by who's in the room follows:

Parents and Adolescent

Who's missing from the session—father, mother, other siblings? Why? Important but absent members may potentially undermine the treatment.

Who's the most active? Often this reflects what happens at home; sometimes it merely shows who's the most motivated or anxious.

Who's got the problem; that is, who's the customer? Mother? Father? Court? School? There may be more than one, but you want at least one in the room.

What is the emotional climate in the room? Angry? Depressed? Anxious? The emotional climate is like taking the family's temperature. Again, one of the tasks for the first session is to change the climate so that the family feels differently when they leave from when they came in.

How does the adolescent respond to the parents, to you? Quiet? Argues back? Silently defiant? If the parents open with double barrels, blasting away at all the things the teen is doing wrong, you're immediately looking to see if the teen can fire back. If he can, this is a good sign of some personal strength, and then your goal is to keep the conversation within bounds and focused.

If the teen cannot defend him- or herself, if he collapses into silence, looks away, or stares at his shoes, the danger is that the teen will walk out feeling beat up and you will be seen as an accomplice. In these cases you need to stop the parental assault and help the teen speak up. If he can't do that with the parents in the room, you need to send them out, and see the teen alone in order to build rapport, show that you are not like the parents, and get a better perspective on what he is really like.

How well can the parents articulate their concerns? What the teen usually hears, of course, is the criticism, the parent on his or her back. Can you help the parents help their child to understand the *fear* and *worry* that underlie their attitude?

Can the adolescent articulate a logical, rational counterargument? Adolescents are like novice lawyers, trying to argue their case with little experience and only the basic skills. Through the arguing, however, by trying to state their reasons and rationalizations aloud, they not only further develop the corners of their brains that handle abstract reasoning, they actually are forced to discover and define what they believe and think, all helpful life skills to have. Teens who complain or get angry about parental limits but little else need to learn to use their emotions as information about what they need or don't like and come up with a counteroffer.

Teens who all too quickly collapse under the weight of parental reasoning (teens who abuse themselves with cutting or eating disorders often do this) also tend to cope with the anxiety of conflict by being good—rather than making the counteroffer, they switch and agree with the parents or backpedal from their own request. They need support in holding their ground. Let them know that their feelings are important, their position is reasonable, and help them articulate it. Coach the parents to back off and listen so that the teen feels safe enough to come out of the corner. Help them understand that what's at stake isn't the details of the argument but their teen finding his or her voice and learning to approach, rather than flee, from conflict. When they hear good, reasonable thinking coming their way, encourage the parents to allow themselves to be persuaded.

Can someone stop when things get out of control? Whether it's one of the parents who calls a halt to escalating arguments or an adolescent who stomps off and slams shut the door of his or her room, what's important is that someone is able to stay sane enough to realize when the process is getting out of control. Some families are unable to do this type of self-regulation, and the results are verbal abuse or even physical violence. If this begins to happen in your office, it's essential that you step in and stop it. If they can't be civil in the same room, separate them, and focus first on teaching them how to stop.

Are the parents presenting a united front or are they split? Splitting leads to teens working the parents against each other or their falling through the cracks and not getting what they need.

Can the parents say positive things about the child? We are what we hear, and research says that we need a 4:1 ratio of positive to negative comments in order for us to be able to even hear the positives. In highly conflictual families, recognizing positives and voicing them can be a stretch. Parents need to be coached and complimented themselves by you in order to change their ways.

How does the family respond to you? What are their expectations of counseling? Some parents are looking for an arbitrator, someone to straighten their teen out, or parenting advice; a few are actually looking for family therapy. Most teens are likely looking to get out of the room as quickly as possible; discovering that you are not just like their parents and that you have some understanding of what life as a teenager is like is often a welcome relief.

The fact that teenagers and parents have different points of view is a given. What you don't want to reinforce by your inactivity, especially in the first session and especially with teens who can't hold their own ground, is an ongoing replication in the room of the dysfunctional dynamics. If the adolescent sees you sitting there watching him or her getting bashed on both sides by parents, the teen's confidence in your ability to protect or even understand his or her point of view is severely handicapped.

Adolescent Alone

How well and willing is he or she to articulate his or her point of view? Some struggle because of developmental delays; some because they get anxious talking to adults; others because they don't want to be there and become passive–aggressive. You need to understand what might be going on and help the teen get his or her story out.

What is his or her theory about the problems in the home? How much self-awareness is present? How much blame, guilt? Again, in the theory lies the solution. Creating rapport and developing trust means understanding the teen's world and problems. While most teens see themselves, in varying degrees, as victims of the adult world, they also vary in their ability to step outside of themselves and empathize with someone else's point of view ("I know my parents are worried"; "I don't expect them to let me do whatever I want"). Excessive blame makes it more difficult to move toward problem solving, while excessive guilt absorbs the energy that could be used for new behavioral changes.

How does he or she relate to siblings? What role does he or she take in the family system? Are siblings an emotional support or stress? The class president, football-quarterback older brother can be an impossible act to follow or be a source of inspiration and support. The acting-out younger sister can be a pain in the neck or someone fun to play video games with and relax. If you haven't seen the interaction among them in a whole-family session, you want to know about relationships with siblings. Teens who have a bond with their brothers and sisters are not only less stressed and less lonely but potentially have in-house support for changes.

Does he or she have friends? Is he or she a leader or follower? How much do friends provide support? How strong and what type of influence and modeling do they provide? Most adolescents will tell you about their place in the peer hierarchy without any trouble. Of particular concern are the isolated adolescents who have few supports or no best friends. They have nothing to hold on to as they try to separate from parents, and are at greater risk for depression and drug abuse.

Does he or she have a boyfriend or girlfriend? How much is it a source of support or stress? Does the current one follow the same pattern as the intimate relationships before? How all-encompassing is the relationship— is there room for relationships with other friends? Does it replicate the parent's history in some way, or the marital relationship? Basically, is the intimate relationship a positive or negative force in the teen's life? Is the teen in that relationship a better person than he or she seems at home, or is it more of the same?

Does he or she use drugs? What kind? How often? Is there an addiction that needs treatment before any further therapy should be undertaken? Just matter-of-factly asking about these drugs often, surprisingly, will give you information, especially if your tone is one of concern rather than criticism. Looking at family history (for example, Dad is an alcoholic) and risk for self-medication through drugs (social isolation, poor social skills, depression, hyperactivity, and so on) should raise your antenna and give you a context for talking to the teen about this: "You mentioned that your dad drinks a lot. How about you—how much do you drink?" It's better to matter-of-factly assume the positive and get a denial than ask if he or she does drink. "Do you worry that you could become a heavy drinker like him?"

Some teens will deny drug use at the beginning, but once they trust you, they will bring it up on their own. As mentioned above, if addicted, the therapy may help to get the adolescent into drug treatment; keep in touch with the teen while in treatment. Also, don't expect to do effective family therapy with an untreated addicted teen.

School—an arena of accomplishment and success, or failure? Are educational goals realistic? Are relationships with teachers supportive or antagonistic? Are there any apparent intellectual emotional barriers to success? How is classroom behavior? Is work completed? Does he or she fit in with a group? Is he or she a loner? Adolescents have a home life, a school life, and a street life. It doesn't take much, it seems, for some kids to give up on themselves as successful learners. Those with undiagnosed learning disabilities, ADHD, family struggles, and emotional difficulties can come to view school as a place of failure and criticism, and their only friends are similarly burned-out types. The challenge is to help teens use school effectively, rather than just marking time until they can quit.

Does the teenager have dreams of the future? Are they realistic? Can he or she plan the steps leading to the goal? How are the goals shaped by the parents' expectations, other siblings, the parents' own history? This is a more sophisticated version of the childhood question, "What do you want to be when you grow up?" The 100-pounder who wants to become a pro wrestler needs help going from passion to practicality. The 17-year-old who sees no point to life needs your help to resolve grief, trauma, or depression. Having dreams of the future provide the escape hatch from the often powerless feelings of adolescence.

How does he or she relate to you? Open? Closed? Suspicious? Accommodating? Passive? Defiant? Anxious? What is the contrast between the content and process from the session together with the parents? Think again in terms of what is missing, and emotional range. Not being treated like the parents is a good sign.

Does he or she understand confidentiality and its limits? Confidentiality is important but so is their understanding of the limits, especially when working with depressed teens.

What would he or she most like to be different at home? This question is particularly important for in it is the therapeutic contract. By asking the question you are telling the adolescent that you are not just dealing with the parent's agenda, but his or her own as well. You're saying that this is the place to work on and accomplish what he or she wants, and offering him or her a stake in the process. Your task, of course, is to link the goals of the adolescent and parent so that one creates the other, or so both can be worked on simultaneously.

Parents Alone

How do they see their relationship with their child? How would they like it to be? These questions can shift the discussion from what is wrong inside the child to the interpersonal interaction. Asking what they would like is beginning to define their side of the therapeutic contract.

Can they clearly articulate the behavioral changes they most want to see? Most parents say that they want their child to change his or her "attitude"; this is too vague a goal. The parents need to be absolutely clear about what they are looking for, behaviorally and specifically, so that the adolescent clearly knows what's expected.

What is their theory of the problems? Is it realistic, balanced? Do they see their own role? Is blame given to outside forces such as teachers, friends? Do they show empathy for their child? If everyone else is to blame, the parents feel like victims who can do nothing to fix the problems. Help them feel more empowered.

Is the adolescent the family scapegoat? What roles do the other children in the family play? Is there a role for the adolescent to move toward? If Mary is the smart one, Tommy the athletic one, Jane the cute one, and Eric the popular one, there may be no role for Brian except to be the delinquent one or Chloe to be the depressed one. Often helping parents see how easy it is for them to lock on to the narrowest slice of their children's abilities and personalities is enough to start to expand family roles.

Who is most involved with the adolescent? How enmeshed is the relationship? How appropriate? Who is more distant? Why? Dad may only show up to yell at Carlos to take out the garbage, but the grandfather is a steady presence. Mom may wind up complaining to 15-year-old Nadine about her moodiness during menopause because she has trouble making friends on the job. Strengthen the hierarchy and get the parents to work together.

How is the marital relationship? How is the adolescent triangled in? How are conflicts resolved? Is the adolescent fulfilling a surrogate role? Is there addiction or other disability handicapping one of the parents and the marital relationship? Most of the traditional schools of family therapy say the marital relationship is the core of the family. If the marriage is strong, then the parents are united, the parental hierarchy is in place, and there's not the need to use the child as part of a triangle to drain off anxiety between the couple.

How empathic can the parents be of the child? Some parents have forgotten what it was like to be an adolescent themselves, or because their child has more materially than they did, they believe the child should be happy. Similarly, some parents expect a 14-year-old to act as responsible as a 30-year-old, and these parents stay in a continual state of frustration. Here's where you educate and reframe their expectations.

Are their goals for counseling realistic? If they think they will drop their teen off for two sessions so you can sit down with him or her and "straighten out" the teen, they are going to be upset when you ask them if they could block out 5:00 p.m. on the next 10 Tuesdays for family sessions. Find out what they expect.

Is the child re-creating the parents' history? How is this fueling the parents' response? What do the parents think the child most needs in order to be a success in life? Children represent new potential and a wide-open future. If their adolescent represents a chance for the parents to correct all their past mistakes or to live their lives over, they are setting themselves up for struggle and disappointment. Help the parents separate the past from the present, themselves from their children.

How do the parents present differently alone with you versus with the teen or the rest of the family? What is the gap between your view and knowledge of the adolescent and their own? What do they need to most learn about their child? Parents can easily wind up showing only one side of themselves to their children, which deprives the children of broader role modeling and an understanding of what their parents really are like as people. Similarly, many parents are not able to see their own blind spots concerning their child and will need help expanding their view.

How do they relate to you? What role have they placed you in? Is there good rapport? Relationship is everything. If you're closer to their teenager's age than theirs, or if they're wary because you don't have any kids, you may have to work harder or differently to gain their trust.

Is there another parent or parental figure who you need to see? If Grandma really is the power in the family, you need to get her involved.

Who else do you need information from? Court? School? Do they understand confidentiality and its limits between you and them, between you and the adolescent? Make sure the adolescent gives consent for information, not just the parents.

Whole Family

Who's in charge? What's the comfortable problem? You can discover both of these answers by watching the process. Who represents the family—the father, mother? Who talks the most or for everyone else and tells you exactly what the problem is? Maybe the kids act up and the parents do nothing, causing you to wonder if this is what happens at home and is part of the problem. What problem or person does the family always return to, especially to break a silence or when you ask an anxiety-provoking question ("So what happens when you both have marital arguments?"). This problem or that person is what everyone is comfortable talking about. This is where the fingers point when less comfortable problems get raised at home.

How do the siblings interact? What roles do they play out? What are the coalitions and competitions? How are they joined or split between the parents? In large families the children may be broken up into camps—the boys with Dad, the girls with Mom; Kevin is Mom's favorite, Tina is Dad's. The family is split, the children have divided loyalties; through sibling rivalry the children may act out the marital tension.

What's the siblings' theory about the problems? What would they like to see changed? How do they see the adolescent differently from the parents? How do they perceive the marriage? When the children are not split into camps, they can often give a more balanced, reasonable view of the problem: "I think my parents are too tough on Ray, but he shouldn't get them mad by staying out late." This perspective gives you something to bounce off the family, such as, "Do you think what Amy says is true?" It gives you a good place to start.

How are conflicts resolved in the process of the session? How are the parents and the adolescent both different with the rest of the family from how they are individually? Who backs down, who is the compromiser, and who sides with the mother? Is there good discussion or are there threats and hysteria? You want to know how the process breaks down so you can help them change it.

If you notice that the family acts differently when they are all together from when they are not, you want to understand why. The differences may say something about the family culture, the way the children get attention, the impact of allies, and divisions among the family members. Dad, for example, may sound strong and stern when talking together with his wife, but in the family session Mom joins with the rest of the kids in discounting him. Simply noticing the change aloud can help the family uncover the dynamics that propel them.

Are there additional family problems that are not being acknowledged? Do other family members have goals that would help break the dysfunctional patterns within the family? Although neither the parents nor the teenager has mentioned it, you discover in the family session that the youngest son has cerebral palsy or a cleft lip. Or maybe the 4-year-old blurts out that Grandma went to jail last month. These are the problems beneath the presenting problems, family stressors that may be precipitating both the struggle the family is having and their coming in for counseling.

Do the parents see the session as valuable or irrelevant to their primary concerns? Back to expectations. Some parents wonder why you want to waste their time and money talking to the 6-year-old twins when the problem is their 15-year-old. Others are surprised by what they learn from the mouths of the other family members, or come to see that the problem isn't just their teenager but their parenting or the fact that Dad drinks a lot. The way to know what they think about it is to ask.

How do you feel about dealing with so many people at one time? Not only may this give a sense of how the parents may feel much of the time, but also how reasonable it may be for you to do whole-family sessions.

Of course, you will not have to ask all these questions—some may be obvious to you as you observe the family, some may be clear through the given background information, and some may not fit your own theory and you will substitute others instead. The point of the questions and the assessment, however, is to see how the lives of the family members overlap and stumble on each other, find the places where functional interactions break down, and discover the ways coping mechanisms and inner and outer resources can be harnessed to solve the problems. They open the door to the treatment possibilities.

Looking Within: Chapter 10 Exercises

1. How comfortable are you with teenagers in general? Are there certain problems, ages, gender, or personalities that are emotionally more difficult for you to understand or work with? Why?

2. When you look back at your own adolescence, what was most difficult about it? What do you most regret about that time? How have those regrets possibly shaped your current life?

chapter 11

The Parent–Adolescent Struggle II
The Return of Ms. Harris and Ellen

Ms. Harris had made the appointment with the therapist at the suggestion of the school guidance counselor, who was concerned not only about Ellen's fighting and poor grades but also her grief. During one interview with the counselor, Ellen started talking about her father and seemed to the counselor to be depressed. In the first therapy session, Ms. Harris herself began to tear up as she talked about how hard their father's death had been on the kids. Ellen looked away and said the school counselor was making a big deal about nothing.

That entire first session was spent seeing mother and daughter together, gathering history and information. It was clear that Ms. Harris was overwhelmed by the changes her husband's death had brought, both economically and emotionally. She spoke freely and painfully about the past year. Most of all she talked about how worried she was about Ellen, and her own guilt that she was not doing a good enough job as a mother.

Throughout all of this Ellen acted stoically. When she wasn't answering a question with a grunt, it was with a simple yes or no, and she usually contradicted what her mother said. The only change she said she wanted at home was for her mother not to complain so much, and let her do more of what she wanted ("All her friends could!"), especially taking her to the mall on Saturdays. She, however, did agree to come back to therapy with her mother.

The second session was split between Ms. Harris and Ellen, to see how each was different without the other, gather more history from Ms. Harris about her marriage, and build some rapport with Ellen. Ms. Harris was seen first so that even if Ellen worried that the therapist and mother were talking about her, at least she wouldn't worry that the therapist was repeating what she'd just told him.

When Ms. Harris talked about her husband her ambivalence was apparent. Sniffling and hunched over she described her husband as 15 years her senior, a longstanding alcoholic, verbally abusive at times, demanding, and controlling of her and the children. Ms. Harris had appeased him as much as possible, served as a buffer between him and the children, swallowed her own anger, and adapted a codependent role. His sudden death knocked her off her feet. Although she had worked part-time before, she now was holding down two jobs.

While she had no trouble with the two younger girls, Ellen's behavior was compounding the stress; having never needed to take a strong role with the children, she now was struggling to reshape her role and image in their eyes. While things certainly weren't great when her husband was alive, now they seemed absolutely awful. What she felt most was that she had to learn to be strong for the children.

Ellen by herself continued to exude her tough air. No, she didn't think about her father that much; yes, things had changed a lot in the past year and a half; yes, school was boring; no, her mother wasn't doing a good job, in fact, she was pathetic the way she whined and complained and gave her a hard time about going out with her friends, but she was even more pathetic because she would eventually give in if Ellen pushed long enough. And Ellen was the one who had to look after her sisters all the time either because her mother was working or she was tired. She didn't mind doing it too much, but her mother sure didn't seem to appreciate it.

The therapist let her vent, empathized with her feeling that things were unfair and that she was taking on more than most other kids her age had to. She just shrugged, but seemed to relax. The therapist talked to her about confidentiality and about therapy as a place to make some of the changes that may be important to her.

One of the traps here, of course, is to be seduced by Ellen's apparent strength and insight, do as the mother does and give her too much power, and ask her what she thinks the mother or her sisters need most. That only reinforces her empowered and entitled role. The therapist's concern should only be on what Ellen needs; it's up to Ms. Harris to be responsible for the rest.

The third session with Ms. Harris and Ellen together, with which we opened this chapter, showed just how the interaction between them is played out. Here they were replicating in the office what happens at home. Even with the therapist's support, Ms. Harris had a difficult time acknowledging her anger and not caving in to Ellen, and Ellen had a hard time not becoming angry and scolding her mother. The third session ended with the therapist talking individually to the mother about specific parenting skills.

DOING WHAT WHEN

So what do we have here? As we saw with Billy, we have another parent who is having trouble setting limits. Ms. Harris is not only having to shift gears from parenting younger children to a teenager, but is having to change roles within the family structure, from an ally and nurturer of the children to nurturer *and* disciplinarian (see the transitional family described in Chapter 4). Ellen, due to her age, personality, and probably past patterns of relationship to her father and mother, has stepped into the father's role and, together with her mother, is quickly replicating the marriage, complete with verbal abuse. The heightened sense of power Ellen has, along with her overresponsibility and concern for her sisters, is enough to keep her in the role; what she's missing is any closeness with her mother or the opportunity to simply focus on her own life. Struggling with Ellen is a variation of Ms. Harris's struggle with her husband. That was familiar ground and less anxiety provoking than making the changes in her current role that she needs to make, especially since she is already so overloaded.

So mother and daughter complement and interlock. Ellen takes charge because her mother doesn't; her mother doesn't because Ellen does. Ellen doesn't get sad; she (as her father) gets angry, tough, and controlling. Ms. Harris doesn't get tough; she gets sad and helpless. Both, pulled by familiarity and pushed by complementarity, stay within their own comfortable emotion and behaviors. The anxiety, what's missing, the need for each person is the same: to expand their emotional range and move toward the underside of what they each cannot now feel, rather than depending on the other to play it out.

What this raises is the question of timing: deciding when it's best to do what, and figuring out the sequence of steps needed to learn new skills and solve problems. Issues of timing run alongside the issue of depth (moving from the least intrusive problem to the more invasive), and alongside questions of priorities determined by the hierarchy of needs (for example, getting the family on food stamps or helping Johnny get back in school before working on "growth" issues like understanding why you feel annoyed when your husband asks what's for dinner). The question of timing is knowing when to approach a topic or task in terms of the family's emotional readiness and foundation of skills. What does the family need to do first before they will be psychologically ready to do more?

If, according to your theory, you believe that it's unresolved grief that is driving the emotional reactions and roles in this family, then the question and the solution lie in determining how to facilitate the grief reaction. Like Billy, it's clear that Ellen isn't comfortable approaching the topic or feelings head-on, and Ms. Harris, for all her sadness, can only go so far—after a year she is still too quickly immobilized by these sad emotions that only trigger Ellen's complementary anger. Like the parents of other overresponsible children and adolescents, Ms. Harris may need to step up before Ellen can step down. Before we can help Ellen more openly grieve we may have to help Ms. Harris get strong. To push Ellen to give up her toughness and look at her sadness while she sees her mother still wallowing and incapacitated may be too difficult for Ellen.

One way of increasing individual power is to help clients become more aware of and able to express their anger. As part of the normal grief process, we can suspect that the Harris family members feel varying amounts of anger over the father letting them down. Anger is an important emotion because it is the beginning of boundary setting (knowing what you don't like), and is a physiological antidote to energy-draining depression. But expecting Ms. Harris to quickly tap her anger as a way of feeling stronger may be too threatening and anxiety provoking for someone who has spent most of her life suppressing such strong feelings. She may need to approach her anxiety more gradually, and take behavioral risks that increase her self-confidence and self-esteem before she feels capable of handling her own anger and entitled to express it.

This way of thinking, this mapping out of sequences and deciding which goals to move toward first, can seem complex but isn't. All it involves is approaching a pocket of anxiety and seeing where the resistance most arises. Ms. Harris's own history with her husband, her difficulty in mobilizing her anger within the session with Ellen, gave the therapist immediate information and feedback about what may or may not work. If the mother had been able to stand firm to Ellen's demands, or if Ellen was able even in individual sessions to let down her guard and approach some of her feelings about her father, these would be clues that more direct routes could be taken. But that didn't happen, and to push either person too hard, so early toward what they most fear, runs the risk of them shutting down or leaving treatment altogether.

What we still don't know, however, is just how pervasive the grief is throughout the family, how entrenched both Ms. Harris and Ellen are in their roles, and the part the siblings play in maintaining the system. This is a good time to see the other children in a whole-family session.

BRINGING IN THE REST OF THE TROOPS

They march in a single file down the hall, Ellen leading the way; followed by Betsy, skipping and jumping; then Marie, slouching, watching her feet; and finally Ms. Harris, once again bedraggled and frail looking. Ms. Harris dumps herself onto a couch alongside Betsy; Ellen sits by herself on the other couch; Marie sits in the chair in between.

"So, did your mom talk to you both about coming here today?"

Both Betsy and Marie nod.

"Momma, can I go over there and play?" asks 8-year-old Betsy.

Before Ms. Harris has a chance to say something, Ellen pipes up, "You need to stay here with us."

"Ms. Harris, I think Ellen spoke for you. Do you want Betsy to stay here next to you?"

"Sure, I guess. Honey, just sit here for a few minutes." Ms. Harris pulls Betsy close beside her.

"Your mom and Ellen and I have been talking in the past couple of weeks about all the changes that have been going on in your family. It sure sounds like a lot has happened in the past year since your dad died."

"My momma has to work a lot," says Betsy with a sigh, "and Ellen is always bossing us around."

"I do not!" snaps Ellen. "You're the one who's always bugging me, always running to Momma, always getting your way!"

"But you hit me!" And she lifts up the edge of her shorts and points to a faint black and blue mark.

"Girls, girls, please don't start," says Ms. Harris, as she limply waves her hand toward both of them.

"Is this what happens at home, Marie?"

"All the time." She sounds bored.

"What do you do when they get into it?"

"Go to my room. Wait till they are finished."

"How are you and Ellen doing?"

"Okay. She tries to boss me around sometimes, but I just don't pay attention to her."

What's happened so far? We see Ellen assuming a parental role, both in the session process and at home, with little resistance from her mother. We could guess that Ms. Harris is closest to Betsy (she identifies with Betsy's helplessness?), is openly favored by her, and Ellen knows it, only increasing the gap between her and her mother, and her retaliation against Betsy. She and Ellen do battle where Ms. Harris does not. And Marie, just as she is seated in the room, is somewhere in between, the neutral middleman, who ducks for cover when conflict breaks out.

What we still need to know is how the family has crystallized around the father's death. After spending some time building rapport with Marie and Betsy, and finding out about their relationship with each other and their mother, this is where the focus turns:

"Betsy, it sounds like you are very close to your mom. How about your dad, were you close to him?" the therapist asks gently.

"Well, sort of, I guess. He would take me to the park sometimes, and sometimes I would sit on his lap when we were watching television."

"How did you feel when he died?"

"I was real sad, especially when I went to the funeral. Everybody was crying. . . . I stayed close to Momma. . . . "

Out of the corner of his eye the therapist sees that Marie is beginning to tear up.

"Marie," says the therapist softly, "what's wrong?"

Marie starts to cry harder.

"She feels sad," says Betsy.

"Are you thinking about your dad?"

Marie nods.

Ellen turns away and starts to get restless. "How about you, Ellen, how are you feeling?"

Ellen ignores the question.

"Ms. Harris, how are you doing?"

"I know this is hard on the girls," she responds. "I don't bring this up at home or try and let them see me get upset."

"Sometimes Momma cries," says Betsy.

"And how do you feel when you see her that way?"

"Bad, sad."

"Who do you all think misses your dad the most?"

Ellen can't handle this anymore. "This is a bunch of shit." She suddenly stands up and walks out of the office.

Grief gone underground. Ms. Harris tries to hold it within, crying secretly, hoping no one will see, making the grief itself a family secret. Marie, too, it turns out, does a lot of her own crying and missing of her father, but like the fights, steals off to her room. Betsy, like the little boy in *The Emperor's New Clothes*, isn't afraid to say what she sees and takes the junior caretaker role, the emotional backup when any sadness breaks out; like her mother she plays out the softer side of Ellen's anger and control. And Ellen, with everyone else morose and collapsing, is boxed in with her anger. Overwhelmed with such strong feelings from everyone in the family, she has no choice but, like her dad perhaps, to leave.

So our hypothesis is checked out. The grief is pervasive in the family, Betsy has stepped in as her mother's support and surrogate to re-create the marital tension; Marie, in many ways like her mother, is most comfortable stepping aside; and Ellen clearly is not able to tackle her own feelings of grief until the family gives her some room and helps her find a place. Ms. Harris needs to become the hub of the wheel, not to re-create her husband's role but to include it within the new reality of her life as a single parent. Unless she can do that the children will continue in their adaptive styles, with Ellen winding up out of the family, Betsy eventually taking care of her mother, and Marie sitting alone, depressed, in her room.

One of the biggest traps with this family, as it was with Billy's grandmother, is the therapist, whether male or female, stepping in and replacing the father as family head. This dynamic can most easily be recognized not only by mentally considering the likely replacement role in advance, but by emotionally feeling the pull to do so in the session process. Ms. Harris could reflexively look to the therapist for leadership, Betsy and Marie would find someone besides their mother to rely on, and Ellen, although she may balk initially at having her position threatened, might be happy turning things over to this seemingly more capable adult, especially if she didn't have to worry about her mother anymore. All of this is important for the therapist to keep in mind throughout the beginning stage, and to even be willing to say aloud in order to counter the possible fantasies, especially for Ms. Harris. The mother needs to hear that the therapist doesn't need to take over like Ellen is trying to do, but can support her in making the shifts she, as the parent, needs to make.

Ellen didn't come back in, but instead sat the rest of the session in the waiting room. The therapist spent the rest of the time giving Ms. Harris and the other two girls some feedback—empathizing with their sadness and the change in the family; pointing out their different coping styles, including Ellen's; and underscoring their secret feelings—the way Betsy worried about her mother, the way Marie missed her father, and the way Ms. Harris worried about the children. The therapist also gave them permission to talk about their feelings, to talk about their father openly at home, ask questions, and bring it all out in the open. Both girls agreed to come back at another time. At the end of the session the therapist then went out and talked to Ellen; she agreed to come in and talk to the therapist individually.

As with Billy, we're at a fork in the path. Several options are open to us, depending upon your theoretical frame of reference, including staying with whole-family therapy so that Betsy and Marie are not excluded. But if it's true that Ms. Harris needs to be the fulcrum of change, she may need some individual work to set her on course. Likewise, Ellen may have an easier time focusing on her adolescent life if she doesn't have the rest of the family as an audience to ignite her role. The therapist decided to see if Ms. Harris could help facilitate grief work at home and to temporarily see her and Ellen separately.

ELLEN ALONE

When Ellen came in the following week, she looked anxious. The therapist suspected that she may have been a bit gun-shy from the family session, afraid that the therapist would once again start talking about her father.

Of course he didn't. Even alone she wouldn't have handled it any better and would only learn to dread therapy itself. Instead the therapist asked her about her school and social life, friends and boyfriends, and dreams about the future. Most of all, the therapist wanted to listen while she talked not about her family but her life as a teenager. And she did. Perhaps it was the relief of not having to talk about something more difficult that spurred her on, or maybe she was feeling more comfortable with the therapist and dropping her tough exterior. It doesn't matter why, so much as that she was able to step out of her role, show her other side and inner life, and be supported and encouraged for doing so.

The session ended with the therapist thanking her for talking and, much as he had at the end of the last session with her mother and sisters, empathizing with the changes she and the family had faced. The therapist worried aloud that Ellen had taken on too much responsibility and that everybody else in the family saw her as mean and angry, but that they didn't really know how she felt or what her world was like. Of course, Ellen had to agree with him because this is what she just spent the session talking about. The therapist suggested that he would like to help her be a better teenager and help her worry less about her mother and sisters.

Ellen said little, but seemed much more relaxed. Essentially, the therapist was giving her permission to step down. This didn't mean she automatically would or could—there was still a lot of power in her role, a need for her behavior to maintain the family patterns, and the underlying grief driving it all. But if Ms. Harris could begin to take up the slack, the new space within the family structure could be created for Ellen, and perhaps then Ellen could be able to grieve. Ellen agreed to meet alone with the therapist a couple of more times, think about specific things she would like help with, and meet with her mother again in a few weeks.

TALKING TYPES

In contrast to sessions with young children, these individual sessions with an adolescent are different simply because of the age difference. Whereas the play becomes the medium for Billy, the means for projecting and healing his inner world, talking becomes the medium for Ellen. Ellen's role and maturity made this easy for her.

Not all adolescents are as vocal as Ellen. In fact, adolescents are notorious for shutting down, sitting in the chair, grunting, and staring at their shoes. Those, like Ellen, who are parentified, seem to be the most willing talkers. Because they sound so much like adults, the danger is in talking to them as though they are. Doing so not only reinforces their role and defenses, but lulls you into believing that they're more mature than they really are and encourages you to gloss over their developmental struggles. Rather than letting them talk on and on about their concerns about everyone else, you need to steer teenagers like this toward their underlying, less easily talked about feelings and concerns about being a teenager.

Some teens are able to do this easily and use the therapist as a confidant. You become the big sister or brother, the good, laid-back parent, their best friend's mother whom they like so much. April, for example, a 16-year-old, would easily and eagerly talk about how she felt left out of the cliques at school, self-conscious about her body, and ambivalent toward her father. She wondered aloud about the purpose of religion and the materialism of our culture—heady but normal expressions of adolescent existentialism and angst. Her isolation made her hungry for the opportunity simply to communicate with someone whom she could trust, and through the process, in a Rogerian way, to discover who she is. Her trusting of the therapist became the template for trusting others around her.

Of course, some adolescents seem to be open like April, but the openness is really an anxiety-avoiding, rather than anxiety-facing, process. What they talk about is no different from what they talk with their best friends about on the phone every night. Sometimes this reflects their misunderstanding of just what therapy is about, how the conversation and the relationship is different from that with a peer. You have the responsibility to clarify your role and the purpose of the process: "Becky, I appreciate your telling me about your friends at school, but I'm not sure why you're telling me about it. What worries you the most? How can I help you with your feelings?" If these superficial topics continue, then it is up to you to ask the deeper questions, and help the adolescent move toward what's missing in the process and toward her anxiety in order to create a new experience.

As with adults, there are important differences between adolescents who won't talk and those who can't talk, or at least can't talk well. James, a 14-year-old, was referred by his school principal because he was crudely propositioning girls in his class at school for sex. He and his mother came in together for the first session and were seen by a woman therapist. James said little in the session, and the therapist thought that James was reluctant to talk because it was the initial session, she was a woman, and his mother was present. So arrangements were made for James to be seen individually by a man on the staff.

Communication was still a struggle. James never initiated conversation and would only answer questions with the fewest words possible. When the therapist tried to talk to James about his sexuality ("So, James, what do you think about girls?"), the communication, although it didn't seem possible, broke down even more. The therapist then tried to talk about the apparent problem of talking ("James, it seems that talking about all these things seems really hard for you"), but this got nowhere. The therapist felt discouraged.

It was only after the therapist received records from the school that he discovered that James had an IQ of 80. James's difficulty communicating may have reflected some of his resistance or embarrassment, but, the therapist realized, it probably reflected a communication problem on his side as well. James couldn't fully understand what the therapist was asking because he was probably talking over the boy's head. The therapist needed to talk more concretely and ask more specific questions ("Did you think that girl liked you?") to help James articulate what he was thinking and feeling. This painstaking process itself was valuable because it was James's difficulty appropriately expressing himself that led to the presenting problem.

There are some adolescents who sound like James who have average IQs but refuse to talk. They may have been dragged in by the parents, ordered to come by the court, or referred by the school, and they want no part of it. Someone else has the problem, not them, and they see no reason to be there or to talk to another adult who is going to give them a hard time.

There are several ways of approaching a grunter like this. One of the best is to see him together with the whole or part of the family. This sidesteps the grueling one-on-one struggle. You can encourage one of the parents to talk with him, which is, after all, their job, not the therapist's. By your exploration of the entire family landscape the adolescent sees that the focus isn't only on him, and anxiety goes down. Better yet, usually someone in the family will say something outrageous enough to ignite some response from the teen. All you then have to do is give him the space to talk and be heard.

Another variation of the family session is to ask the teen to bring in a friend to the first family session. Sometimes these friends serve as advocates and help the teen speak up to the parents. But more often a friend confronts the teen for keeping quiet or lying or doing self-destructive things like taking drugs or skipping school. Again, such confrontation has the effect of clearing the air quickly and getting the process moving.

Peer confrontation is, of course, the value of adolescent groups. The focus keeps moving around to each member of the group, and the comments of one are likely to spark responses in the others. If there are peers in the group who easily talk, and/or are familiar with the group process, they can be the cotherapists, and leave you out of the power struggle.

While most teens will generally warm up once they discover that you're different from their parents and teachers (better yet, that you have a sense of humor), are empathic to their point of view, and are interested in helping them change what they want to change, truly oppositional adolescents will cling to their corner of the ring at the slightest movement you make toward them. In that case some therapeutic aikido—"You know, if I were you I wouldn't say anything you don't want to say here, especially anything important"—is enough to challenge them to open up.

Some therapists prefer to move from the physical to the verbal. A quick game of Nerf basketball in the office or Frisbee outside, especially with boys or younger teens, at the beginning of the session burns up that initial anxiety, builds rapport (especially if you lose), and can break the tension. Playing cards while casually asking questions can provide something for the teen to focus on while thinking or getting anxious. Other clinicians prefer to wait the adolescent out. After they map out the terrain of therapy, it's up to the adolescent to make the first move. The client's growing anxiety from the silence and the sitting usually is enough to start something. Other times it's fine to say that it's okay to be quiet here. Again, for the oppositional teen, it has a strategic effect and gets her to talk; for others it genuinely gives them a chance to settle in and collect their thoughts. What's important for the clinician is to avoid the power struggle, to convey the need not for compliance, but choice.

Finally, some adolescents who may clam up in front of parents or alone with the therapist (who seems like another parent) do well when paired with a sibling. Invariably the quiet teen has a sibling who is not. This mini-family group not only gives the therapist a different perspective on family life, but the sibling at least provides something for both the therapist and adolescent to respond to—"Your sister and I were talking about your Uncle Max last week. How do you get along with him?" This allows the teen to wade into therapeutic waters on a buddy system. Once the adolescent feels more comfortable, generally within a session or at most two, the sibling can be phased out and reappear again in whole-family sessions. What you do want to avoid is the teen becoming dependent on his brother or sister, allowing the sibling to be his voice, or reducing his anxiety by making the sibling the focus of therapy.

Over the course of the two individual sessions Ellen was able to talk about specific problems at home (Betsy's constant intrusion), as well as at school (having an argument with her best friend). In each case the therapist helped her clarify what her feelings were (for example, feeling rejected and hurt by her friend) and *her* problem was (for example, Betsy's feeling bored is not Ellen's problem, but Betsy's). In each case Ellen was encouraged not to be responsible for problems that are not hers (for example, working harder than Betsy to fix her boredom), and to be assertive toward her sisters, her mother, and her friends, rather than suppressing her feelings or getting angry and creating a cutoff.

While Ellen's problems were upsetting but overall relatively minor, sometimes more serious problems are revealed in individual sessions. After a few sessions a teen may talk about heavy use of marijuana, reveal a previously undisclosed incidence of sexual abuse, or admit to a 2-year history of bulimia—problems obviously overriding the initial treatment plan. A more thorough substance abuse evaluation may be necessary; ethical and legal requirements mandate that protective services be notified of the sexual abuse; further exploration is needed to map the triggers and specific behaviors surrounding the eating disorder. Guidance from your supervisor is essential. Impact on the therapeutic relationship, parent–adolescent relationship, and therapeutic goals have to all be anticipated and planned for. The focus shifts, new priorities are set, and new contracts and action plans need to be developed.

This was, fortunately, not the case with Ellen. The next week she was able to report that she talked to her mother about Betsy, and had called up her friend and worked things out.

MS. HARRIS ALONE

Ellen's age, her ability, and her willingness to express herself and to think through realistic solutions to problems helped her take concrete steps at home and change the interactional patterns between her and her mother much more quickly and easily than Billy was able to do. When Ms. Harris was seen individually a couple of weeks later, she seemed less stressed; she reported that Ellen had been less demanding and angry, and actually had come and talked to her about Betsy.

Upon hearing such news it could be tempting for the therapist to let Ellen continue to take the lead and initiate the changes at home. This would not only slow down the change process but would re-create and maintain the reactive role that Ms. Harris had learned. In order for there to be long-term change in Ms. Harris and in her relationship with her other daughters, she needed to make individual changes herself.

The therapist asked Ms. Harris about her relationship with her husband. Once again she sighed and seemed to collapse, but then slowly was able to talk about her loss and the first edges of her anger. His alcoholism and his violent temper had overwhelmed her at times, and she admitted to retreating into a passive accommodation to avoid conflict. Relinquishing any intimate relationship with her husband, she made the children the focus of her concern and needs. When asked, she acknowledged feeling responsible in some way for his drinking and even his death. Perhaps she could have tried harder, helped him to get sober, and made sure he had gone to the doctor for a checkup. If she had, she and the children wouldn't be where they are.

Even though she may not have voiced her guilt aloud before, the feelings themselves were familiar and part of the constellation of emotions that kept her in her passive, reactive role. Rather than letting her sink into these emotions yet again, the therapist stepped in and did some light education about alcoholism and grief, stating that both feeling guilty and responsible are normal reactions for families. There was silence for several minutes, and then Ms. Harris shifted gears and talked about Ellen.

Ms. Harris had never used threats in an effort to make Ellen behaviorally comply, but many parents do. Those who view their teenager as the problem, and/or whose own frustrations have reached their limit, come to rely on threats as the only means they feel they have of controlling their child. Over and over the message to the adolescent, and to the therapist, is that the teen better shape up or else, the else usually being shipping the child out to foster care somewhere. Usually the threats don't work—the adolescent feels the power move and fights back, or feels the rejection and says she doesn't care.

Once you help the parents find other ways of responding to the adolescent's behavior the threat usually stops. But some parents need backing and need to know that the community, and not just the therapist, is behind them. This support can usually come through the schools, if the teen is having trouble there, or through the courts, if the adolescent is acting out in the community. The teachers, principal, or probation officer can be invited to come to meetings with the parent. They can clarify their role, their concern, their limits, and work with the parent to create a united front to the teen. The principal can stress the consequences of cutting school or offer rewards for completing work; the probation officer can let the teen know that she will personally bring the teen before the judge if she continues to ignore the parent's curfew. In many cases this is essential to keep the adolescent from splitting the adults and undermining the changes the parent is trying to make. Even with this backing some parents still lapse into threats. When changes are occurring they let the teen and the therapist know that placement outside the home is always in their mind. This kind of talk can undermine the teen's willingness to work on changes, pull the process back into power struggles, and sabotage any sense of security.

One of the best ways for handling the periodic making of such threats is to simply call the parent on it, that is, to take the parent's threat as a serious option, and confront them individually. Whether you see this as a paradoxical move, a way of calling the parent's bluff, or a sincere acknowledgment of what the parent is saying, the outcome is the same. Saying something to the effect of "Mr. Neal, I've been hearing you say to Tom on and off for months now that if he doesn't change, you don't want to deal with him anymore. Maybe I haven't been taking your feelings seriously enough, and we need to talk about whether we should make plans for Tom to stay somewhere else for a while."

The message here is that what you say will be believed, rather than minimized, that it's all right to consider placement if the parents need a break. By your taking a clear, strong stance, you not only draw out the issue of commitment and what it means to love someone, but provide a strong antidote to ambivalence. The clients are essentially pushed off the fence they have been sitting on. Your clarity forces them to clarify their own position, and challenges them to match words with intent and to take responsibility for their feelings and decisions. The discussion can quickly tap into the parents' own history—the way their parents managed their adolescence.

The net effect of this type of confrontation is to get all of their feelings and intentions clearly on the table, and help the parents separate threat and need for control from their true feelings. Most parents will recommit themselves to the process and stop the threats. But some parents may actually need to sort out their emotions about the possibility of the teen's leaving the home. The therapist's job is to help the parent place this decision in a context and to make it a decision, rather than a frustrated reaction.

Ms. Harris had already demonstrated in her marriage a high tolerance for turmoil and so, not surprisingly, had never reached this point with Ellen. The therapist used the sessions with the mother to map out, with role playing and brainstorming, specific responses for specific situations that she could use should Ellen become too demanding or out of control. To offset the mother's greater setting of limits, they also talked about ways she could spend more quality time with Ellen and new, different ways Ellen could help her at home, creating for Ellen (and herself) a new role to replace what was being taken away.

By focusing on Ms. Harris's parenting skills, on what she as the mother could do, rather than her tales of victimization or on what was wrong with Ellen, the session experience was one of empowerment, the goal one of action rather than reaction and helplessness. By not moving too quickly and overloading her, by staying alert to her becoming too passive and merely accommodating the therapist, Ms. Harris could be led to have successful experiences at home that could help her see herself as a capable parent.

THE RETURN OF THE FAMILY

After three individual sessions each with Ms. Harris and Ellen, home life was beginning to calm down. Although she could easily fall back to her old ways when she was under stress, Ms. Harris was more and more able to set limits with Ellen. She found, to her amazement, that Ellen, after a lot of initial huffing and puffing, was willing to do as she asked. And Ellen spoke of spending time with her mother alone, something that she had not done in years, and hadn't realized how much she had missed.

It was time to bring the rest of the family back in, to find out the impact of these changes on the other girls, and to see what effect it was all having on the family's grief reaction. So in they trooped again, this time Betsy leading the line straggling down the hall, with Ellen and Ms. Harris walking together, taking up the rear. Ms. Harris sat by herself in a chair with Ellen on one couch next to her and Betsy and Marie together on the other. Betsy seemed a bit less rambunctious than last time, and her mother asked her to take her feet off the cushion. Marie still seemed quiet and depressed.

After touching base with Betsy and Marie ("How have you been?"; "How was the field trip you told me about last time?"), the therapist asked about how things have been going at home. True to form, Betsy immediately piped up that Ellen had not been fighting so much.

"And you like that?" asked the therapist.

Betsy nodded her head. Ms. Harris smiled. "And Ellen even let me borrow her sweatshirt."

"You looked like a dork," said Ellen with a smile. "It went all the way down to your knees."

"It wasn't quite her size," chimed in Ms. Harris, "but it was nice of Ellen to let her use it." Ms. Harris looked at Ellen and smiled; Ellen smiled back.

The hierarchy had shifted. Ellen and Betsy were relating more as siblings. Ms. Harris was more in charge and positive toward Ellen. Marie, however, was still quiet.

"How about for you, Marie? Things feel any different at home? Not having to hide out in your room so much?"

"Yeah, I guess," she said flatly.

"How are you and Ellen getting along?"

"Okay."

"I asked her to come to the mall with me the other night, but she didn't want to go," said Ellen.

"Marie and I talked some the other night," said Ms. Harris. "I think she is still having a hard time about her dad."

Marie's eyes began to water.

"Is what your mom is saying true? Have you been missing your dad a lot?"

Marie nodded her head.

"I bet it has still been hard for all of you." The therapist looked around the room, making eye contact with everyone.

"We went to his grave this past Sunday and brought flowers," said Betsy. "I felt sad."

"We hadn't gone in a long time. I decided we needed to do that," said Ms. Harris.

The mother again was taking charge. Ellen so far was staying in her chair and didn't seem to be getting anxious or angry. The goal now was to help everyone in the family stay with the process and allow the emotions to come out. The content itself wasn't important; it was only a medium for the emotions.

"Marie, how did you feel at the cemetery?"

"Sad." She was on the verge of tears.

"I picked the flowers," said Betsy.

Betsy was trying to distract from the emotions to help Marie. Appropriately, the mother reached over and gently touched Betsy's knee and put her finger to her lips. Betsy leaned back and got quiet. Ellen was staring at Marie.

"What do you miss most about your dad, Marie?" asked the therapist, quietly.

"I miss going with him on Sunday mornings to get the paper." Her voice was barely audible, and tears were welling up.

"If your dad were sitting here right now," said the therapist, as he pulled an empty chair alongside of her, "what would you say to him?"

"I'd say that . . . " Marie started quietly crying. Ms. Harris was tearing up, as was Ellen. Betsy was sitting quietly with her head down.

"I—" started Betsy, but Ms. Harris reached over and touched her knee again. Betsy leaned back again and was quiet.

The only sounds in the room were the sniffling and crying of everyone. The therapist said quietly that it seemed that everyone had been feeling sad for a while and missing their father, and that it had been hard to talk about, and probably was making everyone feel lonely. Again, the goal was to facilitate the process, not to interpret. In contrast to the last family session, everyone was able to stay in the room together.

After several minutes Ms. Harris spoke: "I think it would be good for us if we took out the old family videos sometime this week and looked at them." Everyone nodded.

"I remember when we all went out West," said Betsy.

"Do you remember that?" Ms. Harris said. "You were so young."

"I remember Dad went horseback riding with us and almost fell off," Ellen said, half smiling.

"Yeah, he had that huge horse. My head was up to its knee," Marie said.

"I think we have movies of that," said Ms. Harris. "We'll have to get them out."

Everyone talked about things they most remembered, including Ellen's bringing up Dad's temper. The therapist guided the process and helped clarify the emotions, asking about other memories and emotions: "What was the happiest time?"; "Who felt scared when Dad got mad?"; "Can you picture him now?"; "It hurts, doesn't it?" Drawing out these details brought the emotions to the surface and kept everyone from veering off defensively.

The therapist also asked if anyone felt that it was their fault that their dad got so angry or even that he died. There was a long, awkward silence that Ms. Harris then filled by saying to the children that it wasn't their fault, that their father drank too much, and that this made his anger worse. His drinking, and his death, she said to them and to herself, had nothing to do with them.

Each member of the family was sorting through her grief. Like Billy finally remembering and talking about his brother's death, this session too was the opening up of the process, not the end of it. This family would need to have more talks like this, more open sharing of feelings as they together and individually worked through the loss. But now that Ms. Harris was empowered, she could serve as a role model for the children of the grief process. Now that they could feel she could support them, and they, in turn, no longer needed to feel responsible for taking care of her, the natural healing process could follow its course.

WRAPPING UP

The family met again the following week, and again it was a mixture of emotion and recollection. The family talked about seeing the family videos, everyone related once again some past memories, but they were also able to shift focus and talk about solving day-to-day problems—Who was going to cook when Ms. Harris had to work late one night?—with the mother taking charge. At the end of the session, it was decided that Ms. Harris and Ellen would each come in individually one more time.

The session with Ellen felt like one of those termination sessions where there seemed to be not much to talk about, no strong pressure to resolve anything. Ellen mostly talked about school, her plans to get a job over the summer, her hope to visit Disney World with one of her friends and her family. The session ended with an agreement that she could come back by herself anytime she wanted.

The session with Ms. Harris was a debriefing of the family sessions, a review of all the positive changes she had been making, with the therapist clearly in the role of consultant. All of the changes in patterns were reviewed, and ways of keeping the door open on the grief process and supporting Marie were discussed. What was most striking about Ms. Harris was her strength and assertiveness. Like Ellen, she too was told to feel free to come back anytime by herself, with the entire family, or with one of the kids.

Of course, there are other avenues that this family and therapist, or even a combination of therapists could have followed: more individual work with Ms. Harris, ongoing monitoring of Ellen, sessions with Ellen and Ms. Harris, individual work with Marie to help her with her sadness, or continued family sessions to help them possibly unravel more of their anger and solidify the changes in the family structure. All of these options, no doubt, have merit and might have helped this family.

But therapy can and often should end with significant but modest changes. This family had moved beyond the place where they were stuck. They are on a solid, more developmentally appropriate path. They learned some skills (particularly the mom) they should be able to utilize as they individually and together face the changes and challenges to come in the next few years. If, after these sessions, they were still lumbering under their grief—if the mother was unable to develop more power in spite of the therapist's coaching, if Ellen remained angry or shifted her anger to another arena (for example, started fighting at school or ran away), if Marie or Betsy stepped in to take Ellen's place as the IP and began to have severe symptoms that Ms. Harris could not help them with, more work would obviously be needed.

Some families are content merely getting to the other side of a crisis; others want therapy to leave them with a firmer sense of stability and some new skills; while still others, building on the momentum of the initial changes, want to continue in order to maximize the family's potential. Where the end is located is determined by your and their expectations for therapy. What you don't want is to leave them feeling fragile, desiring and needing more help and not getting it, and resolving the initial problem but being left staring at the one or several that have taken its place.

Why did this case turn out seemingly better than that with Billy? Probably because the trauma was not so great, Ellen at her age was able to verbalize her feelings and direct her behavior more deliberately perhaps, and Ms. Harris's level of depression wasn't as great as Billy's grandmother's and she didn't feel as isolated. In addition, the therapists were different, in their personality, clinical strengths and weaknesses, and ability to join with the family—101 variables that affect the course and outcome of a case that are beyond anyone's awareness or direct control. This, of course, is part of what makes for the art of therapy and the challenges that come with each new case.

Looking Within: Chapter 11 Exercises

Adolescence is a bridge between two different worlds. During those few short years we consolidate and build on the lessons learned in childhood about ourselves and life. We are forced to look ahead to our future and our "grown-up" selves while struggling to discover who we are in the present. How well we master the challenges of adolescence and learn the lessons that it needs to teach us often becomes the template on which we shape our adulthood for years to come. As you do these exercises, think back and remember your life as a teenager.

1. Think about your own attitudes about adolescents. Should they, in general, be given more freedom? More discipline? What does your answer tell you about what you believe adolescents need to learn most?

2. How might a therapist have been helpful to you when you were a teenager? How would individual therapy have been useful? Family therapy? What would have been your attitude toward each? How would your family have reacted?

3. In what situations and with what types of problems or families with teenagers are you apt to overidentify, project, resist?

4. How might a psychoanalyst, a Rogerian individual therapist, or a biologically oriented psychiatrist have handled the case of the Harris family differently? What do you see as the major advantages or disadvantages of each?

5. Comparing the contrasting cases involving younger children and teens, which do you feel more confident about? What specific skills do you most need to develop?

6. How do you determine just how good a job you are doing with a particular family?

chapter 12

Getting to the Core

Couple Work in Family Therapy

The room seems empty, and quiet. It's just you, Eric, and Cathy. No kids, no fighting over blocks, Play-Doh, or puppets; no stretching out of a parent's arm to rein in one child before he has a chance to go clobber his brother. You're wondering what they did with the kids (stuffed them in the trunk of the car? Dropped them off at Grandma's?) to come alone, but then you decide you really don't want to know.

Your mission: to help this couple gain some control over the bedlam at home. With four children between the ages of 4 and 12, two of them at any one time are fighting in some sort of a tag-team arrangement. Actually, this should be pretty simple: Find out where things break down, help the parents clarify their rules and their responses, and make sure they are working together as a team. Straightforward child management.

"So how was your week?" you casually throw out to give yourself time to grab your coffee cup behind you and settle in.

"Didn't I send him to his room, didn't I?" Cathy snaps. "I specifically told Danny to stay in his room for 10 minutes."

Whoa, did you just miss something, you wonder, as you barely swallow your first sip of coffee.

Eric, nervously pulling on his shirt collar, apparently knows what Cathy is talking about. "Then 3 minutes later he's out there in the kitchen with me, telling me that *you* told him his time-out was over!" Frail, quiet Cathy of last week suddenly is sounding angry and tough. She's now glaring at Eric, who is taking a deep breath and getting ready to swing into his defense.

" I thought you were being too hard on him, I—"

"But you do this all the time, Eric, ALL THE TIME!" Now she's getting hot.

"No, I *don't* do this all the time." Eric's cranking up too. "You're the one who always lets Allison off easy, but do I say anything about it? No, I don't, because—"

"Don't give me that. I don't treat her any different than the boys. I'm the one—"

So much for a quiet, peaceful session.

THE COUPLE IN THE MIX

Most families enter therapy around problems with children and, as we've discussed in previous chapters, your assessment involves understanding the dysfunctional family patterns, skill base of the parents, individual needs of the children, and environmental stressors. As with Billy's grandmother, Ms. Harris, and now Cathy and Eric, some portion of your work may involve working alone with the parent or parents to build skills and shift roles.

Just as it is helpful to create for yourself and the family a vision of how they together would want to be, it's helpful to create your own vision of how the couple ideally needs to be. This vision comprises clear communication, respect, flexibility, problem solving, and decision-making skills. Also included in this image for the couple is a united front with the kids, a willingness to compromise, and a commitment to each other and their parental relationship. The parents also need the ability to separate their issues as a couple from those of the children, and to see themselves as the building block and central core of the family—all of these attributes readily come to mind. Basically, when the couple is sound, the rest of the family is sound.

When the couple is not well grounded, things begin to fall apart: rules are unclear and the children are constantly testing; parents aren't united and the children quickly learn to split them; problems are never solved or communication is poor and the household is in a state of tension as the same problems come up over and over again; and parents are always battling and the kids learn to lean on each other for support, withdraw or escape, or (especially young children) blame themselves for what they believe is happening.

Some clinicians, especially those not trained to work with children, are tempted to take a reductionist approach when facing a family: They relieve their anxiety about what to do with the kids by assuming that all the real issues in families lie within the couple relationship of two adults. They see the family for a couple of sessions, uncover some marital problem, throw the kids out, and focus instead on this smaller, more manageable unit. Family therapy gets pushed aside and is replaced by couple therapy.

This is understandable perhaps, but often a mistake on two counts: While it's true that in the long haul children will generally do okay if the couple is doing okay, one or two of the kids may have developed individual problems (for example, cutting, extremely aggressive behavior) that need specific parental and professional attention. To ignore such behaviors or assume that they will automatically get better may result in the children only continuing to do worse, or the couple being dragged back into their old patterns. Secondly, even if the problems with the children aren't severe, the couple needs to be able to apply their improved relationship skills to parenting. If they don't, or if you as the therapist aren't sure how well they can, parenting issues may remain the couple's Achilles' heel and eventually erode the gains that they have made.

STARTING OUT: COUPLE VERSUS FAMILY

Occasionally you will run across couples that state upfront that it's their relationship that's creating problems in the family—they can't ever agree about the kids and their marital problems are making the kids upset. They drop the subject of children within a few minutes of the first session. When you ask them why they think the presenting problem is happening, they immediately begin their tales of woe and rage about each other. The children, it turns out, were merely the ticket of admission into the therapy system. The focus from the start is on the relationship.

Other couples may feel the same but are less explicit: They may hint at problems through side comments or joking remarks: "I think Carlos would settle down if she (his mother) would just support me sometimes"; "Of course, I don't get any help with this, he (the father) is never home!" Picking up on these comments—"So you feel you need more support from your wife?" or "If your husband was around more, do you think it would help Carlos do better?"— is enough to open the door and get the couple talking about their relationship.

Just as they can polarize around parenting, so too can couples polarize over the impact of their relationship on the children: Phil feels that the state of their relationship is the heart and soul of the family problems, while Angela believes it has absolutely nothing to do with the kids. Obviously their problem is being replicated right there in the room, and you can usually start with that: "It seems like you have a difference of opinion about whether this is important enough to bring up. Phil, maybe you can tell Angela why you think your relationship problems are affecting the kids?" or "Angela, Phil's bringing up things that it seems like you don't agree with and that seem to bother you. Does this happen a lot? How do you think about it differently?"

One step back from those couples that declare from the outset that their relationship is the problem, are those cases where an individual parent comes in because of a problem with a child, but then quickly switches focus to the other parent: "I think the kids are having so much trouble these days because my wife and I are just not getting along." The parent is openly leading the way into the relationship. At this point, depending on your theory and the client's expectation, you may decide to invite the other parent in, coach the parent on ways of talking at home to his spouse about the problems, work with the parent individually to increase insight into his role in the relationship and the problems, help him become the change agent in the family, or offer to help him with the child's problems and refer the parent to someone else for individual or couple work.

Finally, there are couples that from the start take a firm stance and make it clear that therapy is only to work on the children, and everything else is hands off. For them it is the children's problems that have dominated their lives and any discussion of their couple relationship feels like a diversion. For others your questions about their relationship immediately raises their anxiety, and their solution is to quickly focus back on the kids. In these cases you want to not only explore their feelings further but educate them about the links between marital stress and its possible impact on children.

Between the extremes of full disclosure and staunch resistance are infinite degrees of variation—from a willingness to explore the relationship only as it pertains to the IP (child), to the possibility that improving communication may help coordinate parenting, to some agreement that yes, the couple issues probably are affecting the rest of the family and couple therapy might be helpful. As a family therapist, your task is to close the gap that lies between your view of the family problems and that of the couple.

Looking at Eric and Cathy, for example, the couple we met at the beginning of this chapter, we find a couple that were by the second session openly acknowledging their divided approach toward the children, and that the sibling groups were breaking into father and mother camps. The fact that both were so quickly and openly arguing about it makes it easy for you to talk about their relationship and the struggle they are having not only with the kids but with each other. After zeroing in on these dynamics, you and they may easily decide that they need to leave the children at home for a few weeks so they can sort out some of these parenting/couple issues. The three of you may then decide to bring the children back in and do whole-family sessions to translate their skills into the parenting structure, or let them do it on their own at home and simply check in with you.

If, however, the dynamic was different—that Eric had refused to talk with Cathy about her concerns, or denied there was any difference in their parenting styles and kept the focus only on the children—and you believed that the children and family cannot get better unless this couple gets better, your charge is clear: that you must persuade them that in spite of what they assume, their relationship is not separate from the world of their children. You would have to create a new starting point for discussing the relationship and linking it to the children.

You might, for example, ask Cathy how she felt about Eric's minimizing of her complaints and wonder aloud if this happens at home as well. Or you may turn to Eric and ask if he's heard this all before, or if Cathy seems to always find problems where he feels there are none. These questions, this empathizing with each partner's feelings, ideally would encourage them to talk about their relationship in a broader way, and be used as a springboard for talking about parenting and the problems the children are having: "I notice that the more impatient you seem, Cathy, to change what the kids are doing, the more, Eric, you say that there's not that much of a problem. I wonder if the kids hear the same thing at home, pick up the split between you both, and wind up playing one of you against the other in order to get their way?" The message to them is clear that their relationship is the hub on which everything else in the family holds.

For other couples the way in to work on the relationship may best be through the family. Tina and Marcia, for example, a gay couple raising two of Tina's children from a previous marriage, came in with the oldest boy, Tim, age 11. Although the couple had been together for several years, it quickly became clear that Marcia's role with the children was not clearly and consistently defined. At times Tina would be upset because Marcia would not take an active disciplinary role with the children, while at other times she casti-gated Marcia for doing precisely that. And when the therapist tried to explore the issues of control and decision making between them, both quickly became resistant.

Rather than pressing the issue, the therapist asked Tim in the family session what it was like to be at the receiving end of all this parenting. Tim was able to say that he was often confused and unsure whom to turn to for permission. The therapist then asked Tina and Marcia to work up some guidelines that Tim could use in order to clarify communication and ease the boy's confusion, and checked to make sure that they were both willing to do this.

The next week Tina and Marcia reported just how difficult the process was. Both felt they were engaged in a power struggle. The therapist asked them if they would be willing to use the session to work together and develop guidelines right there and then. By monitoring the process in the room, the therapist helped them rec-ognize when they were starting to get into a power struggle, and by focusing on their communication and encouraging them to com-promise, helped them come up with boundaries that both of them could live with. The guidelines they developed, and the negotiation experience itself, laid a foundation not only for helping Tim with his school problems but for making decisions about the other children in the family as well.

Another therapist, however, might have taken a different path—exploring Tina's unresolved past marital issues, for example; dis-cussing the stresses they felt about being a same-sex couple; exam-ining the children's own response to Tina and Marcia's relationship;

or spending play therapy time with the boy to uncover his inner struggles, loss, or adjustment to the family transitions. All of these are valid and possible, and may be met with more or less resistance based on the couple's anxiety and expectations that the therapist would need to negotiate.

These scenarios raise a larger question: Are there times when it would be beneficial for the children to be part of the couple work? Some therapists would say that as soon as the focus shifts to the couple's relationship, the children shouldn't be included in therapy. Their exclusion helps demarcate for the couple the boundary between couple and parenting issues, and if the interaction between the parents is openly hostile and destructive, it's easy for children to feel overwhelmed or blamed (even hearing their name mentioned a lot is enough to cause little kids to think what is happening right then is their fault), and they need to be spared from further trauma. And of course if there are topics to be discussed that are clearly adult topics (for example, sex, money, adult relationships), if the parents feel inhibited or too easily distracted around the children, or when you feel you can't manage all those people in one room and you can't get a cotherapist, it makes sense to make it easy on everyone and send the children out.

The other side of this issue is that there is value in the children, especially older children, like Tim, or teens, for staying put and seeing adults communicate and work out problems. This can be good modeling for communication and problem solving in relationships, or the process can help the children see the underside of the tension in and between the parents and can come away with a more balanced view of a parent (for example, Mom isn't just angry all the time, but is worried or sad about Grandma). They can discover or see right before them (and with your support) that they are not to blame for the family's problems, and that problems, in fact, lie elsewhere. With your direct blocking, they can learn that they don't need to step in, take sides, or try to fix what is happening, but can instead let the parents work it out themselves.

Your decision to include children or not ultimately rests on your confidence that the session will be positive, rather than hurtful for the children; you will not be inadvertently re-creating the dysfunctional structure in the session (pulling in children and triangulating the couple's relationship rather than helping the couple work out their own problems); and your approach fits both your values and operating theory. Similarly, whatever way you decide to integrate couple work into the family work, it's best that it be integrated both with the other issues in the family and your own view of the system.

ASSESSING THE COUPLE

Determining how the couple sees their role in the children's problems is one important element in assessing them and developing your treatment plan. But just as there were key areas that we focused on in assessing the family, so too are there other key interrelated and overlapping areas to help you and the parents distinguish their needs and concerns as a couple from those as parents.

A quick checklist of questions to ask yourself and them follows:

What Is the Role of Children in the Couple Relationship?

Here we are looking at the structural elements of the family. Is there a hierarchy between the adults and children or is one parent unempowered and allied with the children? Has one child, like Ellen, become entitled, and is basically running the family? Is one or both of the parents using a child as a surrogate partner? Is there intense sibling rivalry suggesting that the children are copying marital arguments or acting out marital tensions? These types of questions help you determine the gap between the structural ideal and what the couple presents.

In addition to the structural assessment is another related question about the role of the presenting problem itself: How has the couple stabilized around the problem? In the 1980s, there was a controversy in the family therapy field over whether people manufacture problems out of some neurotic need for stability; ultimately the field came to reject that notion. Most people's problems are oppressive, and people would do anything to get rid of them. Nevertheless, problems arise, and families and couples often stabilize themselves around the existence of certain problems. This stability can serve as an impediment to addressing underlying problems directly.

Denise's drug use, for example, creates enough of an ongoing crisis and distraction that the couple argues about how to handle their child rather than arguing about the ways they treat each other in the marriage. Denise's problems have become a "comfortable" focus and an emotional garbage can for other couple issues that the couple can't face directly, a distraction from a long worn-out marital contract. The answer to the question about the role of the problem in the family tells you what you may need to work on in the relationship if the presenting problem were to solidly change (for example, the couple would need to acknowledge their conflicts; they would need to find positive rather than negative ways of interacting). Usually you can find clues to the answer right within the session process, such as when Denise acts up and distracts just at the point that tension arises between the couple, or the way the father switches topics to complain about Denise when you ask him a sensitive question about the marital relationship.

How Has the Relationship Changed over Time?

Is there less affection, more affection, more arguments? Are there changes in individual moods or personality (she's more irritable, he's more controlling)? Are there changes over time (how are they different from when they first met), and changes in the family (environmental, situational stress)?

Imagine the start of marriage being like moving into a new, large house. There's room to explore, places to decorate and make your own, and space to move around. But over the years the rooms become dusty and dirty and slowly filled with junk—resentments, half-finished arguments, unexpressed needs, and memories of hurt. Rather than getting up the courage and cleaning out these rooms by talking about what is difficult to say, one by one the couple simply shuts and locks the rooms. Over and over this happens until the once beautiful and large house now seems narrow and cramped as the couple finds themselves living in the hallway by the front door. The only safe topics are the weather and that no-good supervisor on the job. Even though both may occasionally look at each other and shift their eyes upstairs, they just as quickly glance away.

Running alongside this inability to solve problems are often natural developmental changes. When Janice, for example, met her husband she was looking for support and stability. After many years of being a single mom, Malcolm fit the bill—a take-charge type of guy like her dad. Similarly, Malcolm found in Janice what he needed—to be needed and to have a sense of control. Together in the first year of their marriage, they worked out the rules and routines that ran their everyday lives: who would take out the garbage, who would initiate sex, and what they would do when one of them was angry. It worked. But now 6 or 7 years down the road, all is not well in Camelot. Malcolm's take-charge attitude now feels to Janice more like control. Janice's depending on Malcolm now feels to him like dependency.

Both have changed because both were able to get from the other what they needed and now that hole is filled. The marital contract has run out. There is a gap between these individual changes and the established rules, routines, and roles of the relationship. Once again the house that was the relationship feels cramped and narrow.

Ideally the couple would at this point openly acknowledge their discontent and work together to bring the relationship contract up to date. But many don't, there is too much trash to clear out, and it is too overwhelming. Instead they may act out their discontent—having affairs, going on shopping or drinking binges—or they may individually or together seriously talk about divorce. Or, instead, they can decide to distract. One way to do this is to become child centered, focusing exclusively on the children and their problems and concerns. The couple silently makes a pact to be good parents, if not good lovers. Of course, not all child-centered couples are automatically in a suffering relationship. Many parents, for example, usually follow the core values of their culture and instinctively make the children the center of the family universe. They may spend more of their energy and focus on the children than many other families you see or even what you personally feel comfortable with, but there is a clear hierarchy, the parents have a good relationship with each other, and they work together well as a team. Their relationship contract is, in fact, very much up-to-date and representative of their needs.

These couples, however, are very different from those child-centered families where similarly the basic structure may seem sound, where there seems to be a clear hierarchy and joint decision making, but underneath, like rotting supports under flooring, there is a breaking down of the couple relationship. These couples may be longing for a different type of relationship or a return to an earlier and better time, but don't know how to get there, are feeling boxed in, and aware that the children have become the glue holding them together. You can ask questions like "What would your relationship be like if your children were grown up and independent?" or "What do you see for yourselves as a couple once all your children leave home?" and then see where the question leads.

There are two dangers that arise from this couple dynamic: one is that the children of such parents will by default use this as a model of their own couple relationships and families. Even though they have a strong model for parenting, they grow up lacking one for adult intimacy. As coupled adults they may think they are doing the right things, but wonder why they feel empty or awkward when they are alone without children. Often they wind up feeling just the same as their own parents did, but which, as children, they were never aware of. They have failed to learn that being an adult in all its roles and forms is something valuable in its own right.

The other danger is that anxiety, even panic, can set in for the couple as the children begin to leave home and the child-centered parents face the prospect of being alone with just themselves. They may either undermine the children's leaving ("Why don't you go to the college right here in town, dear?") or scramble to find other replacements—for example, adopting children, acquiring pets, becoming a workaholic or alcoholic, and so on—to fill in the holes and provide a distraction. If you ask the parents of teens what they are most looking forward to once the kids leave home, and they don't say much because they expect that the kids will be living right around the corner, or Dad says he's planning on spending most of the winter in his fishing shack up on the lake, you have a good sense of possible couple-transition distress. Healthier couples will say, if pressed, that they are indeed worried that because their lives have been so wrapped around the children, they fear they will have little in common or that, in fact, really don't know each other well.

For those struggling couples that decide not to work out issues in therapy, they may essentially live separate lives—emotionally, if not legally divorced. Again, a hierarchy seems to be in place, the parent relationship is seemingly solid, there is little or no conflict, but the infrastructure is weak. The couple is estranged from each other. They take turns being parents, or one of the parents is often *the* parent, while the other is somewhere else (at work, outside in the garage, out with friends). Distance has replaced intimacy. While the children's basic needs are met, the children rarely have a chance to see how the parents interact with each other. In their own couple relationships as adults the children re-create these patterns and struggle with the same emotions.

The goal, regardless of the configuration, is to help reshape the relationship so that it can better represent the individuals within it. So you ask about such changes: "How are they each different now from when they first were married?"; "What do they each need most right now?" Talk to them about this being a common developmental shift in their relationship and help them see that it both represents their own growth and the ability of the other to fill their needs and the need to revisit those needs once again.

Obviously relationships change not only from the inside but from the outside as well. Even the strongest relationships have deteriorated or collapsed through the impact of serious illnesses, the death of a child or other family member, a job change, or financial stress. Although it's tempting to see these stressors as only pushing on cracks already established in the foundation of the relationship, it's also reasonable to believe that without the stressors the couple may not be sitting on your couch. So you explore this: see if they can work as a team rather than falling into their individual bunkers, and help them see how while they may react differently on the surface, they both share the same emotions and worries.

How Adult Are the Adults?

We asked this same question when assessing the family: the question of whether the adults are differentiated in that they are able to regulate their emotions and not react in kind to the other's anxiety or anger, be calm and thoughtful in decision making, and take personal responsibility for decisions and themselves? Obviously this is important for the overall running of a family, but can severely undermine the couple relationship where emotions and dynamics are easily intensified.

What most often undermines the ability to become or stay adults are two common dynamics: emotional wounds and the relationship triangle. Understanding and exploring them with couples can help you set goals for repair, as well as help them see their couple problems in new ways.

Emotional Wounds

We discussed emotional wounds in Chapter 2, the notion that learned childhood ways of coping lack the flexibility that the adult world demands, and these wounds are reactivated in present-day adult relationships. Our example in that chapter is of someone being highly sensitive to criticism from his supervisor because he was wounded by the criticism of his parents. The intimacy of the couple relationship makes such rewounding an almost inevitable occurrence.

So Tony cleans the house to surprise Michelle and instead of her enthusiastically thanking him, she, having a particularly bad day, says little, stirring in Tony an old wound about not being appreciated and ignored. Reflexively he slips into his learned child-hood coping mode of getting angry, which triggers Michelle's own wound and sensitivity to anger and like Tony falls back into being an 8-year-old and withdraws. Her doing this immediately intensi-fies Tony's feelings, he becomes even more angry, causing Michelle to withdraw further.

The adult goes out the window at this point. Each is feeling wounded, the little kid in each is activated, and both are engaged in a rapidly intensifying negative loop. And as mentioned earlier, even though each of the individuals hates feeling this way, they each also have a high tolerance for it. Over time one of them may finally get fed up—tired of feeling ignored, scolded—tired of feeling this way her whole life. She is done. They divorce, 5 years later they remarry, and through no fault of their own start the process again. But many other couples don't leave (or at least not yet). They replay these cycles over and over, each blames the other, and issues are made all the worse when combined with developmental changes. Resent-ments stack up, their intimacy is eroded, and the family structure deteriorates.

The Relationship Triangle

This is our other dynamic that like emotional wounds can easily afflict couples and undermine their ability to be self-differentiated adults. The model is based on the drama triangle of Steven Karp-man (1968), and provides a useful way of understanding a number of presenting problems.

Begin by imagining or drawing an upside-down triangle. (Do it now, it will help.) At the top at each corner are two letters: *P* on the left-hand side, *R* on the right. At the bottom, the tip of the triangle is the letter *V*. Got it?

This upside-down triangle represents the relationship between two people. The *P, R,* and *V* represent different roles that the people can play; it is not the people themselves, but a role. The roles interlock and there is always someone on top who seems to have more power, and someone on the bottom. The relationship moves about in a circle as follows: The person in the *R* position is, by Karpman's terminology, the rescuer. The person in that role essentially has "nice-guy" control. He hooks into the *V,* or victim. The person in the victim role feels overwhelmed at times. He feels that problems are falling down on his head. The rescuer steps in and says, "I can help you out. Just do what I say, and everything will be fine." Often, couples will begin their relationship in some form of this. They psychologically cut a deal: The rescuer agrees to be big, strong, good, and nice; the victim agrees to be overwhelmed and unable to manage. Everyone is happy. The rescuer feels needed, important, and in charge. The victim has someone to take care of him.

And it works fine, except that every once in a while one of two things happens. Sometimes the rescuer gets tired of doing it all. He feels like he is shouldering all the responsibilities and that the other is not pulling his weight, not giving anything back, and not appreciating what the rescuer is doing. The rescuer periodically gets fed up, angry, and resentful. Bam! He shifts over to the *P,* the persecutor role. He suddenly blows up, usually about something minor (laundry, who didn't take out the trash), or acts out (goes out and spends a lot of money, goes on a drinking binge, has an affair). The *P* feels he deserves it, "Look, after all . . . ," he says to himself, " . . . at what I've been putting up with!" The message underneath the behavior and anger that usually does not come out very clearly is "Why don't you grow up? Why don't you take some responsibility? Why do I have to do everything around here? Why don't you appreciate what I am doing for you? This is unfair!" The feeling of unfair is a strong one.

At that point the victim gets scared and moves up to the *R* position, and tries to make up and calm the waters. "I'm sorry," he says. "I didn't realize. I really do appreciate what you do. I'll do better." Then the rescuer/persecutor feels bad about whatever he did or said and goes down to the victim position and gets guilty and depressed. Then they both stabilize and go back to their original positions.

The other thing that happens sometimes is that the victim gets tired of the other one always running the show, always telling him what to do. He gets tired of feeling micromanaged, criticized, and being looked down on because the rescuer is basically saying, "If it wasn't for me, you wouldn't make it." Every once in a while the victim gets fed up and Bam!, moves to the persecutor role. Like the rescuer, the victim in this role blows up, gets angry, or acts out, usually about something small.

The message underneath that doesn't get said is "Why don't you get off my back!" "Leave me alone, stop controlling my life!" "Back off, I can do things myself!" The rescuer hears this and at this point moves to the victim position. He says to himself, "Poor me, every time I try to help, look what I get." The victim/persecutor then feels bad about whatever he did or said and goes to the rescuer position and says something like "I was stressed out, off my meds, and tired from the kids. I'm sorry." And then they make up and go back to where they originally were.

While everyone gets to move among all the roles, often one will fit more comfortably in one role more than another. This has to do with personality, upbringing, and learned ways of coping. The rescuer as a child was often an only child, oldest, or grew up in a chaotic family. He usually did not have many buffers between him and his parents, and learned early on that he could avoid getting in trouble and avoid conflict by being good: "If I can stay on my toes and just do what my parents (and teacher) want me to do all the time, I won't get in any hot water."

This type of person learns to be very sensitive to others as a means of survival. He develops good radar and can pick up the nuances of emotions. He is hyperalert, spends all his energy surveying the environment, and stays on his toes, ever ready to do what the parents want. Essentially he takes the position of "I'm happy if you're happy, and I need to make sure you are happy." He gets rewarded for being good and his head is filled with shoulds.

And once again, what works for the child, however, doesn't necessarily work so well for the adult. Rather than just two or three important people to pay attention to, the rescuer adult has many more: the boss, the IRS, the president of the local Rotary Club or Veterans of Foreign Wars. He now feels pulled in a lot of directions, stretched thin, as he scrambles to accommodate what he thinks others want from him. He easily feels like a martyr, he is always at risk of burnout.

He also has a hard time knowing what he wants. Because he spent so much of his energy as a child looking outward and doing what others wanted, he never had the opportunity to sit back and decide what he wanted. Wanting, unlike following shoulds and rules, is a feeling, and he is often not aware of what he is feeling. As an adult if you ask him "But what do you want?" he hesitates and gets stuck. He worries about making the right decision and not offending anyone in his life or the critical voice in his head.

He also has a hard time with anger and conflict (which is why he became good in the first place) and tends to stuff anger down until he gets fed up and begins to gag on it. Then he blows up, and because he is so uncomfortable with it and it creates so much drama, he feels like his worst dream has come true. He feels guilty, and shoves it all back down again, only to have it build up again.

The victim, in contrast, as a child was often the youngest in the family, was overprotected as a child by his parents or had older siblings who stepped in and took over all the time when he was stuck with a problem, or was abused and micromanaged. What he missed in growing up were opportunities to develop the self-confidence that comes from learning to manage problems on your own. Now, as an adult, he easily gets overwhelmed and feels unconfident and anxious. To handle these feelings he looks to the rescuer, who takes over and helps him feel better.

There is a persecutor role that some people stay in most of the time, and this person can be thought of as the evil twin of the rescuer. Whereas the rescuer controls by being good and nice, the persecutor is angry, critical, and blaming. This is the abuser, and obviously some couples start with this persecutor–victim relationship, playing out childhood models and roles. The persecutor learned early on that when I get scared I get tough. If I can negatively control everything going on around me, no one can sneak up behind me and get me.

The counter to each of these roles is, of course, the adult—what we are aiming for—who says:

> "I'm responsible for what I think, do, and say. If something bothers me, it is my problem. If you can do something to help me with my problem, I need to tell you, because you can't read my mind. If you decide not to help me, I'll need to decide what I'm going to do next to fix my problem. Similarly, if something bothers you, it is your problem. If there is something I can do to help you with your problem, you need to tell me. And if I

decide not to help you with your problem, you can work it out. You may not handle it the way I might, but you can do it. I don't need to take over."

The adults can also be more intimate than those in the triangle. The rescuer cannot let down his guard, or get too vulnerable because he is afraid that the victim will not be able to handle it. Similarly, the victim cannot ever get too strong because the rescuer will feel threatened and out of a job. The long line between the victim and rescuer is real. It represents the emotional distance between them.

What drives the relationship triangle is the power imbalance, the over and under responsibility of each, the complementarity of the roles, and the seeming repair of wounds (the rescuer initially feels needed, the victim taken care of) that quickly can turn to rewounding and the negative cycle. The way out of the dynamic is through helping both individuals move toward the adult, to once again cope in ways opposite of what they usually do—speak up rather than withdraw, calm down and use anger as information rather than exploding it at others, and focus on wants rather than shoulds. And both need to set boundaries and be responsible for their own problems while remaining sensitive to the needs of the other.

If you can begin to think in terms of the dynamics of the triangle, you can look for the playing out of roles:

"I wonder, David, if you ever feel like Nancy isn't doing enough, or not appreciating you, or if you feel overwhelmed at times by responsibilities? I wonder, Nancy, if you ever feel like David is running the relationship or whether you feel controlled at times? Do either one of you feel resentful or angry at times about this and if so what do you do?"

What the dynamics of the triangle help you see are flare-ups in the couple relationship. The moving to the persecutor stance quickly explains to you, and the couple, the possible source of arguments, affairs, drinking binges, shopping therapy, and other forms of acting out. By showing this model to the couple, just as talking about developmental changes or emotional wounds, you are normalizing their patterns and problems, reframing for them the source of behaviors that lead the list of presenting problems, and placing them within the structure of the relationship rather than the personality of the other.

Like the structural models for families, the concepts of emotional wounds and the relationship triangle help you assess what keeps the adults from moving toward the ideal of the adult: emotional hotspots of childhood wounds that trigger escalating, negative-cycling arguments; or the imbalance in power and complementary roles of the triangle that lead to acting out or overreactive arguments. Not only can you use them to help you uncover and define the sources of conflict, but they each point to a treatment road map for goal setting and change within the couple relationship; by comparing the couple against these healthy models, you can gauge the gap between what they present and what you observe, and see what they need to move toward.

How Are Decisions Made—about Children, Money, Household Chores, and Sex?

This is a logical offshoot of questions about the adult, and about changes over time. Because most couples have, without openly discussing or even being aware of them, evolved rules and roles for making decisions between them, to ask about decisions is to not only ask about communication and problem solving, but also about how the decision-making process itself works. You are also exploring power in the relationship, the dynamics of the triangle—Who is in charge of what? and Who has the last word? Questions about parenting, money, sex, and household chores are the most common power issues in the family. Finding a fair or effective solution to a problem ("Why don't you pay the rent from your check and I'll pay the child care from mine?") can often give way to battles over whose way is going to come out on top ("It's my money and you aren't going to tell me what to do with it").

Needless to say, these decision-making questions can arouse anxiety in the session and in the couple, so it's important to consider your pacing. Hold off if the couple is wary or hostile of therapy itself, is clearly untrusting or still uncomfortable with you, or is already so anxious that any more stress is likely to make them head for the door or shut up. But you shouldn't be reactive and wait for them to raise the issue.

Once they seem committed and settled, ask matter-of-factly how decisions are made and how disagreements are ended (someone gives in; someone walks away and it's not discussed anymore; someone becomes violent). You want to help them become curious about the limits of their anger and ability to compromise, the underlying power structure and struggle, and the emotions that fuel them. Resentments that have been tucked away within these issues and that warp the family structure are often exposed. More important, perhaps, by raising these issues and their anxiety you're testing the waters. You're able to see right there and then in the session how this couple will respond to the anxiety of change itself, where they may resist, and how quickly or carefully you may have to go.

What Emotions Are Presented and How Are They Handled?

Another offshoot of questions about the adult. Sarah is seething throughout the session while her husband, Mike, scarcely responds and seems depressed. It's safe to assume that the process you see in your office replicates to some degree what happens at home. You want to notice not only the mood of each partner, but the mood in relationship to the other and perhaps the children. Does Mike always seem depressed and unresponsive, or is it his way of coping with Sarah's anger? Does he cope through using alcohol or drugs? Does one of the children act out his anger? Does Sarah get angry because Mike is depressed? Is this her way of trying to get him to respond, or is it some internal response independent of Mike or anyone else? How else does she manage her emotions—through the use of drugs, or overeating, or having affairs? How does any of this possibly tie into the presenting problem? For example, does Mike's depression make it easy for Michelle, their daughter, to walk all over Sarah? Does Jeff boss his siblings around because he feels like the parents aren't going to parent?

Through this brainstorming—filtering what you see and hear through the lenses of the adult, family structure, relationship triangle, and your own theoretical model—you are attempting to link the emotional lives of both the individual parents and of the couple as a unit with the rest of the family and the presenting problems. You can check out your hunches by directly asking questions to the couple: "Sarah, you seem angry. How do you feel about the fact that Mike is saying nothing back?" or "Mike, you seem depressed. Do you sometimes feel this way at home? Sarah, is this how Mike seems to feel around you at home?"

Again, your immediate goal is to open the communication. You want to explore both the emotional outlets and each partner's emotional flexibility. You want to track the way emotions bounce off of each other and drive the emotional wounds and behavioral patterns (for example, Mike feels depressed and withdraws, Sarah feels overwhelmed by the children and gets angry, causing the children to run to Mike and drag him back into the family's interactions), and fuel the presenting problem (for example, Jeff acts out Mike's anger toward Sarah). You're looking for where emotions need to be expanded (for example, Mike needs to get in touch with his anger), where emotional triggers can be used by the couple as signals of a dysfunctional pattern (for example, when Sarah starts to get angry Mike needs to step in rather than ignore her), and how to help the couple once again see how their moods spill out over each other and the rest of the family.

How Severe Are the Relationship Problems?

This follows logically from the rest of the key areas of assessment above. If you suspect there are couple problems, developmental changes, the taking on of roles in the relationship triangle, and frequent rewounding, the next question you are likely to ask yourself is "How bad is bad?" Have there been separations, divorce action, abuse, arrests, or affairs? What's the worst the couple's arguments have ever gotten? What you are trying to learn through these questions are the chronicity of the problems and patterns, the prognosis for the relationship, and the need to focus on these issues before expecting any lasting change in other family patterns. Some couples will be up-front about this information, but many won't. If they seem reluctant, you need to show sensitivity, gentleness, and a sense of concern rather than judgment. Help them understand your intentions behind your questions by connecting your assessment of their relationship to their primary family concerns.

All of these assessment questions are, again, similar to those you used in assessing the entire family and, as you did with the family, you are looking to uncover both the couple's relationship structure and process. You are trying to discover where and how the couple gets stuck in solving their own problems; whether change, even though difficult, can be accommodated; whether emotions have appropriate outlets; whether the couple is able to see their relationship as different from that of the children; and whether they both have a commitment to it and each other. By asking yourself these questions you can begin to separate the couple from the family and can see by their response just how open they are to such exploration. By asking the couple these questions you are letting them know that their relationship is important in itself, is linked to the presenting problem, and is vital to its solution.

What to do about the couple is part of your assessment of what to do about the family and the problem. You don't want to replicate the problem (for example, ignore the couple issues the way the couple does), or become swept up in the dysfunctional patterns and roles (for example, giving in to the husband just like his wife does). Remember, you're in charge of the therapy.

COUPLE REPAIR

So does couple work seem a bit intimidating? Does the countertransference seem a little too concentrated? Does it remind you too much of treating your parents, yourself? The easiest way to think of couple work and stay reasonably objective is to see it as a smaller version of family work. You are still dealing, after all, with the basic family therapy elements of determining who has the problem, defining and blocking the dysfunctional patterns, looking for what's missing, tracking the process, and changing the emotional climate. And like family therapy you are being proactive and showing leadership, being careful along the way of not igniting their individual wounds by once again taking on the role of the ideal partner.

Guidelines and goals for family work translated into couple dynamics follow:

Improve Communication

Regardless of your theoretical orientation, improving communication is always a good place to start; it is the groundwork for deeper conversations. So you start with Therapy 101 basics—facilitating the process so that each person can learn to take turns, helping the couple to talk about themselves rather than just blaming or criticizing the other, encouraging them to talk about their emotions rather than just their ideas and rationalizations, and pushing them to talk about what they haven't talked about before. Give them communication exercises (have each repeat what she thought the other said before saying something else), teach them about "I" statements, educate them about the differences between male and female communication styles (for example, men tend to want to come up with solutions to a problem and be done with it, while their partners are hankering for them to shut up, listen, and discuss the problem together), or try having them communicate nonverbally—sculpting with clay or drawing pictures. You can see your job as a coach or traffic cop, a teacher, a role model, or all of the above.

How much do you need to control the communication between the couple? It depends. As in family therapy, you initially want them to talk to each other so that you can see just how well they can communicate: where things go well, how and where communication starts to break down, and when you have to stop them from trying to direct all their communication through you so they don't become too dependent on you and even more anxious about talking to each other at home. Once you've figured out their communication patterns, you can begin to block and change the patterns ("Hector, you sound like you're blaming Teresa and she's feeling scolded and getting defensive. Try telling her how you feel and what you'd like her to do").

Obviously, if their communication is really destructive, you will want to take more control over the process and ask her to talk to you rather than the partner, or see them separately in order to decrease the verbal and nonverbal triggers that set the other person off. But as they improve, give them more leeway (you can stare at your shoes when they are communicating well) and enter the conversation only enough to keep them on track and keep the communication open and honest.

A common mistake that some therapists make in teaching couples how to communicate better is failing to match their teaching with the couple's expectations—doing formal communication exercises (for example, starting a series of statements with "I feel . . . ") may effectively teach skills, but will be met with resistance if the couple feels emotionally pressured to talk about the argument they had Thursday night, or if the husband sees this as confirming his worst fears about the stupidity of therapy. Wait until the emotional turbulence subsides or connect your exercise to the husband's concern. You want to lead, but not do a forced march.

Teach Problem-Solving Skills

While most couples will come in with a handful of problems they need help resolving, your job isn't so much helping them solve them as teaching them the skills they need to solve those and other problems that will come along in the future. Good problem solving involves good communication, a realistic view of the way relationships work, and the ability for both partners to be clear and assertive about their needs and to know what the problem really is.

So as you help the couple work through the problems and arguments they bring to the session, identify the skills ("You both did a good job talking about your feelings"), help them generalize the process ("You both were able to talk about Jane without getting angry. What did you both do that made it easier this time?"), and assist them in getting over communication hurdles ("Bill, you seem to be just passively going along with what Lynn says. I wonder if you are reluctant to disagree. What do you, yourself, really want here?"). Look at your role as more of a coach fine-tuning what they present, rather than a lecturer merely dumping out a lot of information. Instead of getting wrapped up in the content of a problem, help them recognize good problem-solving processes.

Stop Violence

In Chapter 10, we discussed the Harris family and Ellen's escalations about the importance of helping families manage their emotions and conflicts by providing clear and firm guidelines to stop violence. The same is true for couples. You need to help them learn to rein in and stop fueling the fire of emotions in the session by strong leadership, or if necessary, separating the couple and seeing the partners individually until you can coach them on anger management and they are able to stay together in the room without escalating. At home they may need your first-aid plan to help them stop automatically moving into destructive patterns. This is why you should ask (as part of your assessment) "How bad is bad?"

Often couples that you would imagine would never fit the profile of a violent couple, may be.

Stopping destructive arguments both in the session and at home is one-half of the violence equation; the other half is solving the actual problem. With children and teens, we talked about the importance of parents to circle back, deconstruct the argument, and problem solve with the child when she is calm. The couple equivalent, and a good homework assignment, is the business meeting.

The idea behind this is that most individuals are able to act "adult" in environments such as their workplace. There, if their feelings are hurt, or if a serious misunderstanding arises, they're not likely to explode or hit someone, but instead can express their feelings and problem solve in a reasonable way. Why can't they do this at home? Because it is home, the intimacy of the relationship, the strong presence of emotional wounds, and the subtle triggers can quickly set each other off.

If the couple can do it once, they can (albeit with more difficulty) do it again. In order to help them learn to separate emotions from problem solving, ask them to have a scheduled business meeting at home. What the couple is instructed to do is write down over the week issues that come up that bother them—Tuesday night's hurtful comment about dinner, a 3:00 a.m. worry about money—or even about practical issues they are too tired or time constrained to talk about during the week such as selecting a time for a family vacation, or deciding whether this is a good year to buy a new car. A meeting time is conveniently set for both when they are not rushed or distracted by kids (early Saturday morning always seems to be a good time). Each comes with an agenda and you ask them to discuss their issues as if they were at work: everyone is on good behavior with a focus on problem solving. The meeting need not be long—30 to 45 minutes is fine—and the rule is that if things for whatever reason get emotional, they stop the meeting and bring it into the next therapy session.

The goal here is to create successful experiences in "adult" communication, moving toward effective problem solving, and consciously moving out of destructive patterns even for a limited time. It also, as a byproduct, helps develop self-regulation. By waiting and talking about issues later, outside the heat of the moment, each partner learns to calm him- or herself and use emotions as information. Knowing that there is a set opportunity to discuss feelings and problems helps the impulsive partner learn to delay, or helps the unassertive partner have time to plan what she wants to say.

If the couple can't do this successfully at home, if the business meeting becomes too emotional and escalates, ask them to bring their agendas to the session and you will discuss them there with you. With the safety of your leadership, you can help them process and control their emotions and provide a successful experience in the session that they can then eventually apply at home.

Finally, there is another form of violence in the home that is not directly a couple issue but is clearly managed by the couple—that of sibling rivalry. Obviously not all sibling rivalry is abusive, and as with other parenting issues, you need to track the patterns and dynamics, and explore the couple's skills and emotions. Often parents will have different tolerances for sibling rivalry and these differences keep them from working together as a team to manage it, and as a result this impacts the family structure. Sometimes a parent will bring this as a presenting problem, or you, as part of your assessment, can ask about conflict between the children and how the couple together react.

If you find, for example, that one parent has trouble tolerating any sibling conflict at all, the question is why: Was he an only child, perhaps, and has no experience with normal sibling interactions?; Was sibling conflict not tolerated in his childhood home, perhaps through repressive measures?; Does any conflict somehow reflect negatively on the parental self-image?; Does the parent become anxious and uncertain of how to respond concretely? On the other hand, if the tolerance seems extremely high (siblings are physically hurt or emotionally abused), are the children acting out of the couple's anger? Is a parent's seeming unawareness due to depression or other emotional preoccupation? Or does a parent's inability to act indicate some basic lack of skill?

The alternative to parents stepping in too late, too heavy-handed, or not at all, is helping them work together and take a preventive approach: Give the kids positive feedback when they are interacting well ("You guys are playing so well together with your trucks!"); keep an ear out for the beginnings of conflict, and if it sounds like it is beginning to escalate, try distracting or separating ("Tony, would you come and help me make dinner?"); be clear about rules (for example, you can get mad, but no hitting) and consequences (time-outs, taking away privileges); talk about the process after everyone is calm ("How come you guys were fussing with each other before? How can you both fix the problem?"). If the parents have trouble following through with your suggestions, again, ask why. Perhaps you need to break down their new behaviors and skills into smaller, more concrete, and manageable pieces, or explore further what function the sibling rivalry serves in the couple or larger family dynamics.

Educate the Couple about Emotions and Relationships

Just as repairing family relationships lies in helping the family change patterns and take responsibility for their own emotions, so too for couples. Explaining to them, for example, the relationship triangle; mapping for them the rescuer, victim, and persecutor roles; and showing how the power imbalance can fuel anger and acting out helps put their problems in a different perspective and moves them away from blaming. Similarly, talking to them about developmental changes or emotional wounds helps them step away from their current way of thinking and offers a path for creating change. This is what your theoretical perspective is always aiming to do. This view not only provides you with a road map for repair but through your leadership helps them adopt the same perspective.

As we discussed in Chapter 11, there are times when individual problems bleed through those of the couple or family—Amy has an eating disorder, Antonio has panic attacks, and Kirsten is clearly depressed and has been suicidal in the past. Here your clinical decision is whether these issues can be incorporated into the family/couple treatment or need to be broken off for individual therapy to treat. As we discussed with teens, there is often a value in teens having their own space and a different relationship with a healthy adult model.

With couples it can be less clear. When serious clinical issues such as anorexia, major depression, or drug addiction affect one of the adults, there is an obvious need to make concentrated individual treatment be the primary focus until the individual is stable. But what about the husband who had his first panic attack on the heels of his possibly losing his job and his worry that the family may lose its home? Maybe not. You can help him understand how anxiety works, you can spend time in the session helping him learn some anxiety-reducing techniques, you can suggest that he see his physician about possible medication, and you can talk openly about ways his spouse can help him when his anxiety ramps up.

Ideally with his partner in the room, she too can learn not only what worries her husband but why he has been acting the way he has. Rather than worrying herself, their discussion of his problems can give her a clear path for helping him. This is good in theory, but may not work ideally in practice. If the relationship is conflictual, if each are doing trench warfare and are in their emotional bunkers, she may hear his problems not as something that she can help with but rather just confirmation that he is indeed the one with and the source of the couple and family problems. Rather than giving him support, the session only digs them in deeper, and weakens the relationship and their ability to work together.

Again, therapy is a pragmatic sport. You may focus on the individual problem one person has and see how the other partner responds. If empathic and you feel that you can help resolve the underlying source without completely derailing the couple and family focus ("Try working on this this week"; "See if together you can do . . . ") and see what happens. If you suspect that this is only fueling the imbalance in the couple relationship, explore ("How do you think about Arnold's sudden panic attack?") and see what happens next. If it is more of the same ("I always thought that he had a major problem with anxiety"), you may decide to move Arnold toward individual therapy for his own sake, while strongly focusing on the couple so that Arnold does not become the new IP.

For all couples it's useful to help them realize that often though their emotional styles may be different, they are both feeling exactly the same: "It seems from what you both have described that you both are feeling ignored and lonely, but you express it differently. Liz, you seem to get quiet and withdraw, while your style, Matt, is to get irritable and demanding. What you naturally react to, of course, is the withdrawal or demands, but underneath you both are feeling the same." In contrast to the differences that they are only too aware of, you are helping them see commonalities.

Sensitize Them to Their Power Issues

It's not only violent couples that need to be able to tell when problem solving turns into power struggling, or when who makes the decision or who gets the last word has become more important than what the decision or word is. All couples need to be able to recognize when discussions are escalating, know what topics are potential land mines for them ("We realize that we can't talk about my mother, your drinking, the affair I had 2 years ago"), recognize when these topics are being used as ammunition in arguments, and be able to stop before things get out of hand. You as the therapist and outsider are the one to set the pace on this. You are often the first to clarify the process and point out the emotions that accompany the power struggle.

Create Positive Interactions

Affection anyone? How about a night out without the kids? As you help push the children back into their appropriate roles and as you cool down the conflict, something needs to fill the space or it will just fill back up again. Couples that have gone for years living with distance, children as buffers, and conflict instead of positive interaction need to not only learn to stop what they are doing but gradually learn to feel comfortable with intimacy and support.

Pacing is the key here and it's important not to move too quickly. The couple that hasn't been out on a date for 10 years is going to have an anxious time when they do. They could easily wind up talking the entire time about what Johnny did wrong this week, or arguing about whether the restaurant is too expensive.

You can begin by increasing intimacy and risk within the session—helping them to talk about each other rather than the children, and about what they like rather than what they don't. You can help them plan together some small exercise in quality time (watch a movie together after the kids go to bed that they want to see, rather than always watching kid movies) and normalize the anxiety they may feel. Again, you need to be sensitive and walk that fine line between approaching their anxiety, and opening up communication and intimacy (go ahead, casually ask them about their sex lives), and scaring them and causing them to back away (okay, maybe that wasn't a good idea; go back and ask them how they feel about your bringing up sexual issues). As they get more positive experience with each other, and you, they'll be able to move on to bigger activities and challenges.

Block the Patterns

Here we return to the basics. Like families, couple dynamics are built on faulty patterns. Like family therapy, your default mode, what you do when you're not sure exactly what to do, is stop the dysfunctional patterns and see what happens.

STEPPING INTO THE QUAGMIRE

Yes, the couple work isn't much different from the family work, but it can seem more difficult for several reasons. By seeing the couple alone you are by definition creating another awkward triangle. Instead of the children, it's you who's in the middle, and like them you may feel tempted to form coalitions, be a buffer or distraction between them, or not take sides so no one gets mad at you. As with family work with children, the easiest way to avoid the tension of such triangles is to define them as they arise, in the room and in the process, in order to keep the focus on the couple and their anxiety.

Balance is essential in couple work. If you decide to see one partner separately, be sure to see the other separately as well. If you talk with one about goals, talk to the other about goals too. Leaving things off balance is dangerous. Spending more time with one partner than the other fuels fears that two of you have joined forces, or that you really believe that the other person is the one with all the problems and most in need of your attention. It stirs old sibling rivalry feelings. Be clear about your treatment decisions and sensitive to possible misinterpretation.

Before you step into the room you need to be sensitive to yourself as well. You may be seduced into playing out a role, identifying with one side over another not only because of the parent's needs and patterns, but yours. How you are doing or not doing in your own relationships can easily color what you see before you in the room.

If, for example, you've just been arguing with your husband about his doing more work around the house, or his taking off every Saturday to play golf or watch football with the guys, you may find yourself identifying with the woman across from you who complains that her husband "doesn't do a damn thing except sit in front of the TV," or with the husband who says he hates the way his wife stays on the phone talking to her family for what seems like 12 hours a day. It's tempting to use their process to express vicariously your depression, your loneliness, your anger—"Doesn't that make you angry, Margaret? Why don't you tell Alan just how angry you feel?" Who's getting therapy here? With rationalizations you may even encourage the couple to play out your own desire for a divorce.

The subtlety of this countertransference–transference process is even more enhanced if you choose to see the partners individually. The man who flirts as a way of coping with his anxiety may successfully re-create with you the affair he has had, is having, or that he and you fantasize about. The woman who "just would like to meet with you alone next time to discuss some personal issues" may help to create the friendship, the intimacy that she, and you, don't have in your current relationships. Each person becomes a blank screen for the other's fantasies and projections.

The solution, of course, is awareness. Ask yourself the hard questions: What do I need from my personal relationship that I'm not getting?; What do I need most from my clients?; How can I tell when I'm overidentifying with a client, when I'm encouraging them to do what I have trouble doing myself? It also helps to have people around (for example, supervisors; trusted, experienced colleagues; your own therapist) who will help you practice what you preach and separate your personal issues from professional ones.

LONG-DISTANCE FEUDS

Mark comes in to see you with his 10-year-old daughter, Maggie, of whom he has custody. He describes Maggie as "wild and disrespectful" for 3 or 4 days after her visits with her mother two weekends a month. He also thinks he knows what the problem is, namely, that his ex just "lets Maggie do anything she wants, and basically neglects her." He says he wants help in managing Maggie after these visits, and by the way, he's thinking of going back to court to stop the visitations altogether. He wonders aloud whether you would at some point consider writing a letter giving your professional opinion about this.

Just as there are infinite points along the continuum regarding the ability of the couple in the home to own their relationship problems, the same continuum can be found in long-distance conflictual relationships between separated or divorced partners and parents.

Doing couple work where there is no couple, where the child is still triangled and caught in a cross-fire between two warring parents is not uncommon, and not easy.

Just as the couple or ex-couple is blurring the lines between themselves and their pasts, and themselves and their children, it can become easy for your role to blur as well. The best defense in these cases is a good offense, namely, defining for yourself and the client as quickly and clearly as possible just what you will and will not do, what you see as appropriate goals and what are not, what is considered therapeutic, and what is a legal matter. In order not to get sucked in you need to do what this couple apparently cannot.

With Mark, for example, it would be important to clarify exactly what he needs help with in relation to Maggie. Is he asking for management techniques or an expectation that you will see Maggie alone to help her work out her tumultuous emotions following the visits? Is he asking for a formal evaluation of Maggie for court testimony or is there an unspoken expectation that through your individual contacts with Maggie you will gather information from her that he can then subpoena to use in court? If your client seems to be trying to corner you into making a legal recommendation, don't hesitate to suggest that the client contact her attorney about this, or request that the attorney make a formal request. Make it clear, get it out on the table; be sure once again that you know who has and what is the problem, and who is your client.

If your initial impression is that the problem is less the child than the ongoing battle between the parents, you can say this. The next step is then to invite the absent parent in and help the parents work together. This may involve helping to come up with some mutually agreed ways of managing the child (for example, both agree to enforce the same bedtimes), move deeper and help them resolve their continuing issues, or farm the whole thing out to trained mediators or other marital therapists. By having both parents in front of you, you avoid getting sucked in and triangled into an ongoing battle between the parents.

Some therapists will refuse to see the case unless they can actually see both parents together; others don't necessarily have to see them in the office, but want to have at least telephone contact with the other parent (for example, when the other parent lives out of state) so they can hear both sides of the story, clarify what the child may need, and encourage the parents to work together. Again, the goal is to avoid taking sides and replicating the triangle that already exists with the child.

Of course, you have some responsibility to advocate for the child if you feel that there is reason for worry. For example, if you learn from Maggie that she is being neglected or being placed in unsafe situations and she talks about potential or real emotional, physical, or sexual abuse situations, you have a responsibility to notify the proper authorities, usually social services, so that they can pursue a formal investigation. There may be times where there is a fine line between your sense of what may be happening to the child and what the child may feel pressure to report by the parent. If the parent reports to you that she thinks the child is being abused or neglected but you have no firsthand evidence yourself, you may want to contact your local protective services to clarify their protocols and tell the parent to make a formal report as well.

If you have any doubt (and in cases like this there may often be doubt), contacting the proper authorities (and your supervisor, if appropriate) is the best approach. They have the mandate to do the investigation, and your role as therapist, rather than investigator, stays clear.

As with other couple work, these long-distance conflicts have a way of emotionally pulling you in, particularly if you have similar unresolved issues yourself. If you are hearing only one side of the story, seeing the poor child caught in the middle, it's easy to emotionally join the bandwagon against one or both of the parents, and easy to overidentify with the child.

Clarity is the antidote—with the client and with yourself through self-reflection and supervision. Bring someone else in to work the case with you, have someone else see the child, have a team behind the mirror observe the session process, gather court records to find out if there is a court order and legal mandates, talk to the guardian ad litem, and clarify roles and gather background. Do what you need to do to prevent yourself from becoming swept up in already emotionally sweeping family dynamics.

COUPLES AND CONTEXT

Parents share two relationships—one as caretakers of their children, the other, their relationship as a couple. While they often enter therapy with the line between these relationships blurred, or with their focus only on one and not the other, your job is to help them distinguish between both relationships, as well as show how each is connected.

As has been said throughout this chapter, this clarity is important in order for the family to remain structurally and emotionally healthy. It's hard enough being a child without having to get dragged into acting like an adult or taking the blame for problems that the adults aren't handling. It's easy, but detrimental, as a parent to turn to your children for support or distraction when you feel overwhelmed or overlooked in your relationship with your partner.

Because the couple's relationship is made of the same basic building blocks of patterns and process as the family's, your other family skills will serve you as you begin work with couples. Keep in mind the basics, don't be afraid to move against their grain and yours and, once again, above all be honest.

Looking Within: Chapter 12 Exercises

Again, the biggest difference between couple and family work isn't the number of people in the room but your own reactions to what the couple presents. These exercises encourage you to become aware of your own personal and professional biases.

1. What did you learn from your parents about the nature of relationships? How has their relationship shaped your expectations of your own? What did you learn about how problems in the relationship should be solved? What mistake(s) did your parents make that you would most like to avoid?

2. Think about your current or past intimate relationships. What issues most trigger your anger? The urge to leave? What topics most easily turn into power struggles or impasses? Why?

3. How do you personally define intimacy? What role does or did sex play in your current or past relationships? How do any of these issues create countertransference problems for you when doing couples therapy?

4. What is your own theory of couple work? How is it different from and similar to whole-family work or child therapy? What are your basic assumptions?

5. What are your personal values regarding relationships? What are the limits, if any, of commitments? Where do you draw the line between the

couple's problems and the welfare of the children? How open should the couple be with the children about the couple relationship? Who, in what circumstances, has higher priority—the partner, the child, the self? How do you personally decide?

6. If you had siblings while growing up, think back to your relationships. How much sibling rivalry was there in your family? How did your parents handle it? What was the cause or what function do you think it may have served in your family dynamics?

chapter *13*

The Power of One
Individual Work in a Family Context

Ann talks with a slow whine, each word barely limping ahead of the one before. She looks drained, and she tells you how she spends hours in the middle of the night pacing up and down, just sitting at the kitchen table, or lying in bed staring up at the darkness. To her everything seems gray; even things that used to excite her—an evening with friends, a new project at work—seem now like another burden, another responsibility. She sighs, one of those long, heavy sighs that stretches out and fills the room.

Major depression? Persistent depressive disorder? Adjustment disorder with depression and anxiety? Whatever you call it, it has DSM-5 written all over it. Individual therapy here we come.

If you're a family therapist, you may feel, or think you ought to feel, uncomfortable with this. Not only is the room a bit too empty, but you feel a flutter of hesitation at the thought of plodding into that swamp of individual pathology and internal dynamics.

Don't fear. In this chapter we explore together how to work with individuals and still consider yourself a family therapist. Family therapy, after all, isn't about how many people you can cram into a room, but about how many people you can keep in your mind. It's less about what you do and more about how you think—looking at problems and people in terms of their patterns and interactions. With this perspective you can help others change one person or help one person change others. They're really both sides of the same fence.

274

"IS IT ME?"

Most clients don't look at their problems in this interactive way; from where they sit the problem and the coin only has one side. In an agency or clinic setting someone like Ann may call up, come in by herself, and be seen by someone in intake who notes on the intake form: "probable depression." When she shows up alone in your office she will talk about her family's problems as being caused by herself ("I am the problem") or by others ("My mother is the problem"). Whatever way clients may present their problem doesn't really matter. What's important is that you offer them a perspective that they don't have.

We're talking again about giving the client a different theory and problem to replace one that has become too familiar and comfortable, about seeing what's missing and moving toward their anxiety. If Ann, for example, only talks about all the awful things she feels she did in the past, goes on and on about the way her husband is always screwing up her life, or laments about her mother who never really cared about her, she's not wrong in her view; she's simply stuck within it. Her internal narrative always leads to the same moral. Her depression is fed by the feeling of being trapped. You will need to start by hearing and acknowledging her perspective, but then you want to encourage her to look at the other side of the coin and focus on what she's not seeing.

If she is only talking about the past, you want to know about the present. Instead of blaming her husband or mother, and feeling like a victim, you want to help her draw lines of responsibility between herself and them, as well as see her own role in the interactions—be adult. By helping Ann recognize what she can and can't control, by encouraging her to talk in new ways about new topics, you are helping her mobilize her energy and resources in a new and potentially more positive direction.

You also want to introduce the client to systemic thinking and the power of patterns by asking about them: "So what does your mother say when you tell her how you feel?"; "What do you say back?"; "How do these conversations usually wind up?" Questions like these can help the clients begin to recognize that there is an interactional dynamic at work shaping their problems and emotions; they may come to see their past decisions in a less self-accusatory, black–white way. By helping Ann, for example, see how her mother and husband are individuals influenced by their own psychological networks of others may not excuse their actions, but can cast them as less villainous and more human. By sidestepping blame and guilt, and by developing a more complete view of her relationships and problems, Ann can gain a greater sense of mastery, which in turn can serve as an antidote to depression.

The answer then to the question "Is the problem me?" is "Yes, at least in part, if you don't think it is," and "No, maybe not," if you feel absolutely sure that it isn't. The goal is not to identify the culprits but expand thinking beyond either/or dichotomies. You are not the victim or the persecutor, but often both and neither; you affect and are affected by those around you.

COME ON IN: USING THE FAMILY TO HELP THE INDIVIDUAL

If you believe that problems are interactional, then it makes sense to bring in all of those individuals who interact and intersect around a problem—this, of course, is the tried and true basis of family therapy. But even if you or the client decide that switching from individual to some form of ongoing family therapy isn't reasonable, there are still plenty of ways to enlist the help of important others.

One way is to bring in significant others for one or two information-gathering sessions. For example, when Cassie talked about her guilt over the abusive way she felt she had treated her sister when they were teenagers, the therapist suggested that she invite her sister to one of their sessions. She did, and Cassie spent the time in a monologue, delivered with much hesitation and anxiety, about the way she felt about those times past. She finally had the opportunity to say what she could not say, and to put into words what she had only grieved inside for years. The proclamation, the confession, was itself therapeutic.

Having the right audience made it even more so. Her sister did what often happens in such situations. She acknowledged what Cassie had said—how she had felt both hurt and confused by Cassie's behavior, and how her memories of that time continued to strain their relationship in the present. But, then when asked whether she herself had any regret or guilt, she turned the corner and apologized to Cassie for not understanding how hard their parents had been on her, for walling her off over the years, and most of all for failing to show her appreciation for all that Cassie had done for her. These recognitions included Cassie's offer to take her in when she was having a difficult time in college, and her reaching out with consolation and support when her daughter had died several years before.

Healing occurred because Cassie not only repented and was forgiven, but because the distorted memories that had lingered for so long were corrected. Cassie discovered through her sister a new way of viewing herself and her actions that would have been difficult to achieve without the feedback of this family member.

Other times the focus of such sessions is less on healing of the past and more on solving a problem in the present. Louis had just started dating Nadine, but he was already struggling with what he thought were her expectations over how much time they should spend together. Because the relationship was still new, Louis didn't feel comfortable suggesting to Nadine that they consider starting couple therapy. He did, however, agree that it might be helpful to have Nadine come to one of his individual therapy sessions just to discuss the topic.

She came into the next session, and the dialogue that the therapist was able to jump-start enabled Louis to deal with his feelings and concerns in a much more direct way than he had in his past and with Nadine. Rather than remaining silent and ruminating, he was able to be assertive in the session; rather than assuming he knew what Nadine wanted, he took the risk to ask her. Nadine came away with an honest picture of the kind of person Louis was, and he had the opportunity to start a new relationship with a different set of patterns.

Sometimes the motivation of having others come into individual therapy comes from you rather than the client. Individual therapy is by definition limited in its view. You may want others to come in to help provide you with a more complete and accurate picture of the past or present, or to help you better grasp the interactional patterns that have occurred or are ongoing.

Those who you invite in essentially serve as consultants. Rather than using the session as a forum for solving problems or disclosing long-held secrets, the focus is on uncovering the important information you feel is missing. The client listens, and in the listening can step back and perhaps hear what couldn't be heard before.

For example, in the course of her individual treatment, Molly talked about the ways she felt favored by her alcoholic father, while he seemed to ignore her other brothers and sisters. The therapist asked if she would invite her brother, who lived in town, to come with her for a session. He did, and in contrast to Cassie's session with her sister, it was the therapist who asked questions of the brother. She asked how he viewed his father's relationship with Molly and the other children, and what sense he had made out of his childhood years.

Not only did the therapist gain a different and more rounded view of the early family life, but Molly, sitting quietly in the corner, heard reactions and feelings and answers to questions that, because of her own blind spots, anxiety, and assumptions, she would never have been aware of. Because the session focus and process wasn't on her, she was able to really hear what her brother was saying, and, like Cassie, was offered a new vision of her past.

While bringing others into individual therapy is clearly a good way of reshaping the past and present, such sessions need to be carefully planned. The guests need to know why they're there. They're undoubtedly anxious about what might happen and probably have all kinds of fantasies about the session turning into an interrogation or trial. They need to be welcomed, you need to make a connection, and either before the session or at its start, you need to know exactly what you are planning. Make clear to them that they have a choice—to talk or not to talk, to stop, to ask questions. By being both respectful and in command you can offset their fear that the session will turn into an emotional free-for-all.

You also want to be in charge in order to support your client as well as the guest. Because you don't really know the guests, you don't know what they may or may not say. Cassie's sister, for example, might have tried to dominate the session from the moment she sat down, or broken into an angry rant caused by emotional triggers unknown to you. While getting things out in the open and working through the process are all valuable, no one should wind up at the end of the session feeling emotionally trampled. Again, be aware of your leadership role.

One way to ensure that the session doesn't go sour is to leave sufficient time and space for debriefing and closure. Cassie shouldn't just deliver her monologue and leave; Louis shouldn't just say what he wants to without hearing what Nadine expects; Molly's brother shouldn't just open his own emotional can of worms and then be thanked for coming. Watch the clock; leave time at the end of the session for wrapping up, discussing the process itself, supporting risk taking. Offer to have guests come back again if necessary.

You need to judge whether your client is ready to handle a live confrontation or confession even with your support. Does she really think it is a good idea, or is the client merely trying to please you by going along with what she thinks you want? Is there any danger that you are unwittingly replicating a problem and dynamic by taking the lead and suggesting this or by the process that may unfold that your client cannot yet emotionally handle or change?

Be honest with yourself whether bringing in others is your way of coping with your anxiety or sloughing off your responsibility. Just like the college professor who fills a course with guest speakers as a way of not having to actually teach the class by himself, you can fill therapy sessions with all kinds of significant others who seem to do the therapy work you yourself should be doing. If you are bringing someone into the session because you don't know what else to do, or are hoping to dissipate the anxiety that the intimacy of individual therapy can create, you're serving your purposes, not the client's. Be clear about your goal and the effect you would like to create, and then plan your sessions accordingly. Be clear about whose problem you're trying to solve.

IN LOCO FAMILIA

When family members can't or won't come in—they think therapy is only for crazy people—they often will if you are convinced that it's important. Making the effort to reach out and personally invite the family members, letting them know that their contributions are valuable, and reassuring them that it will not be an interrogation or free-for-all is often enough to get them to participate. Even for family members who live far away, a conference phone call, or Skype, though not ideal, may be just as useful.

If they refuse and really won't come in, there's always the opportunity to reach out and communicate long distance. You can suggest to your client, Ned, that he call and talk to his brother about how disappointed he was that his brother didn't come to his son's wedding, or encourage Alice to write a letter and mail it to her boyfriend, putting into words what she would have said if he could have been there in the session. Such long-distance methods are often easier for the client than the face-to-face meeting. The client may feel less intimidated and less put on the spot: Ned can write down what he wants to say before he makes the call; Alice can shape the words in a letter with thoughtful consideration.

Your job is to counteract the limitations of the media—the absence of nonverbal feedback, the one-sidedness of the letter. Encourage the client to talk or write completely, that is, to make sure he says not only what he wants the other person to know, but also explains why he is saying it, anticipating the other's possible questions or reactions and building the person's response into the planned phone conversation or letter.

As an example, here is a letter that one woman wrote to her father who was dying of cancer:

> *Dear Dad,*
>
> *I've wanted to come see you and I'm sorry that I haven't been able to do so. I hope to come at the end of the month.*
>
> *I've wanted to write to you for some time because I guess I need to get some things off my chest. When I look back on my teenage years, those early years of my marriage, I still get filled with anger and regret—anger that you left, regret that you weren't part of my life for so long. For a long time I blamed myself, blamed Mom. Much of the trouble I got into, some of the bad decisions that I made I thought would have never happened if you had stayed.*
>
> *Slowly I'm beginning to see that you didn't leave because of me, but because of you and Mom. I wish we hadn't lost that time.*

This is a pretty clear letter, but she needed to talk more fully so that her father could better understand why she was saying what she was. Here is the revised letter that she wrote after she and I talked more about her feelings about her father and what she hoped the letter could convey:

> *Dear Dad,*
>
> *I've wanted to come and see you and I'm sorry that I haven't been able to do so. I hope to come at the end of the month.*
>
> *I've wanted to write to you for some time because I guess I need to get some things off my chest. I've been doing a lot of thinking lately about some of the decisions I've made, about my time growing up, trying to understand my past better so that I don't make the same mistakes in the future.*

*When I look back on my teenage years and those early years
of my marriage, I still get filled with anger and regret—anger
that you left, regret that you weren't part of my life for so long.
For a long time I blamed myself, blamed Mom for your leaving.
I used to think that somehow you were the reason I got into so
much trouble, the reason I made some bad decisions. If only you
had stayed, my life, I believed, would have turned out so much
different.*

*And maybe it would have, but I also know that I need to
take some responsibility for the life I've led. Finally now I'm
beginning to realize that you didn't leave because of me, but
because of you and Mom.*

*It's taken me a long time to figure this out. I'm not writing
to make you feel guilty or to hit you over the head with the past.
I know you've got your own regrets. I just want to let you know
that I'm sorry I've pushed you away for so many years when
you did try to come back in my life. I'm sorry that we lost that
time between us. I just want to let you know that I love you.*

When connections with family are not possible, others can step
in to facilitate the change process. Both the systemic notion of interactional patterns and the concept of transference tell us that while
people are unique, our relationships with them are not. Each of us
re-creates over and over the same patterns across relationships.
When changes occur in the patterns between friends, coworkers,
bosses, and even strangers, these changes can flow out to change
other family members, and flow in to change the client.

This, of course, is the basis of group therapy, where the group
members project on one another unresolved emotions and re-create the dynamics of their past relationships. Over time the group
becomes a surrogate family. As the interactions are played out, challenged, and changed within the group process, so too are the individual's cognitive and emotional responses that held the patterns
in place.

When formal group therapy isn't possible, you can create a
mini-group. Have friends, roommates, coworkers, cousins—any-
body who the client feels comfortable inviting—come into the session with him. By focusing on the process, rather than the content,
by looking for replication of patterns (the way John is just as unassertive with his roommate as he is with his sister; the way Cynthia
holds back how she feels when her friend hurts her feelings, just

as she does when her mother does the same), you are tackling the same problems from a different angle.

Again, you need to be clear about the expectations and goals for the session or sessions, confidentiality, and the role of the guest. You need to be in charge, be sensitive to the process, and leave time to debrief so that there are not any loose emotional ends left dangling.

Finally, there are cases where neither family nor family surrogates are available. How else can you expand the client's perspective to include the viewpoint of others and create individual change? Some change will naturally come about from your relationship with the client through your tracking of the client's transference, as he projects on you significant others from his past.

The Three-Letter Exercise

It's also possible to expand the client's perspective by bringing others in through the client's imagination. A variation on letter writing when someone is deceased or not available at all is to use a three-letter homework assignment. Here the client is asked to write the first letter to the individual (divorced former partner, deceased parent, a supervisor who fired them). You instruct your client to imagine if the person were to come back for just 1 hour (in the session, point to an empty chair). In this letter the client gets off his chest whatever he ever wanted to say: "Dad, I remember the time . . . "; "I hated it when you . . . "; "I miss you so much . . . "

In the second letter the client writes what he thinks the other would say back after getting the letter, knowing his personality: "Son, got your letter. I always felt that you hated me" or "Got your letter, we don't need to talk about this." Finally, the third letter is the most important. Here the client writes down what he would like the other to ideally say: "Son, I am so sorry for the way I treated you when you were young. I guess I was . . . " or "Thank you for your letter. I realize I never said how proud I was of you and how my problems interfered with our relationship. I hope you can forgive me."

Write down the instructions, tell clients to take their time doing this, and bring the letters in when they are done. Expect that they will put it off due to a busy week, or no quiet time, and so on. It's about anxiety. Inquire but don't harangue. Eventually they'll bring them in and hand them to you. Hand them back and ask them to read them aloud. Get ready with the mop; expect a lot of tears and anger. When they've finished, if you feel they too quickly glossed over potentially important events, ask about them: "So what happened when you mentioned that summer when you were 6 years old?" The goal here is to stimulate the release of emotions.

You can also do a similar exercise through empty chair work—having the client role-play both sides of a dialogue between herself and another person from the past or present or guided imagery. Help the client imagine a conversation between herself and an old mentor; assist the client to create the dialogue she wishes she had the last time she saw her mother; or facilitate the client to imagine one's life as a play, with different periods of time (childhood, adolescence, early marriage) as specific scenes on a stage. These techniques and any others that you can create increase your understanding of the client's inner and outer worlds and expand the therapeutic ground that you both have to work upon. Through the experiential process you are providing opportunities for catharsis, closure, and healing to take place.

HELPING THE INDIVIDUAL BECOME THE CHANGE AGENT

Frank comes to see you, saying that he wants his wife, Suzanne, to stop crabbing at him all the time. At her first appointment Jane states that she wants to get her 14-year-old son, Paul, to stop talking back to her and to come home on time. Tamisha complains endlessly, it seems, about the way her mother stirs guilt in her every time she calls. She wants her mother to just stop doing it. What do you say to these people?

You can tell them that they need to bring these others into the sessions, and that you need to see them to help them change. You may coach your clients on how to talk to the others about coming in, or you may offer to call the other persons and invite them in, but be clear that changing family interactions requires that you see the family.

You can also help them solve their problems by coaching them on ways to change their behaviors at home. The systemic way of thinking says that if Frank changes what he does, Suzanne *must* do the same; as old patterns are broken, new ones will take their place. This is what Billy's grandmother and Ellen's mother, Ms. Harris, were doing as parents—changing their parenting approach in order to effect change in the children. But this can apply to any relationship within a family. You as the therapist can coach the client to become the change agent within the family.

Essentially, what you do is teach the individual how to think systemically. Patterns of interactions are tracked down and mapped out, and strategies are developed specifically to change the patterns: "So, Frank, what would happen if you didn't snap back when your wife starts complaining?"; "Tamisha, when your mother calls on Sunday and starts her usual spiel that makes you feel guilty and angry, try telling her how you feel, rather than staying quiet or trying to change the topic"; "Jane, if Paul doesn't come in on time on Saturday night, what do you want to do about it? What kinds of consequences can you set that are different from what you have done before?"

"Different from what you have done before" is the key to changing the patterns. Just as you would do in a session, you're pushing the individual to go against the grain, to do something that stirs her anxiety, which in turn will stir the anxiety in the other. In order to help the client sustain the change you must think ahead and help anticipate what she can do in the face of the other's resistance and opposition—help Frank envision how Suzanne may react, help him decide what he can do when she becomes even more irritable or angry; assist Tamisha with what she can say if her mother switches roles and begins to sound guilty herself; work with Jane to plan what she can do when Paul blows up or ignores her when she says he's grounded for the next 2 days.

You also want to coach them on being adults, and how to focus on process—ways of managing their own and the other's emotions, especially during times of conflict, rather than so easily getting caught in content. Finally, because you're focusing on breaking patterns and changing the emotional climate, map out with your clients concrete issues and behavioral steps they can take in a given week. You're aiming for success, not a massive, 1-week overhaul.

This type of change making is a slower process than whole-family or couple work because you're only able to work with one side of the interaction. You want to help your client to stay the course, especially in the beginning, as the other half of the couple escalates as a way to quell her own anxieties and attempts to push the client back to the old patterns and role ("It gets worse before it gets better"). Predicting the opposition, framing it as the beginning of change, and helping the client know specifically and behaviorally how to respond are essential.

There is also the challenge of maintaining a new stance over the long haul when increased stress can cause all of the family members to waver and fall back. Frank or Tamisha or Jane may, with job pressures or illness, collapse back to their old responses during those fragile transition times when new patterns have been planted but not yet firmly taken root. Just as the individual needs to hold a clear vision of what she wants and stay committed to it in the face of resistance, you need to hold a clear vision of what your role and tasks are. When the client starts to waver, you need to make sure you don't.

INDIVIDUAL DANGERS

This one-person approach to problems and family change can start to sound pretty simple—too simple perhaps—give me any problem, any individual, and I, as the therapist, can coach her into getting what she wants. Yes and no. Yes, you can help stimulate change by helping your client change, but no, you and the client can't absolutely direct its outcome in others.

The bigger issue is that there is a bigger issue. The goal isn't only to change patterns and behaviors in another person, but to create change in a relationship for a purpose and help the other person fully understand what that purpose is. Beyond the changing of patterns is the need to move toward honesty and intimacy. At some point Frank doesn't need only to stop overreacting to Suzanne, he needs to be clear with her about what he wants, and what he needs from her and the relationship so that she can do the same. At some point Tamisha must not only teach her mother not to trigger her guilt, but leave enough room in the conversation to tell her mother how she needs her. At some point Jane needs to ask herself why Paul seems so angry at her and how she and he can have a better relationship.

Without this honesty, this bare-bones declaration of who and what is really needed and wanted, without proactive behavior toward positive change, the stopping of dysfunctional patterns merely focuses on the worst symptoms. The client may feel more in control, but without self-responsibility, commitment to the relationship, and caring for the other person, he is merely being manipulative. The shifting of patterns merely becomes another form of a dysfunctional interaction.

Your job is to help the client formulate larger, positive goals and take the risk of intimacy. To do this you need to be alert and honest about your therapeutic relationship with the client. Just as couple work becomes more difficult than whole-family work because the couple's issues can more easily tap into your own personal weak spots, individual work often creates an intimacy that can make the therapeutic relationship more important than the change you're trying to establish. Rather than helping Frank look at what he needs from Suzanne, there's the danger that Frank and his therapist will join forces in seeing her as a problem. Rather than helping Jane expand her relationship with Paul, the therapist and she may spend session after session spinning around the problem so they have a reason to keep their relationship the same. At some point the therapeutic relationship, while seemingly working to change family patterns, becomes inadvertently another way of replicating them.

These powerful countertransference forces are what make individual therapy so different from other formats. Just as bringing people into the therapy can become a crutch for the therapist to avoid the anxiety of doing the therapy himself, excluding people can be the rationalized trap for getting your intimacy needs met through your clients.

And if the potential intimacy isn't enough of a seduction, power can be. The dependency of the individual client on the therapist, even when the therapist is helping the individual to change his relationships, can be strong, and stronger still can be the therapist's need for the dependency. Again, it's not that this collusion can't happen in other formats, because it can; it's a subtle way the process can be so easily distorted through the narrower, less-distracted focus of the individual therapy. Even though the goal may be problem solving, the problems somehow never seem to end; the dependency may be recognized, but it is rationalized as a necessary step to further future growth.

The fact that the danger is there doesn't mean individual therapy isn't valuable, or even an approach of choice in its own right. What it does mean is that you need to be curious about the different qualities of your therapeutic relationships, question inconsistencies in your approach, and be willing to use supervision to challenge your decisions and plans. If you can, the dangers can be avoided and once again you can serve as a model of honesty and clarity.

BACK TO ANN

So where does all this take us in regard to Ann? Here are some possible therapeutic options you might consider to help her with her depression:

• Bring in family members to help solve the problems that she's having difficulty solving, increase their support for Ann, help her to be more assertive and more powerful within her relationships, educate the family about depression, and discourage whatever blame or guilt they may be heaping on her.

• If she is relatively isolated, explore dormant family relationships—the sister "who is too busy with her own life to care," or the aunt who she's been long out of touch with.

• Bring in nonfamily members or have Ann start in a therapy group to increase support around her, develop her social skills, help her unravel and change the patterns that undermine her power, maintain her stress, and compromise her decision-making and problem-solving abilities.

• See her individually to help her see how she can change, rather than being victimized by the forces and people around her. Coach her on changing interactional patterns, help her draw clear lines of responsibility around her problem and those of others, between what she can change and what she cannot. Serve as a morale booster, and an emotional cheerleader for promoting change in her life patterns.

• Refer her for antidepressant medication, coordinate services with the physician, and monitor the results along with the physician; be responsible and see if there's a need for more intensive services, for example, hospitalization or increased supervision. Once she is stable, negotiate with her about her goals and needs for further therapy.

• See her individually to help her learn to apply cognitive-behavioral principles. By helping her track her self-talk ("I always screw up; it's never going to get any better"; "I'm just a basket case") and change the statements ("I'm having a hard time, but I can get help to solve this problem"), she can alter the emotions these statements and this language creates. Teach problem-solving skills and encourage her to be proactive rather than reactive.

• See her individually to resolve issues with people from her past and present; use the support of the therapeutic relationship to help her experiment with risk taking and assertiveness in order to increase her self-confidence; help her increase her emotional awareness and emotional range, especially of strong emotions like anger.

All of these and probably more are possible paths to take. The choice once again depends on the severity of the symptoms, Ann's stated goals, her perception of her problem, her expectations of therapy, and the agency and community resources available, as well as your own framework for viewing the problem—your values, comfort, and skills with various approaches, options, and formats. Once you decide on a particular approach, try it and see what happens.

If your plan doesn't seem to be working for her, don't be afraid to try something else. If you start to slow down, feel helpless, feel like your options are getting narrow or that your world is taking on the same hue as Ann's, seek out some supervisory help to pull you out of the therapeutic quagmire. Most of all, listen to your inner voice and teach your client to do the same; respect your intuitions, trust your and the client's creativity.

Looking Within: Chapter 13 Exercises

1. What are your reactions to your values regarding the notion of helping others become change agents? When is it therapeutic and when is it manipulative? How do you know?

2. Does your focus on the past or on inner dynamics change when seeing an individual rather than seeing a family? Why or why not?

3. Imagine if your intimate partner were to come to your individual therapy to present her view of a major problem between you both. How do you think you would react? How might it help or hinder your solving of the problem or saving your relationship? How do you feel about bringing in others to the sessions as consultants? What would make you hesitate about doing this?

chapter 14

Staying Sane

Survival Tips for Therapists

One of the goals of this book has been to show you how to apply some of the basic assumptions and principles of family therapy in your practice. The other has been to encourage your creative thinking, to help you see that there are many therapeutic roads to the same end. If you can be clear about your goals, flexible in your approach, and pragmatic in your philosophy—and have the humility to make mistakes and the courage to fly by the seat of your pants—you can be effective in your clinical practice.

"Fine," you say, "but how do I do this over the long haul?" How do you stay sane in the face of endless tales of abuse, despair, chaos, and frustration? How do you stay committed, rather than numb, bitter, cynical, or even hostile?

This is a challenge for even the most seasoned therapist, and the answer is that you need to treat yourself the way you treat your clients: to be sensitive and supportive of your needs, while at the same time occasionally pushing yourself out of your comfort zone and against your grain in order to reshape your personal and professional world and stay creative. Once again, the therapeutic buck stops with you. But this doesn't mean you need to grind it out all alone. Like your families, you can get help and support along the way.

In this final chapter, a catalogue of sorts, we consider the idea of self-care for the family therapist, ways to keep your creative juices flowing and your options open, and ways to stay grounded and sensitive without becoming emotionally overwhelmed. We also return to where we started by looking at the bigger picture of life as work and creating a life of integrity.

STAND BY ME:
THE SUPERVISOR–CONSULTANT CONNECTION

Clients come to you for help with their children, their marriages, and themselves. You go to your supervisor for help with the assessment, to develop strategies, or help you become less emotionally entangled. The parallel is obvious. A good supervisor or consultant isn't there to solve your personal problems, but like a good therapist, is there as a support, parent, teacher, sounding board, brainstormer, coach, cheerleader, storyteller, and friend; she is there to push or pull you up when you need it. And, just like a therapist, the supervisor's individual personality is less important than how she interacts with you. It's not the person, after all, who helps us to change and grow, but the relationship that you both create together.

The best kind of supervisors are those who have the skills and knowledge you lack. But they are also more than walking textbooks or catalogues of therapeutic skills. The good supervisor not only fills you up with information, but helps you shape that information into a professional self and style that ultimately becomes the very best you.

In order to develop your techniques, you need a supervisor who appreciates your learning style, whether by watching him in action first; planning, preparing, and mapping out your sessions with him carefully in advance; or jumping right in and asking questions about supervision later. Only by supporting your way of learning, rather than pushing you to follow his, can your supervisor help you develop your own approach, voice, and unique weaving of personality and skill.

A good supervisor also needs to be sensitive to your level of professional development. Learning to do therapy is in many ways like learning to speak a foreign language. Competence is more than the ability to memorize a list of words or clinical interventions; it is measured by an ability to use these tools—to *think* in the language of therapy—and adapt them to a wide range of situations. But this takes time, and moves in stages. The novice, for example, will need more direction and straight-ahead information than someone more advanced; the performance pressure of the beginning may give way to the therapist's true dependence on the supervisor, and this may in turn eventually lead to an adolescent stage of testing, questioning, and separating from the supervisor's own model before the therapist can reach a more integrated self. A good supervisor is flexible. Like a good parent, she is able to anticipate your changing needs, flexible enough to provide the variety of support that you require over time, and able to change her supervisory style and skills to match your own.

This is where good supervision most emulates good therapy. The good supervisor appreciates the organic nature of the relationship. She, like the good therapist, knows that it's through the process itself—the negotiating, sorting, and solving that goes on between you both—that growth occurs. She believes that in the development of the relationship between you and her comes the development of the professional self within you both.

And like good therapy, the good supervisor helps you clear out the emotional underbrush that can get in the way of your taking risks or becoming successful. Often it's your anxiety, doubt, anger, or worry that is the main problem with a case. You're anxious about what to do, or what to do right, worried about doing it right, or angry that the family isn't changing the way you want them to. The good supervisor helps you sort and sift out these feelings and agendas so you can best use and trust what you already know.

Bad supervision or consultation is the opposite of responsiveness and collaboration. Like bad therapy, bad parenting, or bad marriages the relationship becomes stale and stifling because both of you are boxed into empty patterns. Rather than developing individuality, the focus is on cloning. Difficult topics are avoided rather than approached. The therapist quickly outgrows the supervisor's rigid learning format, and the supervisor comes to resent the therapist for doing so.

It's your job to make sure you get supervision that both supports and challenges you, that helps you learn and use what you learn. Most of all, find someone who gives you the permission and courage to make mistakes, and who teaches you not only how to correct them but helps you learn the lessons that the mistakes hold.

Yes, there are burned-out or controlling supervisors out there, and you may get routinely assigned to one at your job. If there is a problem, if you feel that it is not a good fit, and if your styles or philosophies are just too vastly different, speak up. Be clear about what you want and need, but don't settle. You don't want clients to do that to you, and you needn't do that with your supervisor.

STEPPING BACK: SELF-SUPERVISION

If you think about supervising yourself, more likely than not, your mind heads for all that's negative: a mental wagging of a finger at yourself for being so tough on that mother; the scowling face of your father, your mother, or your old mentor scolding you for missing the signs of depression in that father; that small, snarly voice saying "Caught you!" whenever you get off track and seem confused.

Some claim that while this harsh, critical-parent image of self-supervision can help keep us on our toes, the self-pummeling can also leave us too cautious and uncreative. Others in the field counter that the danger isn't that we are too hard on ourselves, but too easy. The blind spots, rationalizations, and contradictions in what we do are impossible for us to see by ourselves, let alone change. We have no business trying to supervise ourselves. We need someone else, someone not necessarily with wisdom, but with a simple outside perspective to help us see what we're doing.

In between the dangers of being too easy or too hard on ourselves is the view that self-supervision can be a means of reflecting, of stepping back and away from your work in order not to scold but to discover. Following the path of your anxiety and emotions can cast new light on your assumptions. By tracking the patterns of your practice, in much the same way we encourage families to look at the patterns in their own lives, you can recognize the themes that run your living and work.

Sit down with any of your colleagues at lunch one day and listen to each clinician describe his caseload—the problems, the assessment, the plans of action. Avoid the temptations of getting swept up in the details of the families' lives or dickering over the right diagnosis, but instead just listen carefully as the stories each tells unfold. Tom, you realize, almost always struggles with resistant fathers "who need to be more responsible"; Nancy sniffs out "fragmentation in the family structure" and is set on getting everyone back and in their proper places; Jamal finds that so many of his clients have "suppressed anger" that needs to be expressed in order to increase their personal power; and Joy uses a genogram like a road map to invariably track down some "unresolved grief," some "unspoken trauma."

The themes and patterns will begin to stand out before you. The fact that you notice them doesn't make their clinical assessment invalid or the work ineffective. Their impressions are, after all, wrapped around their favorite theories. The pause comes only with curiosity and questioning: Why does that particular theory seem so true to them?; Why do all their clients seem to have such consistent underlying problems and needs?; What is it that your colleagues see in their families that may tell them what they need? These are the questions that if asked and answered can help keep the projections down; they can keep the therapy from twisting and becoming a vicarious outlet for the therapist's own unexpressed emotions.

What you do and see in your colleagues you can do for yourself. Take the time to reflect on your own work. What is that treatment plan that you instinctively find yourself writing over and over?; What kind of cases or problems are most difficult?; How much do your solutions reflect a working on autopilot rather than a carefully tuned, road-tested plan of action?; How much are the unique aspects of the family blurred so that they all conveniently fit into the same few boxes?; What is the hot diagnosis of the month? Why?

Taking the time to purposefully reflect in this way helps you slow down and see each family and client more clearly. Rather than the family turning into the "2:00 p.m. appointment with the ADHD kid," you have time to sort through your wider impressions and reactions. You have a chance to step back and evaluate how you are responding to everyone in the family, rather than just getting caught up in "getting the parents to set some structure." Small cracks in your approach (for example, your failing to get the father consistently involved) can be noticed and fixed before they develop into something larger (the father undermining the behavioral changes you are suggesting).

Such self-reflection is also vital to your creativity. To be creative requires a stirring of the intellectual and emotional pot, so to speak, and then a letting go so that the bits of impressions and images can settle, sit, and eventually recombine, producing new insights and new approaches. When you cut this process off by shutting off your thoughts at the end of the hour, your work is more likely to reflect your clinical habits and formulas.

Finally, self-reflection helps you realize your own counter-transference. Often, your pushing the session out of your mind after it's over is a way of pushing away uncomfortable reactions and emotions. By taking the time to dwell on them in a deliberate way, you may discover exactly the problem that's causing you to feel stuck.

How you make time for self-supervision depends on your working style. Some therapists take time when they are writing up their session notes to look back over the work on the case so far. Others set a time aside each week, an hour perhaps, specifically to reflect on their entire caseload; make specific time for it at the front end of your weekly planning. Consider an annual year-end review of your work in order to discern the larger patterns. Read through old cases and remember the ones long gone. What patterns do you see and hear? What are common assessments, struggles, and goals? What kinds of clients did you seem to hold on to, while others fell away after a few sessions? How flexible was your own style and approach, how rigid? How has your perspective changed now? What developmental issues of yours—breaking away from parents, becoming a parent, establishing one's own sense of mastery, dealing with death, becoming a wise man or woman—are reflected in your work, coloring your perspective, changing the shape of your practice, and recasting your values?

Tap into your emotions. So you are frustrated with Mr. Jones and angry for some reason at Mrs. Wilson. Go ahead, imagine Mr. Jones sitting there across from you in the chair, and see Mrs. Wilson in her frumpy dress with that half smirk on her face. Tell him what you are thinking; tell her how you feel. Now switch chairs. What would he say back, how would she translate that smirk into words? Switch back again; respond back. Switch again. Notice how the conversation has changed, how you are feeling less frustrated and angry, perhaps, and more depressed or compassionate, how he looks less critical and more helpless. Who else from your past or present could you put in the chair that reminds you of these people, this dialogue, and these emotions?

Write a brief short story about those clients you're having a hard time with. Use them as characters, making them as dramatic and sympathetic as you can. See what you learn about their motives, or their dreams. Put yourself and therapy in the story. What can the fictional process tell you about the real one?

You're sorting out your countertransference, owning your projections, and separating yourself from the family. Use those lagging emotions and that afterburn following a session to discover something about you and them. Self-supervision can help you recharge yourself and the therapy.

TRAINING AND EDUCATION

Do you want to learn how to work with sexually abused children? Are you trying to integrate motivational interviewing into your work with teens? Are you interested in learning how to apply mindfulness to couple therapy? Then get yourself to a conference or workshop, plug into a webinar, and get some training.

Short-term training opportunities obviously help you increase your skills, and keep you on top of the latest and maybe greatest developments in the field. They also provide those invaluable side benefits of getting you out of the office and to a city where you haven't been before, giving you a chance to meet and remeet colleagues who you would probably never see otherwise. When you are feeling burned out or discouraged, short trainings can recharge you by helping you see that there is more that you can do, and that there are ways to overcome the places in your practice where you feel the most stuck. And sitting in a room or online with hundreds or thousands of other therapists not only validates that you are not the only one struggling or wanting to increase your skills, but that you, in fact, belong to a larger therapy family.

Should you desire to delve even deeper into any subject, there is always the extended trainings: the 3-week or 1-month variety, or the extended online course. Rather than just getting a taste of a particular skill or approach, you can get a whole meal. Beyond that is the intensive, ongoing training, usually leading to some certification: the 2-year program in hypnosis, imago or internal family systems, or the 3-year investigation of object relations. Not only is your commitment of time and money obviously greater, but also is the commitment to that approach. You need to be clear about your objectives: What is it that you most want to learn? Why now? How does it fit or conflict with your values? How does it fit with your internal image of whom you want to be?

The questions are important because the answers, which on the surface seem so transparent, quickly turn murky with a bit of reflection. For example, you are burned out on what you are doing, or are at that stage of development where you are beginning to outgrow your supervision and feel restless. You may have the feeling that you want something else, something more, such as increased energy or a new perspective that cuts through your hodgepodge of techniques. This feeling may be strong, but undefined. It's tempting to grasp on to something that at least points toward a direction, some release from the tension or depression that you feel.

And the program may do just that—catch you up in something that's new, that gives you a new way of defining yourself and what you do. But it also may be a mistake if you're not honest with yourself about what you are really seeking and feeling. The restlessness or burnout may merely be a symptom of a larger problem and not the problem itself.

Often the best course is to wait, rather than jumping in, and to sit through the transition period and see what happens, rather than becoming impatient and grasping something just to have it to hold on to. You may discover that the problem has nothing to do with your professional practice and more to do with your personal needs.

Once you've clarified your clinical needs and goals, however, these extended trainings can indeed help you feel more grounded, solid, and expert in your work. In contrast to a conference or workshop that gives you new ideas or techniques to supplement your work, immersion in the more intensive training format can literally transform it.

Like good supervision, long-term training should challenge you to discover a deeper level of yourself than short-term training usually does. At its best, extended training shouldn't only give you a few more details about what you already know, or reconfirm what you already believe, but push you to look at what you're doing with fresh eyes, help you to see yourself in a new context, and discover what makes you tick. In fact, any good, rigorous course of study, even if it is outside your field—literature, mathematics, music, rock climbing—can be worthwhile if you come away from it intellectually and emotionally stretched.

TEACHING

The learning process can be divided into four stages:

1. You know what you don't know.
2. You don't know what you know.
3. You don't know what you don't know.
4. You know what you know.

In the first stage, as a beginner, you're filled with anxiety because you're only aware of your incompetence: you know what you don't know. Much of what you do feels like you're barely keeping your head above water. You mistakenly believe that others see your incompetence as well and are not mentioning it in order to be polite.

In the second, you've gained ground, you've learned more, but pieces of what you've learned remain scattered in your mind: you don't know what you know. You haven't been able to bring them together to give you a solid framework from which to practice. Instead, you often wind up winging it—pulling out bits of theory here, samples of techniques there—and feeling once again like a beginner.

In the third stage, your knowledge and skills consolidate and your sense of confidence and power grows. In fact, like an adolescent, you're aware only of your power and you see only what you know— your way is the best way. You feel on top of things, but in this haughty frame of mind, you don't realize the limits of your knowledge and experience: you don't know what you don't know. Your vision is myopic, you're often not aware of the subtleties of your approach, and you can easily ignore the larger implications and effects of what you're doing. Your sense of self-importance and your uncritical loyalty to your beliefs may make you take unnecessary risks.

In the final stage, you come back down to earth, and you're more humble about your skills and knowledge. Like everyone else you have your own strengths and weaknesses: you know what you know, but you're less cocky, more flexible. There isn't one way, you realize, but many. There's always more to learn, but you also know you can trust the foundation of knowledge and skill that you have worked hard to acquire.

In all of these stages the challenge is in defining and using what you know and believe, and honestly admitting what you don't. But there's more to this than simply glancing over your shoulder and tallying up what you have and what you don't. Learning to be a therapist involves bringing together all the aspects of who you are. It's an ongoing, developmental climb of building up and peeling away, supporting and confronting, giving yourself a break, and looking at yourself squarely in the eye.

One useful way of clarifying what you know from what you don't and uncovering the gaps in your knowledge is through teaching—formally, through a classroom, seminar, short course, or writing a journal article; or informally, through a brown bag lunch topic, 2-hour staff development for colleagues, or taking on a student in supervision. Teaching forces you to consolidate your bits of knowledge, pinpoint and name your hunches and intuitions, and shape them both into something more integrated and substantial. In the process of sorting through for others what is important to learn, you have to sort through for yourself what you already know.

The teaching process is also a great antidote to the feeling that you're intellectually treading water. It's easy to become dulled by your own practice and feel that you "just do what you do." You need the opportunity to rediscover your uniqueness, reconfirm for others and yourself that what you do works, and that your approach represents a unique blend of personality and skills. Teaching, and the feedback that others give about what you say, can do this.

So arrange to have a regular staff development time where each therapist presents her own unique approach to helping families. Think about a case or technique that was particularly successful and expand on its implications. Do a literature review, define your own unique perspective or application, and write it up for a journal. Contact your local university and see if you can serve as a field instructor for graduate students in social work, or clinical or counseling psychology. See if they need adjunct teachers. Offer to teach a course on marriage and family at the local community college, or one on parenting through the county continuing adult education program. Make up a flyer of the topics and workshops that you can teach and mail them out to all the departments of Social Services and family courts in your state. You may be surprised by how much you have to offer.

THE QUICK AND EASY:
MISCELLANEOUS SURVIVAL SKILLS

Finally, there are everyday antidotes to therapy's wear and tear. Here are a few.

Diversify

A caseload filled with 20 hyperactive 8-year-old boys may help you refine your skills, but may also drive you insane. If at all possible, diversify your caseload—see a mix of families, problems, personalities; have a stable of core clients, perhaps, of what you do best, and one or two cases that lead you to learn something new. Create a mix in your daily schedule: seeing four depressed clients in a row on a rainy Wednesday afternoon is going to leave you feeling dull and empty. Put a couple of those hyperactive kids in the middle of it all, see a couple after doing some play therapy, or schedule an individual adult after three teenagers. If your clients start to sound the same, you'll start to react the same.

Don't be afraid to diversify your work responsibilities as well. Talk to your supervisor about taking part in a community assessment or treatment team, help with agency public relations and marketing, and do follow-up research on your clients' satisfaction. These additional activities can break up the grind of doing back-to-back therapy and can give you another perspective on your work.

Control Your Time

This is relatively easy to do in private practice, though, of course, even here some of your time is going to be generated by client demand. In agency work, however, where others may schedule your appointments, you could wind up with the most chaotic family at the time of day when you are most sluggish and least able to manage them. You know how the case flow over the course of the day affects you, you know when you are at your best, and when you need a break to regroup. Set your own schedule.

Be Proactive about What Scares You

Do you walk around with the dread that you too could get subpoenaed and wind up having to testify in court? Do you worry that

that retired gentleman who you just started seeing could easily turn actively suicidal and make you feel panicked and helpless? Do you wake up at 2:00 a.m. wondering if one of the clients in your anger management group is actually getting too excited and could possibly turn explosive at the next group meeting?

Everyone has some fear about something that 'he's not yet encountered but eventually could. The dread comes from worrying that this shoe could drop at any time, and most likely, you imagine, when you're unprepared to handle it.

So spare yourself the worry by preparing yourself for the worst. Talk to your supervisor now about protocols for dealing with subpoenas. Follow one of your more experienced colleagues to court to see what happens and how she manages those situations. Sign up for a suicide prevention training or intervention skill training for managing aggressive or violent clients. Be proactive so you can be confident.

Allow Yourself to Relax in Sessions

Beginning therapists often feel that they have to be hypervigilant with clients—never breaking eye contact, and constantly making those cow eyes and appropriate sighs and nods of the head to let the client know you are listening. Usually, this is attention overkill. Some of the best therapists allow themselves to relax and stare off into the space just above the client's head. It can be a huge relief and it helps you to listen and think better.

Make an Effort to Spend Time with Colleagues

Therapy is isolating. Offset this by scheduling a regular time to have lunch with a colleague upstairs, a weekly meeting with everyone in the practice every Thursday morning just to check in and touch base, or have an informal supervision lunch meeting with a group of folks whose work you respect on Wednesdays twice a month.

Make Your Work Space as Comfortable as Possible

Is that rickety chair driving you crazy? What about the drawer that always sticks, the bland beige walls, the couch with the dark stain and the sagging cushions that you feel embarrassed about every time a new client sits down on it? You spend a good amount of your time in one place, so try to make it your own.

Try to make it attractive as well. Take a look at the offices of friends and colleagues to give you creative ideas. How about a pleasing picture on the wall that reflects your personality or the mood you want to create. Get a small aquarium and a few fish. Shut off the overhead florescent lights and get some attractive lamps. Put down carpeting, or throw down a small patterned rug over the grayish, industrial carpeting that's there. Set up the toys in a bookcase rather than heaping them in a cardboard box. Bring in some plants, even fake ones, to help the place look less sterile. Use your imagination. Make it look more like home and less like an office.

Do Something That Helps You Feel Centered

Because therapy so easily pulls you into others' lives, it's important to have something in your life that can pull you back out, helps you feel centered, and activates another portion of yourself—meditation twice a day, running, cooking dinner, playing the piano, writing a novel, rafting, gardening, or singing. Whatever it is, find something that puts you somewhere else (preferably legal and not addicting), that lets you drop the day's events from your mind, and that makes you feel competent, healthy, powerful, or positive about who you are and what you do.

Take Vacations

I'm not suggesting working vacations, but real vacations that help you either relax or stimulate you, but certainly are different from your everyday life. Go to the beach for a week and bring novels, not journals. Go to Pennsylvania, but instead of going to see your mother or Aunt Rosie, stay in Philadelphia and take in the sights. Or go see your mother and Aunt Rosie, but stop off in Philadelphia anyhow.

Have a Balanced Personal Life

This is easier said than done, of course. But if you want to avoid the dangers we have been talking about—the vicarious acting out through your clients, the need for their intimacy, all the ways that therapy can be distorted because you have come to personally need more from it than the rest of your life provides—you need to discover and stay involved in the rest of your life. If you need to do therapy more than your clients need the therapy, everyone is in trouble.

Have Realistic Expectations

Like any other craft or art it takes time—8 to 10 years is probably reasonable—to hone your skills and style, begin to master the subtleties of practice, and feel confident in what you do. Some therapists, often the most sensitive ones it seems, give up too quickly. They get so frustrated and critical of themselves in those early years over what they're aware they don't know, that they leave the field before they have a chance to develop their skills and get really good. Be patient with yourself and don't box yourself in with unrealistic expectations.

These survival skills, along with good supervision, training, and opportunities to teach what you know can help you stay sane, stable, and even steadily enthusiastic about your work over the long haul. The overriding theme here is one of balance and diversity— of putting your emotional eggs in several baskets so that you don't have to clutch too tightly to just one, and finding many ways of expressing yourself, working, and discovering what lies within.

Finally, it's also important to find balance in your therapeutic role. One of the important and often subtle shifts that good therapists make as they gain experience is in seeing their responsibility as less fixing the presenting problem that the family brings in and more helping the family fix it themselves. As we asked early on, "What keeps the family from solving their problems on their own?" You want to help them move forward to their goals, not yours. You can help the family understand how and why the problem came about, point out what they're doing to one another and themselves and speculate on how it might be connected to their concerns, and then give them a place and way of talking about ideas and options and supporting them in what they decide to do. And then you're done; you've done your best. What they ultimately do next is up to them. As was said in the first chapter, therapy is only one way of approaching problems. Your sanity and satisfaction, and that of your clients as well, comes in accepting and appreciating your limits.

LIFE AS WORK

This unity of life and work is what we most often associate with the artist: Mary Cassatt, struggling to capture on the canvas the vision that fills her mind; Mozart and Beethoven, driven to translate the feelings inside into notes on a page so that others may hear the sounds and experience the emotions; Virginia Wolfe, who dedicated 5 years of her life to create the perfect novel, one that carries the reader so completely into the world that she alone creates within her. It's easy to be drawn to this way of life not only because it seems so unstructured compared with the nine-to-five routine into which most of us feel wedged, but mostly because it seems so passionate, committed, and creative.

Doing therapy is work that flows from the inside out, rather than from the outside in, work that soaks in all of who and what you are. It is work that goes beyond the boundaries of a "good job" with its means to other ends, or the "career," that track we follow to some ultimate level or publicly recognized success. This is work as a calling.

While the notion of calling conjures up the sound of celestial choirs and beams of radiant light falling down on you from above, it most often begins with only a whisper of some inner voice telling you that this is something you should do, the flicker of an image across your mind that gradually over time grows into a vision that pulls you forward. A calling is realized when you step back from what you are already doing and sense that this work is something that you are not only good at, but were meant to do. You have found a medium for expressing who you most are. Like the artist, you become caught up in the flow of the work, can lose sense of time, and are absolutely engaged. You do the work not because of what you might get for it at some time in the future, but because of what the *doing* does for you in the present.

So what is that calling for you? Why do you do therapy or want to do therapy? What does it offer you as a medium, how does it actualize your values and beliefs, and your sense of purpose and creativity? Why do you need to do it?

And if you are not sure that therapy is your calling, then what is? What is it that you can't wait to do when you wake up in the morning? What do the dreams, visions, and fantasies that you have tell you about what you need to do most?

Obviously, everyday practicality and reality have a place in this discussion. Sure, you need to have a job for money, a place to live, pay off the college loans, send your kids to college, and survive in the real world. But . . . unless you have the courage to periodically ask these bigger questions, the gap between your work and yourself will gradually widen. You will feel cynical, tired and burned out, frustrated and fed up. You will find yourself one day in the middle of a 20-, 30-, or 40-year crisis, filled with fantasies and ready to run away toward dreams that have only become more desperate and powerful by your neglect. If you don't build your work around your life, you can easily wind up building your life around your work.

A LIFE OF INTEGRITY

Actually, *building* may be the wrong word. Do we really build our lives? Many would say yes, especially considering the society we live in. Images of American pioneers, those self-sufficient, hardworking, brave, frontier men and women who created their lives out of nothing more than hope and sweat and guts is incorporated within each of us. We have, we're told, roughly 40 years—20 to 60 years old—to do the same, to grab hold of our lives in our two hands and make something out of it. At the end of that time you and everyone else will take stock and look at just how much you've accomplished, how well you have done, and how successful you are.

But there is another point of view, another way of looking at our relationship to living. Rather than building our lives we discover them. This is the notion of a life unfolding, the sense that our lives are led, the image of it staying always a few steps ahead of us, around the corner, gently waving its hand, urging us to follow. It's an image that tells us that by staying close to ourselves, with our ear pressed tight against the ground of our lives, listening—to our intuitions, emotions, and fantasies—we will discover our purpose, our calling. We will live the life we were meant to have.

The split between these two perspectives is like that of context and process; they are two sides of the same reality. Building at its worst becomes a left-brain-driven forced march to success and accomplishment. Discovery at its worst lacks grounding: weightless visions and fragile dreams float forever within our heads but never enter our lives. The best view is the combination of both, where discovery becomes the thin lines on a sheet of blueprint paper and building becomes the nailing of rafters and beams into the solid structure that we call our life.

Both are important, but like its sister, process, it is discovery that leads the way. To give credence and respect to this side of our lives is to only do what we do with our families. We are helping them to give full voice to whispers and nods, helping them to step aside for a moment from the pain that their problem may be creating in order to hear what their problem is telling them about what they need to learn, and asking those "miracle questions" to help them draw out the answers within them that they didn't know were there. Even when our clients feel victimized and battered by life, we say to them that life, their life, is ready to give something back to them if only they have the courage to open their eyes and live it.

When we scrape down to the bottom of this way of thinking, we find ourselves resting once again on assumption, values, and even faith—a faith in which we cannot only find our purpose, but that there is a purpose. Problems not only have solutions but lessons to teach us, and once we learn them, the problems miraculously disappear. This is not the calm, sedentary faith that reassures us that everything will turn out all right, but the wild, robust faith that comes from living by the seat of our pants.

If you are able to live this way, to wait and listen and then go, to work to make your inner and outer life mirror each other, then your life is filled with gut-sure honesty and with true integrity. It will be a different life from the carefully built one that keeps discovery locked away, and sets its marker early on and moves steadily forward. To bring faith, discovery, and honesty into your life and into your work, is to walk out on a trail on a crisp morning following the sound of the hawk flying above rather than the painted sign on the tree. You may suddenly find yourself sitting out on a limb or looking over the edge of a cliff and not know why or how you got there. You may look down and feel afraid, but if you look inside, you will find courage; if you look up, you will see visions.

Looking Within: Chapter 14 Exercises

1. How do you learn best? What do you need most from supervision or consultation? How have your needs changed over the past year? What would be most difficult to talk about in supervision? Why? How can you repair or expand that relationship? How can you change it to better meet your clinical needs and personal needs?

2. How can you change your work environment—physically, socially, emotionally—to make it less stressful?

3. Be honest—how's your personal life? How is it affecting your work life? What can you do to change it?

4. Draw a picture of your life. Get crayons, pencils, paint, and a large sheet of paper and write at the top "My Life." Let your unconscious lead you—follow the images that come to mind, the memories that may be stirred up, and the feelings that you have. Give yourself about 15 minutes. Let the picture sit for a day, and then look at it carefully again.

5. How do you look back on your past now than how you did 5 or 10 years ago? How has this image changed your sense of the present and the future?

6. How close is the gap between your inner and outer worlds? What would it take to bring them together?

Suggested Reading

CLASSICS

These are the texts by the grandmothers and grandfathers of family therapy. Each offers its own particular theory and slant on the systemic process.

Ackerman, N. (1995). *The psychodynamics of family life: Diagnosis and treatment of family relationships.* New York: Jason Aronson.

Originally published in the early 1970s, this was one of the first books to chart the course into family therapy waters. You can tell from the title that Ackerman came from the psychodynamic, psychiatric school.

Bowen, M. (1992). *Family therapy in clinical practice.* New York: Jason Aronson.

Theory, theory, theory, said Bowen in his Georgia accent. If you had a good theory, you had the lens through which you could see and understand any family. Here's his theory—the world of undifferentiation, influence of history, start of genograms, and therapist as coach and change agent.

Burnberry, W., & Whitaker, C. (1988). *Dancing with the family: A symbolic–experiential approach.* New York: Routledge.

Carl Whitaker, the crazy uncle of family therapy who seemed to fly by the seat of his pants, who always seemed to be fooling around but wasn't. Here you find out what all the fooling around was really about.

Haley, J. (1991). *Problem-solving therapy: New strategies for effective family therapy.* San Francisco: Jossey-Bass.

Bowen liked the past and Minuchin created structure; Haley took a different course. This book describes the beginnings of strategic therapy:

learning to think not only in patterns and circles but from different heights; understanding how solutions turn into problems; telling a client that he or she needs to wax the floor on hands and knees before he or she goes to bed each night—if nothing else, just learning to think the way Haley does can open your mind to new possibilities.

Minuchin, S. (1974). *Families and family therapy*. Cambridge, MA: Harvard University Press.

The original book on structural family therapy that first described, well, structure—those enmeshed and rigid families with diffuse boundaries, distant parents, and unresolved marital issues.

Satir, V. (1983). *Conjoint family therapy*. Palo Alto, CA: Science and Behavior Books.

The grandmother of family therapy, the one person in a club of men to bring out the softer side of the family therapy movement, and the first to write in a consumer-friendly way. This new edition of Satir's classic provides useful, practical information about communication and emotional patterns in families.

OTHER FAMILY THERAPY BOOKS

Here is thinking from a variety of new/next-generation family therapists— some offshoots of the classics, others combine various approaches into one, still others give food for thought from different schools that you can apply to your family work. Given the changing and creative nature of the field, undoubtedly some important contributions may be left out. My apologies.

Alexander, J. F., Waldron, H. B., Robbins, M. S., & Neeb, A. A. (2013). *Functional family therapy for adolescent behavior problems*. Washington, DC: American Psychological Association.

This evidence-based model tackles teen problems with a home-based approach.

Boyd-Franklin, N. (2003). *Black families in therapy: Understanding the African American experience* (2nd ed.). New York: Guilford Press.

Race and ethnicity shape families—it helps to know how to best approach the work.

de Shazer, S., & Dolan, Y. (2007). *More than miracles: The state of the art of solution-focused brief therapy*. New York: Norton.

Solution-focused therapy can be applied to a variety of clients, but its start was family therapy. For a period of time it had a reputation for being somewhat simple and mechanistic in its approach. This book does a good job of retaining a can-do positive approach while underscoring its underlying principles.

Falicov, C. J. (2014). *Latino families in therapy* (2nd ed.). New York: Guilford Press.

What to know about working with Latino families.

Henggeler, S. W., Schoenwald, S. K., Borduin, C. M., Rowland, M. D., & Cunningham, P. B. (2009). *Multisystemic therapy for antisocial behavior in children and adolescents* (2nd ed.). New York: Guilford Press.

This is another evidence-based approach to working with a special adolescent population. The focus here is on the environment and community supporting the struggling teen.

Hughes, D. (2007). *Attachment-focused family therapy.* New York: Norton.

Attachment has become a new focus in recent years and here Hughes moves it away from the individual approach and incorporates the family.

McGoldrick, M. (2008). *Genograms: Assessment and intervention.* New York: Norton.

Genograms are the work horse of family techniques. Here's how to do it and use it.

McGoldrick, M., & Hardy, K. (2008). *Re-visioning family therapy: Race, culture, and gender in clinical practice.* New York: Guilford Press.

This makes for a broader societal look at families and family therapy. Both authors are heavyweights in the field and they bring a different and invigorating perspective.

Minuchin, S., Reiter, M. D., & Borda, C. (2014). *The craft of family therapy: Challenging certainties.* New York: Routledge.

The grandfather keeps going. Here Minuchin not only breaks down structural techniques but does a good job of focusing on a session process.

Napier, A., & Whitaker, C. (1988). *The family crucible: The intensive experience of family therapy.* New York: Harper & Row.

This is a classic in its own right and another reader-friendly book. Includes good descriptions of the family process and the layers of problems.

Nichols, M. (2009). *The lost art of listening* (2nd ed.). New York: Guilford Press.

As the title says, this book can make you look again at the power and practice of good listening.

Nichols, M. (2012). *Family therapy: Concepts and methods* (10th ed.). Hoboken, NJ: Pearson.

Now in its tenth edition, this is the go-to book in graduate school programs. If you didn't read it there, check it out now. Includes a history of the family therapy field as well as good summaries of various schools of thought.

Schwartz, R. (1997). *Internal family systems theory.* New York: Guilford Press.

Schwartz applies family systems concepts to individual work where clients dialogue with different internal selves. This is a creative approach and work.

White, M. (2007). *Maps of narrative practice.* New York: Norton.

White set up a new way of thinking about problems by externalizing and separating them from the self and family. Here are concepts and tools to help you think this way.

PLAY THERAPY

Bailey, E. (Ed.). (2005). *Children in therapy: Using family as a resource.* New York: Norton.

Rather than breaking the child's treatment off from the family, here the family is part and parcel of the approach. Includes lots of techniques.

Gil, E. (2014). *Play in family therapy* (2nd ed.). New York: Guilford Press.

This is a bible of sorts about play therapy over the past 20 years. There are good reasons that it is.

Lowenstein, L. (Ed.). (2010). *Creative family therapy techniques: Play, art, and expressive activities to engage children in family sessions.* Toronto: Champion Press.

This is sort of the reverse of Bailey's focus—here, children are incorporated into the family therapy process. Lots of techniques and tools are included.

Thomas, B. (2009). *Creative coping skills for children: Emotional support through arts and craft activities.* London: Kingsley.

You can't get enough techniques. What is unique in this book is that the author links specific activities for different emotional problems, such as worry and grief.

COUPLE THERAPY

Dattilio, F. M. (2010). *Cognitive-behavioral therapy with couples and families.* New York: Guilford Press.

Dattilio does a great job of applying the concepts of Beck, the father of cognitive-behavioral therapy, to couples and families.

Gottman, J. M., & Silver, N. (1999). *The seven principles for making marriage work.* New York: Three Rivers Press.

Gottman, originator of the Love Lab, did for couples what Masters and Johnson did for sex. This book is geared for general audiences, but the authors lay out the concepts for Gottman's communication-based approach to couple work.

Gurman, A. S., Lebow, J. L., & Snyder, D. K. (Eds.). (2015). *Clinical handbook of couple therapy* (5th ed.). New York: Guilford Press.

Now in its fifth edition, this book covers every aspect of couple therapy— various approaches, special populations, and problems.

Johnson, S. (2004). *The practice of emotionally focused couple therapy.* New York: Routledge.

Johnson feels that Gottman's approach misses the attachment issues that help sustain good communication skills. Her concepts and techniques are presented.

Scharff, D., & Scharff, J. (2014). *Psychoanalytic couple therapy.* London: Karmac.

We need to have a least one book on psychoanalytic approach—here it is.

References

American Psychiatric Association. (2013). *Diagnostic and statistical manual of mental disorders* (5th ed.). Arlington, VA: Author.

Anderson, C. (1983). *Mastering resistance: A practical guide to family therapy.* New York: Guilford Press.

Arcelus, J., Mitchell, A. J., Wales, J., & Nielsen, S. (2011). Mortality rates in patients with anorexia nervosa and other eating disorders. *Archives of General Psychiatry, 68*(7), 724–731.

Bowen, M. (1993). *Family therapy in clinical practice.* New York: Jason Aronson.

Ekstein, R., & Wallerstein, R. (1958). *The teaching and learning of psychotherapy.* New York: Basic Books.

Giedd, J. (2008). The teen brain: Insights from neuroimaging. *Journal of Adolescent Health, 42,* 335–343.

Gilbert, R. M. (1992). *Extraordinary relationships: A new way of thinking about human interactions.* New York: Wiley.

Karpman, S. (1968). Fairy tales and script drama analysis. *Transactional Analysis Bulletin, 7*(26), 39–43. Retrieved March 5, 2014, from *www.karpmandramatriangle.com.*

Taibbi, R. (2013). *Boot camp therapy: Brief, action-oriented clinical approaches to anxiety, anger, and depression.* New York: Norton.

Index

315